AFRICAN PERSPECTIVES ON [illegible] TICE

AFRICAN PERSPECTIVES ON TRADITION AND JUSTICE

Edited by
Tom Bennett
Eva Brems
Giselle Corradi
Lia Nijzink
Martien Schotsmans

intersentia
Cambridge – Antwerp – Portland

Intersentia Publishing Ltd.
Trinity House | Cambridge Business Park | Cowley Road
Cambridge | CB4 0WZ | United Kingdom
Tel.: +44 1223 393 753 | Email: mail@intersentia.co.uk

Distribution for the UK:
Hart Publishing Ltd.
16C Worcester Place
Oxford OX1 2JW
UK
Tel.: +44 1865 517 530
Email: mail@hartpub.co.uk

Distribution for the USA and Canada:
International Specialized Book Services
920 NE 58th Ave. Suite 300
Portland, OR 97213
USA
Tel.: +1 800 944 6190 (toll free)
Email: info@isbs.com

Distribution for Austria:
Neuer Wissenschaftlicher Verlag
Argentinierstraße 42/6
1040 Wien
Austria
Tel.: +43 1 535 61 03 24
Email: office@nwv.at

Distribution for other countries:
Intersentia Publishing nv
Groenstraat 31
2640 Mortsel
Belgium
Tel.: +32 3 680 15 50
Email: mail@intersentia.be

African Perspectives on Tradition and Justice
Tom Bennett, Eva Brems, Giselle Corradi, Lia Nijzink and Martien Schotsmans (eds.)

Cover photo: *People gossip and smoke waiting for the sun to come out, Chencha Village, Southern Ethiopia* (© Marcin Bartosz Czarnoleski/Dreamstime.com)

ISBN 978-1-78068-059-0
NUR 828

British Library Cataloguing in Publication Data. A catalogue record for this book is available from the British Library.

ACKNOWLEDGEMENTS

This publication was completed in the framework of the research project 'Addressing Traditional Law in Post-Conflict Legal and Judicial Development Aid in sub-Saharan Africa', with the financial support of the Belgian Ministry of Science Policy within its programme 'Society and Future' 2007 [TA/00/17 AFTRALAW]. The editors wish to express their gratitude to the programme administrators, Mrs. Margarida Freire, and her predecessor, Mrs. Zakia Khattabi, for their enthusiastic support to the project. They also wish to thank Dr. Marleen Renders for her role in designing the research project and the members of the Scientific Support Committee for their valuable inputs and critical comments as the project moved on: Mrs. Lara Deramaix, Prof. Marie-Claire Foblets, Mr. Renaud Galand, Prof. Em. Luc Huyse, Mr. Robert Olbrechts, Prof. Barbara Oomen, Mr. Dick Oosting, Prof. Stephan Parmentier, Prof. Filip Reyntjens, Mrs. Heidy Rombouts, Dr. Stef Vandeginste, Mr. Marc Van Wymeersch and Mr. Pierre Vincke. The authors of the chapters especially deserve our thanks for accepting our invitation to contribute to the volume and for addressing our comments and adjusting their chapters accordingly. Finally, our thanks are due to the University of Cape Town for the organization of the international forum 'Traditional Justice and the Role of External Actors in sub-Saharan Africa' in March 2010, which planted the seeds out of which this publication grew.

CONTENTS

ABOUT THE AUTHORS AND EDITORS

Joe A.D. Alie is an associate professor of history, head of the Department of History & African Studies and former dean of the Faculty of Arts, Fourah Bay College, University of Sierra Leone. He holds BA and MA degrees in history from the University of Sierra Leone, and a PhD in African History and Certificate in African Studies from the University of Wisconsin at Madison, USA. Dr. Alie is a leading textbook writer on the history of Sierra Leone.

Tom Bennett holds a BA LLB (Rhodes) and a PhD (UCT). He is a Professor in the Department of Public Law, a Fellow of the of the University of Cape Town and the recipient of the Alexander von Humboldt Fellowship. As a member of the special project Committee on Customary Law of the South African Law Reform Commission, he was actively engaged in the Report on Customary Marriages (1997), Report on Application of Customary Law (1997), Discussion Paper on Reform of the Customary Law of Succession (2000). His other major publications include: The Application of Customary Law in Southern Africa: the conflict of personal laws (1985), A Sourcebook of African Customary Law for Southern Africa (1991), Human Rights and Customary Law under the South African Constitution (1995) and Customary Law in South Africa (2004).

Eva Brems studied law at the universities of Namur (candidat 1989), Leuven (licentiaat 1992, PhD 1999) and Harvard (LLM 1995). Before joining Ghent University as a professor of Human Rights law, she was a researcher at the University of Leuven (1992–1994 and 1995–1999) and a lecturer at the University of Maastricht (1999–2000). Her research interests include most areas of human rights law (Belgian law, European law, international law, comparative law), with special emphases on women's rights, children's rights and cultural diversity. Since July 2010, she is also a member of the Belgian Parliament.

Giselle Corradi is a PhD candidate at the Human Rights Centre, Ghent University Law School. Her doctoral research focuses on the role of legal development actors at grassroots level regarding the relationship between human rights and customary justice in sub-Saharan Africa, with case studies in Sierra Leone and Mozambique. She holds a Bachelor in Law from the University of Buenos Aires and a Masters in Comparative Studies of Culture from Ghent University. Before joining the Human Rights Centre as a researcher, she worked as a consultant in fair trade projects in Guatemala and Peru for the Durabilis Foundation.

Daniel Komakech holds a MA Philosophy and a BA in Political Science and Philosophy, both from Makerere University, Uganda and is a PhD Candidate in Philosophy, Makerere University. He is a lecturer in African political philosophy at Gulu University in Uganda and acting Director of the Institute of Peace and Strategic Studies at the same university.

Kenan Tilombe Manda is a Judge of the High Court of the Republic of Malawi. He holds an LLB (Hons) from the University of Malawi and an LLM from the University of Warwick (UK).

Maria Paula G. Meneses, a Mozambican scholar, is currently a senior researcher at the Centre for Social Studies, University of Coimbra, integrating the Research Group on Democracy, Citizenship and Law. She holds a PhD in Anthropology by Rutgers University (USA) and a MA in History from St. Petersburg University (Russia). She has carried out research on legal pluralism in Mozambique and Angola. Her current research focuses on the struggles over citizenship in Mozambique in the 1970s, with the transition to independence.

Alphonse Muleefu is a PhD researcher at Intervict, Tilburg University. He holds a Law Degree (LLB) from the National University of Rwanda and a LLM in International and European Public Law from Tilburg University, The Netherlands. He has participated in short courses on Transitional Justice, International Criminal law and International Criminal Investigations. He worked as a research student and legal researcher at the International Criminal Tribunal for Rwanda and as a legal intern at the International Criminal Court (ICC). In Rwanda he worked as a legal officer in the National Service of Gacaca Courts and is a Founder of Together Against Impunity in the Great Lakes Region (TAI/GLR).

Felix Mukwiza Ndahinda is an Assistant Professor at the International Victimology Institute Tilburg (Tilburg University – The Netherlands). He holds a law degree from the National University of Rwanda (2003); an LLM from the Raoul Wallenberg Institute of Human Rights (Sweden, 2006) and a PhD from Tilburg Law School (2009). In 2001, he worked as a trainer for the elected *gacaca* judges. He also worked for the Office of the Auditor General for State Finances in Rwanda (2004), as an intern (2003) and a legal officer (2009) at the International Criminal Tribunal for Rwanda in Arusha, Tanzania and has been a visiting lecturer at the Kigali Independent University/Université Libre de Kigali (ULK) in 2005 and at the Independent Institute of Lay Adventists of Kigali (INILAK) in 2009, teaching Rwandan Criminal Law.

Lia Nijzink is a Senior Researcher with the Law, Race and Gender Research Unit, University of Cape Town. Previously, she held the same position with UCT's Department of Public Law, where she conducted research on the role of traditional justice in international justice sector aid in Africa and coordinated a research partnership with the universities of Dar es Salaam (Tanzania) and Warwick (UK). Nijzink holds an LLM from the University of Maastricht (NL) and an MA in Political Science from the University of Amsterdam (NL), has lectured in UCT's Department of Political Studies and has worked as a researcher for various South African and African organisations. Nijzink is the co-editor of Electoral Politics in South Africa (Palgrave/Macmillan 2005), Accountable Government in Africa (UCT Press 2012), Trajectories of One-Party Dominance in African Democracies (Lynne Rienner Publishers 2012) and Political Parties, Party systems and Democracy in Africa (Palgrave/Macmillan, forthcoming).

Martien Schotsmans is a PhD candidate at the Human Rights Centre of Ghent University on globalisation and localisation in transitional justice, with a focus on tradition-based justice. She holds a Master in Law and in Criminology from the KU Leuven University. After having practiced as a lawyer in Belgium, she worked in Rwanda, Chad and Sierra Leone and with Avocats Sans Frontières, among others. Since April 2008, she is a researcher at the Ghent University, looking into the role of international actors regarding the use of tradition in the framework of transitional justice in post-conflict Africa.

CHAPTER I
INTRODUCTION

Giselle Corradi and Martien Schotsmans

1. BACKGROUND TO THE VOLUME

This volume presents contributions of six African authors, who offer various perspectives on the relationship between tradition and justice on the continent. The publication originates in a research project conducted by the Human Rights Centre of Ghent University in Belgium (UG) in partnership with the University of Cape Town in South Africa (UCT). The research project on "Addressing Traditional Law in Post-Conflict Judicial and Legal Development Aid in sub-Saharan Africa" (AFTRALAW) was funded by the Belgian Science Policy Office (BELSPO), and carried out under the supervision of Professor Eva Brems (UG) and Professors Thomas Bennett and Christina Murray (UCT). The results of this three-year policy-supportive research project are published in Brems, Corradi, Nijzink, Schotsmans (eds.), *On Tradition and Justice: the Role of International Actors in Africa*, also with Intersentia Press. The project focused on the role of donor states as well as multinational, governmental and non-governmental organisations regarding the role of traditional justice in sub-Saharan Africa in the framework of both transitional justice and justice sector aid. In both fields of intervention, these actors are confronted with the fact that traditional or customary justice plays a prominent role in the normative life of major segments of the population on the African continent. The research comprised six case studies in Sierra Leone, Mozambique, Zambia, Malawi, Rwanda and Uganda.

In the context of this research project, an international forum was held in Cape Town in March 2010, during which a series of focus group discussions were held on the preliminary findings of the research, with representatives of donors, governments and civil societies from the countries in which case studies were conducted. The forum also included presentations by academics of the same countries on the role of tradition and traditional justice in their societies. The current volume originates from the discussions and reflections at that forum and its aftermath.

Reflecting the double focus of the research project and of the international forum (justice sector aid and transitional justice), the first part of the book focuses on tradition in the framework of the democratic state, whereas the second part examines the role of traditional practices and values in transitional justice processes. Human rights surface throughout these contributions as an issue that still sparks debate. Before providing an overview of the chapters, we will situate these themes in a broader historical context and highlight important current approaches.

2. HISTORICAL CONTEXT AND CURRENT APPROACHES

2.1. TRADITIONAL JUSTICE AND DEVELOPMENT IN AFRICA

As recent conferences, publications, the contributions to this volume and the various discussions held during the international forum in Cape Town underscore, we currently witness the emergence of a new international position towards the role of traditional justice in the African legal landscape.[1] This development is progressively being brought about by the – often collaborative – work of scholars and practitioners from the Global South and North reflecting on issues such as access to justice, human rights, the rule of law, state building and legal pluralism in Africa and beyond.

Amongst the main ideas included in this new approach we find a critical examination of the 'tradition vs. modernity' dichotomy. The latter is unpacked, showing that tradition cannot be understood as the remnant of an archaic past, but needs to be conceptualized as part of the dialectic power dynamics that constituted traditional and modern institutions during the colonial and post-colonial periods (Meneses n/d). This perspective highlights the relevance of focusing on mutually constitutive official and unofficial interactions between actors from traditional and modern legal institutions and the dynamics of legal pluralism that shape the African legal landscape as a whole.

---

1 See for example the conferences 'Access to Justice and Security – Non-State Actors and the Local Dynamics of Ordering' Copenhagen, Denmark, 1–3 November, 2010 and 'Customary Justice and Legal Pluralism in Post Conflict and Fragile Societies', Washington D.C., 17–18 November 2009 and Isser (2011); IDLO (2011); Toomey (2010); ICHRP (2009); Wojkowska (2006) and Stevens (2000) amongst others. It is not so much the ideas about traditional justice that are new, but their inclusion in discussions about access to justice, state building and transitional justice.

This exercise goes hand in hand with the need to scrutinize whose interests legal institutions serve, regardless of their traditional or modern character (Kyed 2009; ICHRP 2009). Departing from the premise that law and power are closely linked, it is crucial to understand the perspectives and experiences of justice seekers who resort to and combine a variety of legal orders as 'resources' in their search for justice. These strategies are strongly linked to the availability, costs, and cultural relevance of legal institutions. Consequently, a renewed emphasis is placed on the role of traditional dispute resolution in improving access to justice (Stevens 2000; Wojkowska 2006). In other words, there is a renewed interest in building on the forms of justice that are locally available and improving their downward accountability, rather than replacing them (Nyamu-Musembi, 2002).

These emerging positions allow for a broader conceptualization of justice that goes beyond positive law. On the one hand, they facilitate a re-assessment of the role of different justice paradigms in the African context. As a result, the complementary potential between retributive and restorative justice frameworks is explored (Toomey 2010; Wojkowska 2006). On the other hand, they lead to the recognition that legal pluralism is an empirical reality that, for good or for bad, is part and parcel of the African legal landscape and needs to be addressed rather than repressed. Amongst the complex issues that are studied in this context we find different processes of 'inter-legality' or 'hybridization', where elements from different legal frameworks are combined in order to respond to people's needs (Santos 2002; Meneses n/d).

At another level, the tension between traditional forms of dispute resolution and human rights begins to be seen as a broad societal issue that is not so much related to the backwardness or progressiveness of a specific system of justice, but is rather embedded in the general values of a society influencing the actions of legal actors (Chopra and Isser 2010). In this context, it is increasingly acknowledged that sustainable changes cannot be attained overnight but need time and a long term commitment. Moreover, these changes cannot be generated from the outside but need to be grounded in a demand 'from within', which requires dialogical approaches (Weilenman 2007).

Though most of the perspectives that start to take root within these waves of thought are not necessarily new, what is innovative is their combination and incorporation in the thinking and practical work of actors active in the field of law and development. As the authors in this volume underline, the current shift in perceptions on the role of tradition in the development of the African legal landscape has the potential to reverse a history of 'subalternization' of African experiences, identities and epistemologies.

A brief revision of the evolution of the thinking on law and development since its inception in the sixties shows that the value given to local forms of knowledge and their manifestation in local forms of law is closely linked to the way development is understood and defined. The Law and Development movement, which started after the second wave of decolonization, was inspired by modernization theory. According to this movement, development was an inevitable evolutionary process, and, in order to accelerate this process, developing countries adopted specialized Western institutions (Tamanaha 1995). It was this movement that introduced the relationship between law and development for the first time: development, understood in terms of state-led economic growth, would result from the modernization of institutions, which would guarantee the legal uniformity and predictability necessary for the development of internal markets (Trubek 2003). Legal development aid during this period consisted mainly of educational programs for legal scholars and professionals, based on legal transplants of Western concepts and rules (ibid). In this context, traditional law was considered backward and was seen as an obstacle to development.

The emergence of Dependency Theory, during the mid 1970s, marked the beginning of a new paradigm. This Marxist theory postulated that underdevelopment was not caused by internal shortcomings, but by external domination and exploitation. According to this theory it is the structure of the global capitalist system, where the developing world forms a 'periphery' producing goods for export to the Western 'core', that forms the source of underdevelopment. The rejection of the modern paradigm by these scholars went hand in hand with the idea of protecting local cultures from the invasion of Western values and the preservation of customs and 'folk law'. However, this was framed in a top down protectionist approach to culture that did not necessarily value cultural diversity or legal pluralism (Hoekema 2007).

By the beginning of the 1990s, with the end of the cold war, the expansion of multinationals and the dismantling of one party authoritarian regimes, the context of development aid had changed again. The economic panorama in the developing world was then characterized by inflation, huge foreign debts, rent seeking authorities and poor productivity. In this scenario, the state-led growth formula was replaced by a neo-liberal market-led one, embodied by the Washington Consensus and the Structural Adjustment Programs imposed on developing countries by the International Financial Institutions as a condition for obtaining loans. According to this paradigm, it was an open global economy guaranteed by a minimal state that would bring about economic growth and development.

This led to a revival of the Law and Development ideas. Western style law was again considered necessary for guaranteeing the efficiency of market exchange, promoting foreign investment and maintaining the necessary macro-economic stability. Authoritarian regimes had to clear the way for the introduction of good governance and the rule of law. During this neo-liberal period, legal interventions not only focused on legal education and professional development, but they also included judicial administration reform and training, substantive commercial law reform, alternative dispute resolution training, and procedural reform of public administration (Newton 2004). Traditional institutions were not totally rejected, as decentralization and participation were part of the good governance package. This led to consultations with local communities, though local interests were not necessarily given priority.[2]

As from the end of the 1990s, critiques started to arise about the lack of distributive effects and positive spill overs of the neo-liberal development paradigm. Hence, the current 'Post Washington consensus' paradigm is no longer about pure economic growth: attention shifted to poverty reduction. Ownership and participation are seen as conditions for sustainability, which eventually led to the adoption of the Paris Declaration in 2005 and the Accra Agenda for Action in 2008. The state is given back a role in facilitating development since social problems cannot be left to the private sector alone. Legal development aid is no longer exclusively concerned with guaranteeing legal security and private property for international investors, but also with more immediate local needs, such as improving access to justice as a means to fight poverty (Piron 2005). This trend is leading development actors to pay more attention to grassroots realities so that a series of issues that might have been overlooked in the past are progressively receiving more attention.

The contributions in the first part of this volume do not directly discuss justice sector aid and the approaches discussed above but all three chapters present case studies of the themes and issues that arise in the context of efforts by international or state actors to reconsider the place of traditional justice in the legal landscape of Africa.

2.2. THE LOCALISATION OF TRANSITIONAL JUSTICE

In the field of transitional justice too attention grew for grassroots realities, local ownership and hence for traditional values of justice and reconciliation. The end

2 See for example the cases of the indigenous population Cree in James Bay, Canada (Scott 2002) and the Q'eqchi of Izabal, Guatemala (Representation (article 24) – Guatemala – C169 – 2007).

of several armed conflicts and authoritarian regimes in Africa since 1990 has brought post-conflict reconstruction and long term peacebuilding strategies to the international agenda. Considering the high risk of conflict recurrence within five years after the end of a conflict (Collier and Hoeffler 2004), attention grew for peacebuilding as a separate transitional policy in between emergency and development in post-conflict countries to consolidate sustainable peace (initiated in Boutros Boutros-Ghali's Agenda for Peace, UN 1992, and further developed in the Brahimi Report, UN 2000). This created awareness of the need to address the root causes of conflict, hence the importance of democracy, good governance, the rule of law, the fight against corruption and finally the need to deal with legacies of abuses committed in the past by previous regimes or during an armed conflict, i.e. transitional justice (Chetail 2009; also: OECD-DAC Guidelines on Peace, Conflict and Development Cooperation 1997).

Transitional Justice as a concept first appeared in the early 1990s. Obviously, mechanisms which are today labelled as transitional justice mechanisms, were already practised before. The Nuremberg and Tokyo trials after World War II, the truth and/or enquiry commissions established in several Latin American countries in the eighties and the South-African Truth and Reconciliation Commission established in 1995 are all transitional justice mechanisms. But it is only over the last twenty five years that transitional justice has emerged as a specific field of multidisciplinary study and practice (Kritz 2002).

Simultaneously with the evolution in law and development aid and the growing attention for ownership, participation and sustainable solutions, peace building in general and transitional justice thinking in particular shifted from one-size-fits-all formulas in the eighties and nineties towards recognition of the importance of local solutions adjusted to the specific context of the post-conflict country around the millennium. Initially, transitional justice was considered a kind of toolbox, with criminal prosecutions, truth finding mechanisms, reconciliation activities and reparation programmes as the main tools, from which countries in the aftermath of conflict, assisted by the international community, could chose. The emerging obligation to prosecute and the prohibition of amnesty for international crimes (Orentlicher 2007; also United Nations 2005) were reflected in the establishment of the International Criminal Tribunal for the former Yugoslavia, the International Criminal Tribunal for Rwanda, the adoption of the Rome Statute in 1998 and the establishment of the International Criminal Court (ICC) in 2002.

Around 2000, the need for context-specific solutions and local ownership started to be acknowledged, both by actors on the ground – who draw attention to the negative perception of the ad hoc tribunals (Stromzeth 2009; Arzt 2006) – and by international bodies. As Kofi Annan acknowledged in 2004: "*Too often, the emphasis has been on foreign experts, foreign models and foreign-conceived solutions to the detriment of durable improvements and sustainable capacity.*" He recommended that: "*We must learn as well to eschew one-size-fits-all formulas and the importation of foreign models, and, instead, base our support on national assessments, national participation and national needs and aspirations.*" (UN 2004). Initially, this evolution maintained the above mentioned tools, but adjusted them to the context or tried to identify an appropriate combination with due consideration to the local situation. An example of this are the hybrid, mixed mechanisms, such as the Special Court and the Truth and Reconciliation Commission established in Sierra Leone in 2000, of mixed international-national composition and combining aspects of international models and rules, national legislation and local processes. This evolution in transitional justice approaches went parallel with the shift in the concept of ownership, as reflected in the above mentioned Paris Declaration on Aid Effectiveness (2005) and later by the UN Peace Building Commission (Peace Building Commission 2010).

In transitional justice local ownership was initially understood as state or country ownership, which is one of the reasons why the *gacaca* jurisdictions proposed by the Rwandan government as an alternative to trials by domestic formal courts were welcomed by the international donor community. With the Accra Agenda for Action (2008), country ownership gradually expanded to national ownership and the involvement of non-state actors as stakeholders in the peacebuilding process. This was not an obvious development since peacebuilding strategies initially focused on statebuilding, and the fear was that working with local structures would undermine this process (Chopra 2009). Non-state actors – civil society organisations, religious and traditional leaders – became important participants in both peace processes and transitional justice mechanisms (OECD-DAC, The DAC Guidelines. Helping Prevent Violent Conflict, 2001). This evolved towards recognition of the importance of local consultations (UN Guidance note of the Secretary-General, March 2010) and even of population surveys on transitional justice. The need for the localisation of transitional justice or, in other words, the fact that top-down planning has been replaced by a process in which the national governments and civil society stakeholders are included and local needs and the specific country context are considered (Roht-Arriaza and Mariezcurrena 2006; Gready 2005; Kritz 2002), has opened the door to traditional and other local views on justice and reconciliation. (Huyse and Salter 2008). In his 2004 report Kofi Annan acknowledged "*that traditional dispute resolution mechanisms are equally relevant*" (UN 2004).

Thus, transitional justice is no longer a mere choice among existing models, but a joint journey of international, national and local stakeholders to find or create the most appropriate mechanisms to deal with the past. Complementarity has become a key concept: each mechanism (criminal prosecutions, truth and/or reconciliation instances, tradition-based practices, etc.) can play its own particular role and complement the other, which poses particular challenges regarding balancing and sequencing (Lutz 2006).

Since more attention and time are given to the process to decide on the transitional justice policy for each specific country and the voice of each of the stakeholders needs to be considered, clashes between their views are to be expected. As in the area of law and development, also in the transitional justice field, the growing attention for the grassroots reality reveals the tensions between traditional practices and human rights. Tradition-based practices raise particular questions regarding the rights of women and other vulnerable groups, the rights of individual victims (Lutz 2006) and the respect of fair trial standards, as Bennett's contribution shows. More particularly, tensions rise when traditional justice and reconciliation methods are mixed with aspects of formal criminal justice, as in the Rwandan *gacaca* jurisdictions (cf. Ndahinda and Muleefu's contribution). Presenting tradition-based practices as alternatives for criminal prosecution by formal courts will lead to even harsher discussion, as Komakech illustrates with regards to the Acholi culture in Northern Uganda and the ICC.

Such clashes between different normative orders (or overlapping semi-autonomous social fields – Moore, 1973) are an obvious aspect of the dialectal processes that occur in situations of legal pluralism. These occur not only between formal law and traditional practices within one country (as is mainly the case in the field of law and development), but also – increasingly – between standards of international human rights and criminal law and national or local mechanisms, i.e. global legal pluralism (Berman 2007). The contributions in this book illustrate the perspective on this dialectal process from those operating on the ground, i.e. authors who contest the dominance of the international normative order over the local order. Other authors have elsewhere presented the opposite perspective by defending the universal character of international criminal justice standards over the 'invented' character of traditional justice (e.g. Waldorf 2006; Allen 2006).

Obviously, the contributions in this volume do not provide the final outcome of the debate. Rather, they are part of it. While each normative order has equal value in itself, and the international, national and local levels are all to be considered as equal stakeholders in the debate on how to deal with international crimes, giving a voice to African authors on these topics will add their views to the discussion. Such exchanges and debates are part of the dialectal process, which is an unavoidable phase in the evolution towards new, hybrid, legal spaces (Clark 2010) that will need to be created on an ad hoc basis for each specific post conflict country as part of a new inclusive transitional justice paradigm (Brems and Viaene 2010).

3. THE CONTRIBUTIONS

The present volume appears at a time when several scholars and practitioners are engaged in producing better understandings of the role of local realities within both law and development and transitional justice in Africa. The volume provides a series of African perspectives on a varied range of issues on tradition and justice. Though the contributions are not directed towards development or transitional justice actors in particular, they provide a rich and critical background that will hopefully inspire future efforts in the field.

The papers are presented in six chapters. The first set of three papers addresses the role of traditional institutions in the future development of legal and political landscapes of sub-Saharan Africa. The second set of contributions deals with the relationship between tradition and justice from the point of view of transitional justice processes. Though the difference in focus is clear, the issues emerging from these analyses cut across these two topics and reveal a series of common themes that are explored at the end of this chapter. Before turning to the latter, an overview of each chapter is presented.

Chapter II, *Access to justice and human rights in the traditional courts of sub-Saharan Africa* by Tom Bennett, considers how different elements of the right to a fair trial relate to African traditional institutions of dispute resolution. Bennett identifies five aspects of this right, i.e. due process, equal treatment, a series of specific rights applicable to criminal proceedings, access to justice and the right to demand that the state respects the litigant's culture. He then examines the applicability of each of them within traditional jurisdictions. He shows that only certain aspects of this right are relevant to traditional courts. According to his analysis, the rights applicable to criminal proceedings and the guarantee of an independent and impartial judge, i.e. an aspect of the 'due process of law', are hardly ever in issue in traditional tribunals. In order to explain this, some essential aspects of 'the traditional African style of justice' are sketched out, such as the reparation of relationships, the voluntary process of persuasion, the participation by the community and the aim to restore peace and harmony. As long as punitive outcomes and the use of force are not involved in these proceedings, certain fair trial guarantees are deemed redundant. Despite the fact that traditional courts may disregard 'equality of arms' requirements with respect to women, children and strangers, Bennett concludes that such non-compliance needs to be balanced against other aspects of the right to a fair trial that traditional courts do protect, such as access to justice and the right to respect a group's unique cultural institutions.

Chapter III, *Courts and the application of customary law in Malawi: Towards the reintroduction of local courts* by Kenan Tilombe Manda, takes us to the complex challenges that arise when formal courts apply customary law. After sketching the background leading to the abolition of traditional courts in Malawi, Manda explains how magistrate courts deal with the administration of customary law at present. This allows him to reflect on a series of difficulties, such as magistrates' lack of training on customary law, their positivist bias, and the development of 'hybrid' jurisprudence. According to Manda, most of the difficulties result from a distortion of customs and customary practices, which cannot be approached from a modern concept of law but need to be understood from the epistemological foundation of traditional justice. Against this backdrop, Manda discusses the proposals of the Malawi Law Commission to reintroduce a system of local courts specifically dedicated to customary law cases. He concludes that despite such legal reforms being potentially 'a step towards the development of customary law jurisprudence' they could nevertheless 'prove a failure if customary law is not given a space for dialogue'.

Chapter IV, *Powers, rights and citizenship: The 'return' of the traditional authorities in Mozambique* by Maria Paula Meneses, offers a critical discussion of the role of traditional authority within the African state. Based on a revision of the socio-historical construction of the modern vs. traditional dichotomy in Mozambique, Meneses shows 'the ambiguities and complexities associated with the notion of tradition' and argues that 'the historical context of its introduction remains central to understanding contemporary social dynamics and policy'. Accordingly, current debates on the future participation of traditional institutions in local politics cannot be read as 'a return to the local' for they are in fact 'discourses about global access'. Through careful historical analysis, Meneses' contribution highlights the different processes of subalternization that local practices and forms of knowledge underwent during the colonial and post-colonial periods. This leads her to the conclusion that current dynamics towards the recognition of traditional authority and their role in local conflict resolution imply the inclusion of 'other epistemic references beyond that of the techno-bureaucratic operation of the state' and 'the denial of a single model of citizenship'.

Chapter V, *Traditional justice and human rights in post-war African countries: Prospects and challenges,* by Joe A.D. Alie, examines the nature and relevance of African traditional justice systems, especially in post-war countries such as Sierra Leone. It highlights the philosophical differences between formal (Western-type) and traditional justice systems and argues that the latter adopt a more holistic approach to justice because traditional justice is multi-dimensional. The author highlights both the social goals and the limitations of traditional justice, especially in dealing with international crimes. Among others he suggests to 'reconsider its reliance on the supernatural and the use of harsh methods to extract the truth'. In his opinion traditional justice can play a more beneficial role in rebuilding fractured communities in Africa, if exposed to basic human rights principles. Since the formal system has its shortcomings as well, he proposes a mix of formal institutions to deal with crimes against humanity and grave human rights abuses, while local practices can complement this by dealing with less severe cases among community residents.

Chapter VI, *Reinventing and validating the cosmology and ontology of restorative justice: Hermeneutics of the traditional Acholi justice system in Northern Uganda*, by Daniel Komakech, interrogates the dominant authority of the modernist retributive justice epistemology and wants to acknowledge and integrate restorative justice aspects as well – as applied in the traditional justice concept of the Acholi cosmology and ontology in Northern Uganda. The author sees this not as a competing frame, but as part of the field building of transitional justice. He urges the International Criminal Court to reconsider its view on the Acholi traditional justice system and to appreciate it not only as a practice of social redress, but also as 'a means for bestowing upon society the dignity and security of living, and the connection of generations'. Komakech encourages a pluralist perspective on justice to which an open-ended, cooperative dialogue is necessary.

Finally, Chapter VII, *Revisiting the legal and socio-political foundations and (Western) criticism of gacaca courts*, by Felix Mukwiza Ndahinda and Alphonse Muleefu, revisits the reasons behind the establishment of the gacaca courts, their historical, legal, socio-political and cultural legitimacy and the various criticisms of this unique mechanism. It argues that while some of the gacaca criticisms are legitimate, others are a result of misconceptions about, or ideological rejection of, a mechanism perceived as contravening the established foundations of the globalised criminal justice mechanisms of Western inception. The authors argue that in spite of some evident shortcomings of the 'essentially experimental' mechanism, the tendency in some studies to generalize their conclusions based on limited findings from specific geographies or the hasty predictions about the legacy of a mechanism still in motion are more a result of subjective than objective evaluations of the process, while failing to prescribe viable and acceptable alternatives.

4. COMMON THEMES

The chapters in this book show a common concern with understanding traditional forms of justice from within their own paradigm. The authors share the view that this entails an appreciation of African epistemologies and their manifestation in the law, and they illustrate how instead of being neutral and universal, law and justice are contested concepts that are rooted in particular contexts, experiences and forms of knowledge.

One of the positions arising from this perspective is that different justice paradigms may serve different needs. Komakech, analysing ontological pluralism in Uganda, draws an explicit relationship between the appropriateness of the intervention of the International Criminal Court and local cosmologies. He suggests that retributive forms of justice may not be the only or most adequate answer for war affected Acholi communities, who place great value on reconciliation and harmony. In a similar vein, Manda, reflecting on the application of customary law by magistrate courts in Malawi, emphasises the need to question the perspective from which judges approach law and justice. According to him, this is often done in a positivist way leading to misconceptions about local customs and a failure to address the local justice needs of most Malawians. Finally, Meneses raises a critical note on the extent to which most Mozambicans identify with official justice, indicating that what is at stake is the right to culture as a space for self-determination.

Other contributions devote considerable attention to a comparison between formal, so-called 'Western', and tradition-based forms of justice coexisting in Africa and show that analysis needs to be carried out at the level of the foundations of any justice paradigm. Bennett departs from a comparison of the logic and objectives of formal and traditional justice in order to develop his argument on the applicability of fair trial guarantees within traditional courts. In his view, endogenous legal cultures of Africa are inclined to restore relationships rather than punish and use force, rendering certain aspects of the right to a fair trial inapplicable or irrelevant. Alie, in his discussion on the prospects and challenges of traditional justice in post-war African countries, clearly disagrees with this non-violent image of traditional justice, but suggests that Western and traditional forms of justice rely on different methods of accountability, truth seeking and conflict resolution, which are all valuable and need to be combined in a complementary fashion. Ndahinda and Muleefu, dealing with the assessment of the gacaca courts in Rwanda, warn us about the ideological rejection of tradition-based justice mechanisms on the sole basis that they may contravene the foundations of globalized criminal justice. They point out that the fairness of such mechanisms needs to be examined according to their own principles and values.

Though the contributions differ in the amount of attention that they dedicate to the definition of tradition, it is clear that all authors avoid a reified understanding of the term but at the same time acknowledge that endogenous approaches to justice remain most relevant to the African continent. The chapter by Meneses pays particular attention to this point, which is central to her argument. By means of a nuanced account of the historical development of traditional institutions in Mozambique, she makes clear that tradition and modernity are mutually constitutive, and yet tradition is not 'a mere byproduct of colonial intervention' since it was 'continuously (re) interpreted, (re) formulated and (re) built'. Bennett points out that despite traditions being greatly distorted and eroded by the colonial encounter, the social and political structures that supported them did not disappear.

It is against this backdrop that we can read Alie's, Komakech's, and Ndahinda and Muleefu's call for greater recognition of the role of tradition within transitional justice processes. Their argument is not that an idealized, out of time version of tradition will contribute to peace building, but that efforts need to be grounded on the experiences and sensibilities of local communities. Likewise, Manda's plea for the inclusion in university curricula of the epistemology of customary law underlies the view that traditional justice cannot be seen as part of the past, but is very much alive and will continue to play an important role in the future.

Another thread running through all contributions to this volume underscores the power that inhabits knowledge. A discussion of past and present developments in the African legal landscape allows some of the authors to question the way hegemonic positive law contributes to the subalternization of traditional justice and institutions. Komakech interrogates the dominant authority of the modernist retributive justice epistemology by showing the capacity of local Acholi resources to establish justice and peace. His account calls for the building of a discipline that allows for 'pluralism in the generation of knowledge'. Manda's critical assessment of the current role of customary law in the legal system of Malawi stems as well from a concern with the suppression of other forms of knowledge about social regulation. Bennett reminds us that it is 'European powers' introduction of a notionally superior brand of justice to their African colonies that has had the effect of concentrating funds and resources in a system of courts that lies beyond the reach of ordinary people'.

Clearly, such remarks are closely related to current international discourses on access to justice and human rights in Africa and the role of customary institutions therein, as well as to the call for the localisation of transitional justice. These concerns are not only shared by the authors of this volume, but their contributions also seem to suggest that access to justice and appropriate, context-specific transitional justice strategies entail a right to diversity and legal pluralism. In this sense, they all stress that dialogical approaches are the way forward. Whether it is in the context of legal reforms, transitional processes in post-war societies or the promotion of human rights in general, the authors all accentuate that it is by means of cooperation, conversation and cross-fertilization between different legal realities that positive achievements can be realized.

BIBLIOGRAPHY

Allen, T. (2006)
Trial Justice. The International Criminal Court and the Lord's Resistance Army, London/New York: Zed Books.

Arzt, D.E. (2006)
Views on the Ground: The Local Perception of International Criminal Tribunals in the Former Yugoslavia and Sierra Leone, *The Annals of the American Academy of Political and Social Science*, 603: 226–239.

Barnett, M., Kim, H., O'Donnell, M. and Sitea, L. (2007)
Peacebuilding: What is in a Name?, *Global Governance*, 13: 35–58.

Berman, P.S. (2007)
Global Legal Pluralism, *Southern California Law Review*, Vol. 80: 1155–1237.

Brems, E. and Viaene, L. (2010)
Transitional Justice and Cultural Contexts: Learning from the Universality Debate, *Netherlands Quarterly of Human Rights*, 28 (2): 199–224.

Chetail, V. (ed.) (2009)
Post-conflict peacebuilding. A lexicon, Oxford: Oxford University Press.

Chopra, T. (2009)
When Peacebuilding Contradicts Statebuilding: Notes from the Arid Lands of Kenya, *International Peacekeeping*, 16:4, 531–545.

Chopra, T. and Isser, D. (2010)
From 'fixing' systems to supporting processes of change: rethinking women's access to justice in fragile states', paper presented at the International Conference on Access to Justice and Security, Non-State Actors and the Local Dynamics of Ordering, November 1–3, 2010, Copenhagen.

Clark, P. (2010)
The Gacaca courts, Post-Genocide Justice and Reconciliation in Rwanda. Justice without Lawyers. Cambridge: Cambridge University Press.

Collier, P. and Hoeffler, A. (2004)
Greed and grievance in civil war, Oxford University Press, *Oxford economic papers* 56: 563–595.

Davidheiser, M. (2007)
Governance and legal reform in the Gambia and beyond: an anthropological critique of current development strategies, Max Planck Institute for Social Anthropology, Working Paper 93.

De Sousa Santos, B. (2002)
Towards a New Legal Common Sense, London: Butterworths Lexis Nexis.

Gready, P. (2005)
Analysis: Reconceptualising Transitional Justice, Embedded and distanced justice, *Conflict, Security and Development*, Vol. 5 (1): 3–21.

Hoekema, A. (2007)
Some reflections on modernity and law today, or: the fall and rise of legal pluralism, *Texts on Legal Pluralism and Development*, Amsterdam: Universiteit Amsterdam.
Huyse, L. and Salter, M. (eds.) (2008)
Traditional Justice after Violent Conflict. Learning from African experiences, Stockholm: International IDEA.
ICHRP – International Council on Human Rights Policy (2009)
When legal worlds overlap. Human rights, state and non-State law, accessible at www.ichrp.org/files/reports/50/135_report_en.pdf, retrieved on 2 September 2010.
Isser, D. (ed.) (2011)
Customary Justice and the Rule of Law in War Torn Societies, Washington, DC, United States: Institute of Peace Press.
Kritz, N. (2002)
Where We Are and How We Got Here: An Overview of Developments in the Search for Justice and Reconciliation, in: Henkin, A.H. (ed.), *The Legacy of Abuse: Confronting the Past, Facing the Future*, New York: Aspen Institute, New York University School of Law, 21–45.
Kyed, H. (2009)
The politics of legal pluralism: state policies on legal pluralism and their local dynamics in Mozambique, *Journal of Legal Pluralism and Unofficial Law*, 59: 87–121.
Lutz, E. (2006)
Transitional justice: lessons learned and the road ahead, *Transitional Justice in the Twenty-First Century. Beyond truth versus justice*, United Kingdom: Cambridge University Press 325–341.
Meneses, M.P. (n.d.)
Toward interlegality? Traditional healers and the law in postcolonial Mozambique. Accessible at www.ces.uc.pt/publicacoes/oficina/202/202.pdf, retrieved on 2 September 2010.
Moore, S. (1973)
Law and Social Change: The Semi-Autonomous Social Field as an Appropriate Subject of Study, *Law & Society Review*, 7: 719–746.
Newton, S. (2004)
Law and development, law and economics and the fate of legal technical assistance, Fourth Aladin Annual Conference 'Perspectives on Law and Development', Leiden, Van Vollenhoven Institute for Law, Governance and Development. Research Report 04/02.
Nyamu-Musembi, C. (2003)
Review of experience in engaging with 'non-state' justice systems in East Africa. Accessible at www.gsdrc.org/docs/open/DS37.pdf, retrieved on 2 September 2010.
OECD-DAC (1997)
Guidelines on Peace, Conflict and Development Cooperation.
Orentlicher, D. (2007)
Settling accounts revisited: reconciling global norms with local agency, *International Journal of Transitional Justice*, Vol. 1: 10–22.

Peace Building Commission (2010)
Emerging lessons and practices in Peace building 2007–2009, Working Group on Lessons Learned of the Peace Building Commission.
Piron, L.H. (2005)
Donor assistance to justice sector reform in Africa: Living up to the new agenda?, in: *Justice Initiatives: Human Rights and Justice Sector Reform in Africa, Contemporary Issues and Responses,* 4–11, accessible at www.soros.org/initiatives/justice/articles_publications/publications/justice_20050207, retrieved on 12 August 2011.
Roht-Arriaza, N. and Mariezcurrena, J. (2006)
Transitional Justice in the Twenty-First Century. Beyond Truth Versus Justice, Cambridge: Cambridge University Press.
Scott, C. (2002)
Co-management and the politics of aboriginal consent to resource development: the agreement concerning a new relationship between the government of Quebec and the Crees of Quebec, Conference Paper presented at Reconfiguring Aboriginal-State Relations / Canada: The State of the Federation 2003, November 1–2, 2002, School of Policy Studies, Queen's University, Kingston.
Stevens, J. (2000)
Access to justice in sub-Saharan Africa, the role of traditional and informal justice systems, accessible at www.penalreform.org/files/rep-2001-access-to-justice-africa-en.pdf, retrieved on 2 September 2010.
Stromzeth, J. (2009)
Justice on the Ground: Can International Criminal Courts Strengthen Domestic Rule of Law in Post-Conflict Societies?, *Hague Journal on the Rule of Law,* 1: 87–97.
Tamanaha, B. (1995)
The lessons of the Law and Development studies, *The American Journal of International Law,* 89: 470–486.
Toomey, L. (2010)
A delicate balance: building contemporary customary and state legal systems, *The Law and Development Review,* Vol. 3 (1): 156–208.
Trubek, D. (2003).
The rule of law in development assistance: past, present and future, accessible on www.law.wisc.edu/facstaff/trubek/RuleofLaw.pdf, retrieved on 12 August 2011.
Ubink, J. (ed.)
Customary Justice: From Program Design to Impact Evaluation, Rome: IDLO.
United Nations (2010)
Guidance Note of the Secretary-General. United Nations Approach to Transitional Justice, March 2010.
United Nations, Economic and Social Council (2005)
Report of the independent expert to update the Set of principles to combat impunity, Diane Orentlicher, Addendum: Updated Set of principles for the protection and promotion of human rights through action to combat impunity, 8 February 2005, E/CN.4/2005/102/Add. 1.
United Nations (2004)
The Rule of Law and transitional justice in conflict and post-conflict societies, Report of the Secretary General, 23 August 2004, S/2004/616.

United Nations (2000)
Report of the Panel on United Nations Peace Operations, A/55/305, S/2000/809.
United Nations (1992)
An Agenda for Peace, preventive diplomacy, peace-making and peace-keeping, Report of the Secretary-General pursuant to the statement adopted by the Summit Meeting of the Security Council on 31 January 1992, 17 June 1992, A/47/277 – S/24111.
Waldorf, L. (2006)
Mass justice for mass atrocity: rethinking local justice as transitional justice, *Temple Law review,* Vol. 79 (1): 1–87.
Weilenmann, M. (2007)
Legal pluralism: a new challenge for development agencies, in: Penal Reform International and Bluhm Legal Clinique of the Northwestern University (eds.), *Access to Justice in Africa and Beyond, Making the Rule of Law a Reality,* 87–93, accessible at www.penalreform.org/files/rep-2007-access-africa-and-beyond-en.pdf, retrieved on 13 July 2010.
Wojkowska, E. (2006)
Doing justice: how informal justice systems can contribute, accessible at www.undp.org/oslocentre/docs07/DoingJusticeEwaWojkowska130307.pdf, retrieved on 2 September 2010.

CHAPTER II

ACCESS TO JUSTICE AND HUMAN RIGHTS IN THE TRADITIONAL COURTS OF SUB-SAHARAN AFRICA*

Tom BENNETT

1. INTRODUCTION

It is one of the sad ironies of Africa that the formal court systems inherited from the colonial era are largely responsible for creating the problem of access to justice.[1] While the colonial powers had set up these systems to provide judicial services of the highest quality, they never in fact catered for more than a small fraction of the continent's legal needs. The vast majority of disputes are heard in various species of informal tribunal.[2]

For the poor and uneducated, these informal tribunals provide a culturally relevant remedy that is quick and affordable, and, of course, lie ready to hand (Wojkowska 2006). Although informal justice systems of this nature are found throughout the world, they are especially important in developing states. Here they are the 'cornerstone of dispute resolution and access to justice for the majority of populations. '*[They] usually resolve between 80 and 90 percent of disputes*' (ibid., 12).

The various institutions included in the term 'informal tribunal' appear in many different guises.[3] This paper, however, is concerned only with one: 'traditional

* My thanks are due to Jacques Jacobs for his invaluable assistance in preparing this paper.

1 The terms used to describe such courts are a matter of some contention. Whether described as 'formal', 'recognised', 'state' or 'official', they are the courts given full state recognition and support.

2 See the proceedings of the conference on *Human Rights and Traditional and Informal Justice Systems in Africa* organised by the UN Office of the High Commissioner for Human Rights 20 June 2007, Windhoek.

3 A more detailed account of such informal institutions may be found in Schärf and Nina (2001) and in Stevens (2001).

courts'.[4] These courts can be distinguished from other, like tribunals by two factors: their source of legitimacy (a tradition ascribed vaguely to the pre-colonial era) and the laws they administer (normative orders generated by the communities they serve).[5]

Traditional courts have various types of relationship with the state. They may have no official link with a formal judicial system, but may nonetheless be tolerated (as in the case of Zambia or Burundi's *bashingantahe*). They may be subject to an outright ban (as in Mozambique after independence from Portugal), or they may be given state recognition and allowed an institutional autonomy, in the sense that they are subject to only minimal regulation (as in Swaziland). Finally, they may be fully integrated into the state judicial structure, whereby they are fully regulated by the state, in the sense that the state controls their procedures and allows appeals and reviews to the formal courts (as in South Africa).

Although critical to providing access to justice, traditional courts are frequently criticised for failing to meet the standards laid down in human rights instruments. For purposes of this paper, the three relevant instruments are the 1948 United Nations Declaration of Human Rights (UNDHR), the 1966 International Covenant of Civil and Political Rights (ICCPR) and the 1981 African Charter of Human and People's Rights. Each of these features a right to fair trial.[6]

Fair trial is one of the most broadly conceived human rights, and is deemed so basic that compliance is said to underpin all other rights.[7] The nature of this right can be gauged from Article 10 of the UNDHR: *'Everyone is entitled in full*

---

4 At its core, the term 'court' denotes an institution that adjudicates disputes according to predetermined rules of law (Walker 1980). 'Tribunal' is a broader term encompassing institutions that may seek arbitration or conciliation of the parties. They may or may not apply rules of law. As such, a 'tribunal' can include various mechanisms of alternative dispute resolution. ADR, however, does not form part of the discussion in this paper (UNDP 2005, 97–100).

5 The term 'traditional' is clearly contentious, for it is a construct used to justify many contemporary social norms, practices and institutions. It, nevertheless, serves here to suggest some connection with a pre-colonial, indigenous institution of dispute resolution.

6 Which is now considered part of customary international law. See Meron (1989) and *Filartiga v Pena-Irala* 630 F 2d 876 (2d Cir 1980).

7 Indeed, according to the African Commission on Human and People's Rights (ACHPR) Dakar Declaration on the Right to a Fair Trial in Africa (1999), it is non-derogable. See para 6 of the United Nations Human Rights Committee (UNHRC) General Comment No 32. The Committee does hold, however, that: 'States parties must respect [the right] regardless of their legal traditions and their domestic law ... [and that] it cannot be left to the sole discretion of domestic law to determine the essential content of Covenant guarantees.' See further para 4 of the General Comment.

equality to a fair and public hearing by an independent and impartial tribunal, in the determination of his rights and obligations and of any criminal charge against him.'

Although the details of fair trial have been fleshed out in later human rights instruments, the right still lacks a precise meaning. Even so, the following five aspects can be identified: (i) due process, (ii) equal treatment, (iii) in criminal proceedings, a series of specific rights, notably, a presumption of innocence, a right to legal representation and a right to be tried without delay[8], (iv) access to justice, and (v) the right to demand that the state respect the litigant's culture.

It is, of course, questionable whether those drafting the international instruments ever contemplated their application by traditional courts. Admittedly, bodies monitoring the ICCPR and the African Charter have declared that traditional tribunals are not exempt from the duty to ensure a right to fair trial, but it seems unlikely that the diplomats and legal advisors negotiating human rights treaties had in mind indigenous African forums for resolving disputes.[9] In fact, it is quite clear that only a Western form of judicature is capable of applying the full catalogue of rights encoded in the ICCPR and (anomalously) the Africa Charter (Baderin 2005).

We may perhaps accept that traditional courts meet the requirements of the first aspect of fair trial, i.e., due process, but the most serious objections are usually saved for the second and third aspects: failure to ensure equal treatment and failure to comply with rights protecting defendants in criminal prosecutions. One of the aims of this paper is to show that the rights applicable to criminal matters are hardly ever in issue in a traditional tribunal. In fact, the very language describing them would in itself suggest that these rights have little

---

8 These rights appear in Article 14 of the ICCPR and Article 7 of the African Charter of Human and People's Rights.

9 The UNHRC in para 24 of its General Comment No 32 stated that fair trial proceedings are applicable to 'courts based on customary law, or religious courts' provided that the state allows them to carry out 'judicial tasks', and further provided that 'the judgments of such courts will not be considered binding unless they are restricted to minor civil and criminal matters …[and they] meet the basic requirements for fair trial and other relevant guarantees of the Covenant …' Para 4 of the ACHPR's Dakar Declaration (1999), which considered this issue, stated that: 'It is recognised that traditional courts are capable of playing a role in the achievement of peaceful societies and exercise authority over a significant proportion of the population in African countries. However, these courts also have serious shortcomings, which result in many instances in a denial of a fair trial. Traditional courts are not exempt from the provisions of the African Charter relating to fair trial.' See, also, the ACHPR *Principles and Guidelines on the Right to Fair a Trial and Legal Assistance in Africa* DOC/OS (XXX) 247 section Q.

relevance to the everyday procedures of simple tribunals serving the needs of local communities.

The general right to equal treatment, however, is another matter. While it is obviously relevant to traditional courts, they have been widely criticised for discriminating against women, children and outsiders. This paper nevertheless contends that failure to comply must be weighed against second- and third-generation human rights: those of access to justice and of culture. Seen from this angle, the debate about traditional courts must shift from outright condemnation to a balancing of interests.

2. THE TRADITIONAL AFRICAN STYLE OF JUSTICE

From the typically Western perspective, the ideal method for dealing with disputes requires an impartial judge to apply a set of certain and pre-determined set of rules to the facts found proved, and then to pronounce judgment in favour of one party. Rules are an essential element in this process, and they have always been a preoccupation of Western jurisprudence (Abel 1973; Roberts 1979a; Comaroff and Roberts 1981).

The concern with law and adjudication, however, is not shared by the traditional cultures of Africa (Roberts 1979a, 45–47). For instance, a penetrating study of the idea of justice amongst the Tiv (an ethno-linguistic group of south-eastern Nigeria) showed how differently they and their British colonisers viewed 'law' (Bohannan 1957, 208–213). The Tiv did not conceive of law as a closed system of precise rules. Rather, they believed that, for all disputes, there was a right answer. Those hearing a dispute were expected to find that answer, and then to persuade all interested parties to accept it (ibid., 213). In this process, Tiv tribunals look to the future, towards the repairing of relationships. They have less interest in the past, i.e., in the wrong that precipitated the dispute.

Subsequent studies have suggested that, if legal cultures in Africa were to be properly understood, we should focus not on rules but on the methods and procedures for dealing with disputes.[10] In this respect, political structures have a clear bearing on preferred methods for handling disputes. In groups lacking central organs of government and the power to mobilise organised force, aggrieved parties must resort to self-help (which might be an outright contest of

[10] Bohannan (1967) poses the two poles of conflict resolution, namely, law and violence. See, too, Roberts' distinction between fighting and talking in (Roberts 1979a). A similar distinction is also drawn between political and judicial modes of dispute settlement (Gulliver 1963, 297–301) and Abel (1981).

physical power or simple negotiation). In groups with centralised structures of state, the state itself may compel disputants to appear before a tribunal. The likelihood of this happening depends, of course, on the physical resources at the disposal of the state. With a police force to back up its commands, a tribunal may assert jurisdiction regardless of a party's reluctance to co-operate. Otherwise, jurisdiction will depend on voluntary submission – and the tribunal's role is confined to mediating or arbitrating (Gulliver 1979, 1973).

Rules are obviously not essential for achieving a satisfactory settlement through mediation or negotiation (Gulliver 1973, 297; Fallers 1969; Hamnett 1977). The study of a Shona-speaking community in Zimbabwe, for example, showed that the people there did not consider justice to be the rational and impartial application of abstract rules. Rather, it was seen as a process of persuasion, with the emphasis on a spirit of give and take. The law thus provided *'a broad and flexible basis for discussion and consideration, but [was] not inviolable and imperative'* (Holleman 1974).

Social structure also has a significant bearing on the ways in which disputes are handled. In this regard, Gluckman's classic work on the Barotse in Zambia, revealed what he called a 'multiplex' society dominated by an intricate network of social ties binding together kin and neighbours (Gluckman 1967). Because relationships were so complex, disputes were equally complex. What might have appeared as a petty quarrel about the infringement of a mere courtesy could be the surface manifestation of a deeper conflict that had been fed by grievances going back for many years. In these circumstances, the judicial process was designed to untangle all the grievances with a view to persuading the disputants to sink their differences so that peace and harmony could be restored to the community (Gluckman 1972).

In such circumstances, a strict division between civil and criminal matters would be otiose, as was evident in a famous case study in Zimbabwe of a dispute between father and son (Holleman 1974, 16–47). The father had long harboured grievances against his son. Eventually, he was driven to perpetrate a series of public outrages – some of which constituted serious 'criminal' acts – in order to force his son to participate in a public hearing of his complaints. The study showed that, in small, close-knit communities, conflicts such as these were quite likely to erupt into public outbursts of anger, because close relationships always generate intense emotion.[11] In an effort to reconcile the parties, however, courts necessarily overlook what Western courts would consider criminal issues.

11 In heterogeneous urban settings, on the other hand, where relationships are less intimate, personal conflict tends to be excluded from the public arena (Merry 1979).

We may say, then, that the prime values of the traditional African style of justice were preservation of peace and social order (Gluckman 1967, 55).[12] The vindication of individual or community claims was a lesser concern, and certainly would not have been superseded by the demand for strict application of the law (Hinz 2010).

The rules and procedures applicable in traditional courts were oral, and hence simple and flexible. Although constantly being adapted by considerations of common sense and community practice, the rules were deemed to be derived from immemorial traditions. Laws of this nature are designed to apply within parochial environments with stable social structures, in which each person is aware of his or her status and responsibilities.

The officers presiding over traditional courts were determined by their position in the community or by inheritance of their office. They drew their legitimacy from community support and dynastic connections, so that failure to achieve the expectations of wisdom and fairness in solving disputes would result in shame and loss of status.

This all too brief summary of the African conception of justice is expressed mainly in the past tense, which poses the question whether the 'traditional' regime still in fact exists. Dramatic changes have swept through Africa since colonial occupation, and indigenous institutions have been both transformed and, on occasion, manipulated to meet colonial demands.[13] Nevertheless, the social and political structures that supported these institutions have not entirely disappeared. One institution in particular – traditional leadership – has proved to be a hardy survivor of colonial and post-colonial rule – and this institution is the bastion of indigenous ideas of justice (van Rouveroy Van Nieuwaal, 1987).

3. DUE PROCESS OF LAW

In its most general sense – which derives from the notion of 'fair' – this right means that individuals should not to be subject to arbitrary or capricious treatment. In other words, they should be tried in accordance with the due process of law.[14] This provision entails certain further guarantees: a full public

---

12 Much depends on the nature of a dispute, the parties' relationship and the social and political structure of a society (Roberts 1979a, 167).

13 Fitzpatrick, for instance, said that colonialism had taken existing social relations, reconstituted them in terms of its demands, '*and then, as it were, [gave them] back to the people as their own. In this process, history was denied and tradition created instead*' (1985, 479). See also, Burman (1979, 129).

14 As in the 5th Amendment to the American Constitution which provides that '*no person shall be deprived of life, liberty, or property, without due process of law*'.

hearing before a court or tribunal, which presupposes a competent, independent and impartial judge.[15] Considered in this sense, fair trial complements the more general notion of rule of law.[16]

While traditional courts comply, by and large, with the requirements of due process and full public hearing, they may infringe the requirements of judicial competence, independence and impartiality.[17] For a start, judges are not obliged to recuse themselves if they happen to be related to litigants or if they have personal knowledge of the cases they hear. To the contrary, personal information of this nature may be considered a virtue, not a vice, because it may assist the court in deciding how best to resolve a dispute so that the interests of all the parties can be accommodated (Bennett 2004).

Traditional leaders may also be thought not fully 'competent', in a Western sense, because they are not sufficiently versed in the rules of the received law. This problem, together with others concerning independence, impartiality and the nature of proceedings before traditional courts, was broached in two cases emanating from South Africa: *Bangindawo and others v Head of the Nyanda Regional Authority and another*[18] and *Mhlekwa and Feni v Head of the Western Tembuland Regional Authority and another.*[19] These were the only reported decisions in which an African court has had to decide a head-on confrontation between all aspects of traditional justice and human rights.

For a start, the courts had to consider the problem of a differential system of justice. *Bangindawo's* case conceded that considerable differences do indeed distinguish traditional courts from the formal court system, but it held, nonetheless, that these differences were consonant with a particular cultural orientation. In consequence, infringement of the right to equal treatment was justifiable.[20]

In both *Bangindawo* and *Mhlekwa's* cases, the courts also had to consider the question of judicial autonomy. They found that judicial independence implies not only freedom from personal bias, but also an institutional autonomy, namely,

---

15 African Commission on Human and Peoples' Rights *Principles and Guidelines on the Right to Fair a Trial and Legal Assistance in Africa* DOC/OS (XXX) 247 section A para 1.

16 See para 1 of the ACHPR Dakar Declaration and (Udombana 2006, 311). Rule of law generally implies: a separation of governmental powers, official action based on predetermined laws conforming to certain substantive and procedural standards, subjecting everyone within a state, on a basis of equality, to the same laws and procedures (Walker 1980).

17 Which, according to para 19 of the UNHRC General Comment No 32, '*is an absolute right that is not subject to any exception*'.

18 1998 (3) SA 262 (Tk). See Koyana and Bekker 1998, 218.

19 2001 (1) SA 574 (Tk).

20 Ibid., 278. This issue is explored more fully below.

freedom from the influence of the executive arm of government. This requirement may pose a particular problem for traditional courts, especially where presiding officers have been formally incorporated into the structures of government.[21] In this event, they may then be expected to perform two or all three functions of government, and so may be predisposed, especially in criminal cases, to rule against certain parties for failing to comply with the state's fiat.[22]

Following jurisprudence from the developed democracies, both cases accepted that judicial autonomy required the actual absence of an unduly close relationship with the executive, together with the *perception* of that absence. *Bangindawo's* case,[23] however, held that the tests evolved abroad for independence were not applicable to traditional courts in Africa.[24] Here, no clear distinction is drawn between the executive, judicial and legislative functions of government. Thus, no reasonable African would perceive a bias on the part of traditional leaders merely because they exercise executive functions. *Mhlekwa's* case, on the other hand, concentrated on criminal proceedings, and held that traditional courts (which *in casu* were very much part of the organs of state) had too close a connection with the executive.

4. EQUAL TREATMENT

In another sense, fair trial denotes simple equality, or non-discrimination, in court proceedings.[25] As such, the right has ancient origins in the principle of *audi alteram partem* and its associated rules, such as giving the defendant proper notice of the hearing so that both parties can prepare their cases in time.[26]

In a procedural context, the rule of non-discrimination refers to what is generally known as 'equality of arms', namely, the right of both parties to be heard according to the same procedures, and to be given the same opportunity to

---

21 A problem evident even in colonial times, especially in British territories (Hailey 1945). In the French colonies, on the other hand, the judicial powers of traditional rulers were progressively diminished (Robert 1959, 129; Hailey 1945, 290).

22 In several cases, the African Commission has questioned judicial independence in terms of the African Charter (but only of the formal courts). See, for example, the *Civil Liberties Organisation v Nigeria case* (2000) AHRLR 188 para 12 and *Lawyers for Human Rights v Swaziland* (2005) AHRLR 66 para 60.

23 1998 (3) SA 262 (Tk).

24 The court held that the idea of judicial independence meant that a reasonable person would consider the judiciary independent if it were free from interference by either the executive or the litigants.

25 See paras 7 and 10 of the UNHRC General Comment No 32.

26 See Udombana 2006, 300. In criminal cases, the requirement of due notice is even more important, since defendants must be made aware of the evidence or arguments that will be adduced against them (Treschel 2005, 85).

question all the evidence and arguments.[27] Significantly, however, it does not mean that both parties must have the same means and resources (a lacuna in the human rights code that provided the basis for the right of access to justice).[28]

Traditional courts may be particular offenders against the requirement of equality of arms, since women and children are usually not permitted direct access to court. Consonant with the principle that they have no capacity to engage in public-sphere activities, neither a woman nor a child has *locus standi* to sue or be sued. On the assumption that only adult males are properly versed in the forensic arts, the rights of women and children must be pursued by their guardians (Bennett 1995).

The problem of discrimination on the ground of sex or gender has attracted much field research, and we now have ample evidence of consistent patterns of bias not only against the participation of women in trial proceedings but also against their representation in the judiciary.[29] Two key international conventions have special provisions in these respects. Article 15(2) of the Convention on the Elimination of All Forms of Discrimination Against Women (1979) provides that: '*States Parties shall accord to women, in civil matters, a legal capacity identical to that of men and the same opportunities to exercise that capacity. In particular, they shall ... treat [women] equally in all stages of procedure in courts and tribunals.*'[30]

Similarly, Article 8 of the Protocol to the African Charter on the Rights of Women in Africa (2003) lays down a list of requirements to ensure that women are given equal access to courts and protection before the law.[31]

By contrast, we have very little information concerning children. In customary law, the general rule is that, if a child has an interest in a dispute, a guardian

---

27 Para 13 of the UNHRC General Comment No 32 continues: the right to equal procedural rules may not apply if there are 'reasonable' grounds for suspending them.

28 Para 13 of the UNHRC General Comment No 32.

29 Such as that by Women and Law in Southern Africa (WLSA), a private NGO based in Harare, which has been conducting a series of studies in southern African states. An example of work of this nature is Griffiths (1997), a study of property claims made by the Bakwena women of Botswana.

30 Article 15(2).

31 See further para 9 of the ACHPR Dakar Declaration, which provides that: '*Judicial processes and institutions reflect societal discrimination against women. Gender discrimination affects women in accessing justice and as prospective litigants, accused in criminal trials, victims of crime, witnesses and as legal representatives before judicial institutions. Women are not adequately represented in judicial positions and legal procedures are not sufficiently sensitive to issues that affect them.*' In the Declaration, judicial officers are adjured to '*[a]dopt measures to ensure the elimination of discrimination against women both as regards their appointment as judicial officials and as participants in judicial proceedings*'.

(normally the father) must speak on the child's behalf. Conversely, a child's rights may simply be treated as those of the parent, as frequently happens in matrimonial disputes, when a wife's interests are subsumed under her father's claim to return of bridewealth.

The UN Convention on the Rights of the Child (1989) sets out to improve the status of children and to protect them from exploitation by their guardians. Accordingly, Article 12(1) provides that children have a right to be heard and have their views taken seriously in all decision-making processes affecting them. Obviously, however, this provision does not oblige states to give those who are under age full legal capacity. Rather it is interpreted as a requirement that decision-makers must hear a child's views in a manner appropriate to the child's maturity (which will vary with age and the cultural norms of the community). Article 40 lays down a comprehensive list of obligations whereby state parties must secure the interests of children in criminal proceedings.[32] Finally, Article 3 covers any other eventualities by providing that: 'In all actions concerning children, whether undertaken by ... courts of law, administrative authorities or legislative bodies, the best interests of the child shall be a primary consideration.'[33]

Another category of persons that very probably suffer similar discrimination in traditional courts are strangers to a community. Although there seems to be no empirical research on their standing before traditional courts, it is quite likely that they may be required to pay extra fees or to make some formal act of submission before being granted a right to sue. Even thereafter, they may well suffer from the more subtle discrimination of local prejudice.

5. RIGHTS IN CRIMINAL PROCEEDINGS

5.1. THE CIVIL/CRIMINAL DISTINCTION

When the application of human rights depends upon how an action is classified, the distinction between civil and criminal suits must obviously be subject to a careful examination.

---

32 The same, or very similar, provisions can be found in Article 17 of the African Charter on the Rights and Welfare of the Child (1999). *'Every child accused of or found guilty of having infringed penal law shall have the right to special treatment in a manner consistent with the child's sense of dignity and worth and which reinforces the child's respect of human rights and fundamental freedoms.'* See, also, para 10 of the ACHPR Dakar Declaration, which provides that: *'Children are entitled to all the fair trial guarantees and rights applicable to adults and to some additional protection.'*

33 See, also, Article 4 of the African Charter on the Rights of the Child.

At the outset, it must be appreciated that a decision whether to classify a dispute as a civil action for compensation or a criminal action for punishment may be quite arbitrary. Especially in the case of minor injuries, the decision may rest with the victim of a wrong. In this event, much will depend on that person's desire for vengeance rather than damages. Even if the decision is made by state authorities, in which event a more objective judgment might be expected, the determination will depend upon whether Western or customary law is used to characterise the cause of action. The two may well not take the same view on a matter.

By all accounts, however, these considerations seldom weigh with state authorities. When deciding whether to prosecute, they operate according to their own criteria, and, in this respect, they favour Western standards for determining the civil or criminal character of a wrong. Such a consistent bias in favour of the one law is due, in part, to the obscurity surrounding customary criminal law.

Throughout Africa, the colonial powers imposed their own systems of law as the general laws of the land. While they were prepared to make an exception for indigenous systems of customary law, they seldom specified whether only civil law was intended. It was, of course, assumed that the European systems of criminal law were be applied to everyone within the colonial territories, settlers and Africans alike (Bennett 1985), but the position of customary-law crimes was usually left unspecified.[34]

If customary criminal law then survived the colonial conquest, it could play a critical role in determining the nature of court proceedings. Herein, however, lies a problem: customary law draws no hard and fast distinction between crime and delict. This is not to say that it denies any distinction between offences that harm the individual and those that are deemed to have a wider impact, and therefore require a community response (Seagle 1941).[35] The violation of certain norms, such as the bar on incest, invite a spiritual sanction, with an obvious effect on the entire community (Van Niekerk 1986; Myburgh 1980, 94–99).

Nevertheless, customary law has no strict – and, what is more, consistent – distinction between the civil and criminal. Rape is a classic example (Bennett 1985, 107–108). Customary law may regard non-consensual sexual intercourse as

---

[34] Even in the post-colonial era, policy has been ambivalent. For example, s 3(3)(b) of the Namibian Traditional Authorities Act 25 of 2000 gave no indication whether these authorities may apply customary criminal law, whereas the Zimbabwe Customary Law and Local Courts Act (Chapter 7:05) allowed local courts (i.e. courts of traditional rulers) no criminal jurisdiction. See Anyangwe (1998, 52–53).

[35] However, he says that this formulaic proposition disguises the fact that there are no universally recognized crimes (Seagle 1941, 228).

a private matter of adultery or as a public disgrace (Moult 2004; Myburgh and Prinsloo, 1985).

The strict separation between crime and delict, which is so fundamental to Western systems of law, is historically linked to the state's assumption of a monopoly over the use of force. Thus, an individual's resort to self-help in order to settle a dispute may be deemed vigilantism, and punished as the usurpation of state power.[36] By arrogating to itself the sole power to use force, the state also assumes power to compel those under its jurisdiction to submit to its judicial process and to inflict punishment (Burchell 2006, 68).

The origins of this claim to an exclusive right of coercion are not altogether clear, although they obviously coincided with the process whereby all powers were gradually gathered together in central organs of state. Prior to this, law enforcement depended on various species of community or individual self-help. Indeed, legal anthropology shows that, before a polity develops the apparatus necessary to regulate resort to physical violence, there can be no absolute distinction between private wrongs and public crimes.[37] The key factor is the institutionalisation and centralisation of power in a bureaucracy whose function it is to maintain social order and to defend itself against outsiders (Service 1975, 11–13).

As it happens, the state's monopoly over the use of force appeared quite late in European history, at the time of the eighteenth-century Enlightenment (Bittner and Platt 1972). Thereafter this power, whether exercised internally or externally, was taken to be definitive of the modern state.[38] Even so, any analysis of state-building indicates that the degree of control varies over time and place, and, in Africa, few (if any) states in fact have the sole right to command force.[39] Thus, the state monopoly seems to function as a statement of ideology rather than a factual proposition.

Even so, the state's exclusive right to use force has had a profound effect on the development of procedural laws. Writing about the history of legal institutions,

---

36 A dramatic example of this proposition occurred in South Africa during the state of emergency in the 1980s, when anti-apartheid forces set up people's courts as a direct challenge to state authority. See *S v Mayekiso* 1988 (4) SA 738 (W).

37 Thereafter, Seagle (1941, 229) says that the number and nature of offences changes.

38 Indeed, Max Weber declared that an entity could be deemed a state only '*if and insofar as its administrative staff successfully upholds a claim on the monopoly of the legitimate use of violence in the enforcement of its order*' (1947, 141).

39 See Baker (2008, 14–18), who notes that, even in the nineteenth century, policing was largely in the hands of civil society. See further Baker (2008, 181–183) commenting on the Western model of policing in Africa.

Seagle said that, at the time of the Enlightenment, a system of public criminal law subject to adversarial adjudication became *'a sort of secular High Mass of advanced civilization'* (1941, 227–228). He noted that the primitive notion of vengeance in earlier times was transformed into public punishment, based on deterrence as well as repression. In order to ensure that this state-imposed 'peace' would not seem arbitrary or inhumane, the law emphasised due process. The further development of the law was then a tug-of-war between state control and due process.

Seagle's account proposes an opposition between interests of state and human rights that is typical of Western thinking. It now provides the basis for enforcing not only substantive criminal law but also criminal procedure. If only the state is entitled to use force, then only the state may exact penalties for wrongful behaviour. The severity of this process demands special protections for the accused, all of which have been encoded in human rights instruments.

5.2. DUE PROCESS IN CRIMINAL PROCEEDINGS

In this section, it is argued that the fundamental rights may well be irrelevant to procedures in traditional courts. For a start, these courts may favour a non-punitive outcome to their proceedings – and, if the aim is reconciliation rather than retribution, the basis of the court's jurisdiction is consent, not force.[40]

In recent years, much has been made of the fact that traditional courts in Africa aim at restorative justice.[41] Indeed, pre-state societies lacked the physical infrastructure to inflict the type of punishments (notably detention) considered necessary in a modern criminal justice system.[42] Conversely, in Western law, conviction for an offence may carry severe consequences, and so, in criminal proceedings, defendants are offered a cluster of interrelated procedural rights to provide some counter to the powers wielded by the state (Ashworth 2006, 83), and to ensure protection against mistakes in the process.[43]

---

40 And, by implication, they do not violate the state's monopoly on coercion.

41 See further Epstein (1969). The case for restorative justice, however, has been somewhat overplayed, since compromise settlements only become the goal when long-term relationships are threatened. See Ashworth (2002) and, especially, Daly (2002) who questions the claim that restorative justice is typical of indigenous and pre-state social orders.

42 Hence, any resort to punishment would have involved the infliction of immediate forms of physical suffering, whether loss of life, beatings, banishment, confiscation of property, reprimands or fines of livestock (Myburgh 1985, 48–51; Prinsloo 1983).

43 See, for instance, Brennan J in the US Supreme Court in *Re Winship* (1970) 397 US 358.

5.3. THE PRESUMPTION OF INNOCENCE

The most basic of these rights is a presumption of the defendant's innocence. By implication, the prosecution has the onus of proving the case. This presumption is now enshrined in all major international human rights instruments.[44] It is, in turn, related to the right to remain silent,[45] and the right not to be compelled to make admissions or confessions that can be used in evidence against the defendant.[46] The seriousness of criminal conviction further requires a special standard of proof: guilt must be established beyond a reasonable doubt.[47]

In traditional courts, none of these requirements would be considered necessary to protect defendants. The rules of evidence are not nearly as strict as under Western systems of law. There are no hard and fast rules about the burden of proof – although it generally rests with the person alleging guilt[48] – or about the standards of proof – although that is generally on a balance of probabilities (Van Niekerk 1986, 43). Considerable weight is attached to confessions and admissions, but with none of the safeguards thought essential under Western law.[49]

In general terms, customary law emphasises duty rather than right.[50] Given this perspective, together with the principle that people must avoid harming others, defendants have to convince courts that they had no responsibility for damage that has occurred, once the fact of damage is established.[51] It follows that the person who remains silent may be taken to have something to hide. Guilt may then be presumed, and judges may question an accused on the understanding that he or she is lying (Gluckman 1972, 231).

This approach to proving liability does not necessarily mean that traditional tribunals are violating constitutional rights. If the principal aim of a hearing is to reconcile the parties, the human rights guarantees – which are aimed at protecting an accused against harsh penalties – become redundant. What is more, although it could be said that customary procedures are inquisitorial (Van

---

44 See Articles 11(1) of the UNDHR, Article 14(2) of the ICCPR (together with para 4 of UNHRC General Comment No 32) and Article 7(1)(b) of the African Charter.

45 Article 75 of the African Charter. This right was the focus of two major constitutional reviews in South Africa: *S v Manamela and another* 2000 (3) SA 1 (CC) paras 24–6 and *S v Singo* 2002 (4) SA 858 (CC) paras 28ff.

46 Article 14(3)(g) of the ICCPR.

47 See para 4 of UNHRC General Comment No 32, Schwikkard (1999, 35) and *R v Downey* (1992) 90 DLR (4th) 488 (SCC) 456.

48 There may, however, be exceptions to this rule (Van Niekerk 1981; Myburgh 1985).

49 Hence a confession may result in the instant closing of a case (Holleman 1979, 123,126).

50 Hence, Article 27 of the African Charter provides that individuals have duties to their families and society.

51 In any event, alleged offenders are not necessarily required to plead (Van Niekerk 1986, 43).

der Merwe 1981, 141–142; Van Niekerk 1981), this term does no more than describe a technique used to test a defendant or witness's credibility. It should not be taken to mean an overbearing exercise of state power. Indeed, the very term 'inquisitorial' is a product of Western jurisprudence, and is therefore to be used with circumspection in other cultural contexts.

5.4. LEGAL REPRESENTATION

In a complex and, for the layperson, inaccessible legal system, the assistance of counsel is critical to the successful defence of a criminal charge. Hence, legal representation is a basic right in international human rights instruments.[52]

Unlike their Western counterparts, however, traditional courts are non-professional in the sense that they are not the preserve of specially qualified practitioners. Instead, simple accessible fora such as these operate on the understanding that all adults know the rules and procedures of the community. Representation in court is therefore unnecessary, unless an individual is considered unable to present a proper case. In this respect, male guardians generally act for women and children. Full-time professional lawyers, however, were unheard of.

In some states, what had, in effect, been the absence of any specific rule about representation was turned into a prohibition. This was done in order to preserve the informality of traditional courts, and to ensure that wealthier parties would not enjoy an undue advantage (Hailey 1945, 297, 299). When this prohibition was challenged in the South African case, *Bangindawo & others v Head of the Nyanda Regional Authority & another*,[53] the exclusion of lawyers was held to be permissible in civil matters. The court argued that the elaborate safeguards associated with Western courts provided 'fertile ground for the raising of technical points', whereas the more informal procedures of customary courts had the advantage of 'leaving less room for such technicalities and of having the real substance of disputes dealt with and laid to rest'. In criminal matters, on the other hand, the court could find no justification for dispensing with the right to representation, since crimes could involve complex legal issues and potentially severe penalties.[54] It could further be reasoned that, whenever civil and minor criminal matters are concerned, both parties can be fairly presumed to know the

---

52 Articles 14(3)(b) and (d) of the ICCPR and Article 7(1)(c) of the African Charter.

53 1998 (3) SA 262 (Tk).

54 Indeed, it noted (at 277) that the right to representation *'applies with more force in respect of the vast numbers of uneducated and illiterate people'* of South Africa. This part of the judgment was confirmed by *Mhlekwa and Feni v Head of the Western Tembuland Regional Authority and another* 2001 (1) SA 574 (Tk) at 631–632.

law and procedures of traditional courts. Professional assistance would not be warranted.

6. ACCESS TO JUSTICE

Access to justice is a relatively recent arrival in the code of human rights law. It did, however, make an early appearance in several instruments under a somewhat different guise. Article 8 of the UNDHR, for instance, provided that '[e]veryone has the right to an effective remedy by the competent national tribunals for acts violating the fundamental rights granted him by the constitution or by law', and Article 7(1) of the African Charter provided that '[e]very individual shall have the right to have his cause heard'.[55] In both these provisions, access to justice appears as a logical outcome of the right to fair trial, an entailment that was even more evident in Article 14(1) of the ICCPR: '*...everyone shall be entitled to a fair and public hearing by a ... tribunal established by law*'.[56]

Initially, however, equality was not construed to mean that parties should have the same resources to litigate.[57] Only with the development of economic and social rights did attention shift to realising the full implications of the earlier right of fair trial. This first-generation right had gone no further than protecting an individual's formal entitlement to sue or defend (Roberts and Palmer 2005, 47). The idea of access, which appeared as a second-generation right,[58] went further. It required the state to provide the means with which individuals might find an appropriate resolution of their disputes,[59] and, to that end, ensure that courts or other tribunals were available on a basis of complete equality (Francioni 2007).

55 See, also, paras 1 and 2 of Annex IV adopted in Tunis in March 1992. The Resolution by the ACHPR on the Right to Recourse Procedure and Fair Trial ACHPR (1992) Res4(XI) also speaks in language reminiscent of access to justice: every person whose rights and freedoms are violated is entitled to have an effective remedy, and '*all persons shall have the right to have their cause heard and shall be equal before the courts and tribunals in determination of their rights and obligations*'.

56 Note, however, that para 12 of the UNHRC General Comment No 32 states that: '*The right of equal access to a court [in art 14(1)] concerns access to first instance procedures and does not address the issue of the right to appeal or other remedies.*'

57 Para 13 of the UNHRC General Comment No 32.

58 Implying a state's active duty – although programmatic in nature – to realise the conditions necessary to allow potential litigants full enjoyment of their rights. Access to justice, however, does not feature in the International Covenant on Economic, Social and Cultural Rights (1966).

59 As Galanter (2005, 147) says, '*[t]his vision of justice in many modalities and diverse institutional settings*' arrived with Mauro Cappelletti's four volume *Access to Justice* (1978–1979). It was accompanied by a shift of attention in legal studies to dispute resolution and ADR.

The access movement began in North America during 1960s and 1970s, when it became increasingly apparent that justice was available only for those who could afford it. In terms of first-generation human rights, the state had no active duties, and hence no obligation to meet public need. It also became apparent that formal justice – although assumed to be equal – was not necessarily effective.[60] Hence, advocates for true access called for quicker, cheaper and more readily available tribunals, marked by less formal procedures (Roberts and Palmer 2005, 45).

Such a right would have been taken for granted in a traditional African society, where, for ordinary people, their rulers were a 'personification of the moral and political order, protection against injustice [and] unseemly behaviour …' (van Rouveroy Van Nieuwaal 1987, 23). Dispensing justice, in other words, was one of the principal duties of a traditional ruler. In the post-colonial state, however,

> [w]ith the increased bureaucratisation and professionalisation of the law, gaining access to justice has become a cumbersome, protracted and costly matter. Ignorance of one's rights, inability to get legal advice and hardened language barriers are conspicuous features of a general legal disenfranchisement, although this malaise affects especially the poor and the powerless (Koch 1979, 1).

Hence the irony: the European powers' introduction of a notionally superior brand of justice to their African colonies had the effect of concentrating funds and resources in a system of courts that lies beyond the reach of ordinary people.

This problem is not, of course, peculiar to Africa. Wherever governments struggle with shortages of finance and personnel, legal needs are bound to remain unmet. In Africa, however, the problem is especially acute. This is partly due to governments' commitment to formal court systems – which, of course, are always the most expensive to maintain[61] – in the persistent belief that only they can dispense an acceptable form of justice. The dualist judicial structure, therefore, has the effect of exacerbating the problem.

Legal dualism went hand in hand with the colonial regime, and criticism of it harks back to the 1930s. Even then, members of the legal profession and liberally-minded politicians were voicing their doubts about segregating courts on racial lines,[62] and the fact that traditional courts violated precepts of due process. The higher courts were in no position to remedy these lapses, because they had only

---

60 Thus access implies an *effective* remedy (Francioni 2007, 24–25).

61 Koch, ibid.

62 In the Belgian, French and Portuguese colonies, however, the possibility of attaining racial equality was available in the form of *assimilation*, i.e., exemption from customary law (Hailey 1945, 277–278).

minimal (if any) appeal and review jurisdiction (Epstein 1951; Brooke 1954). It was as if two different legal systems were operating independently (Robinson 1949).[63]

Shortly before independence, African nationalist movements joined the call for fair procedures, known laws and a separation of judicial and administrative powers. In addition, however, they demanded greater respect for customary law (Elias 1956), going so far as to call for complete unification of the legal system, a blending of customary and received laws, together with a single hierarchy of courts open to all citizens (Allott 1965, 366).[64] This principle proved to be the point of departure for post-colonial legal developments (Brooke 1954, 69).

Almost immediately, however, ideals had to be compromised. A return to customary law and indigenous legal institutions was the first to founder, because no one was prepared to give up the received systems of European law.[65] Unification of the courts was thought to be a more workable option, but it was evident that, even here, any meaningful reform would require more than simply connecting the African courts to the superior courts through rights of appeal and review: new and properly trained personnel had to be recruited.[66]

Unification met another obstacle in the resilience of traditional authorities. Where local polities were stable and well organised, they were quite capable of withstanding any reforms imposed by the central state (Roberts 1979b, 37). In fact, most countries simply lacked the resources to replace traditional courts, and so these courts had to be retained.[67] In consequence, post-colonial legal systems were only partially unified.[68] Indeed, as the optimism of decolonisation

---

63 For these reasons, the influential Bushe Report roundly condemned the entire system of indirect rule: Great Britain *Commission of Inquiry into the Administration of Justice in Kenya, Uganda and Tanganyika Territory in Criminal Matters* (1934) HMSO para 21. See Morris and Read (1972, 295–308).

64 In 1953, for example, a judicial advisers' conference at Makerere College adopted the principle that every country should have one body of law and one judicial system, applicable to all persons in the state.

65 Instead, the problematic element in the legal system was seen to be customary law, which therefore had to be adjusted to meet the demands of the received law (Anyangwe 1998, 48; Hailey 1945, 41; Spalding et al. 1970, 79; Opoku 1974, 65).

66 This was the finding of a 1963 Conference on Local Courts and Customary Law (for a report of which see Cotran 1965).

67 In some countries, however, customary courts were abolished (Nwogugu, 1976), in others, they were more closely integrated into the general court system (Pauwels, 1973), while, in others still, little happened other than a change of name (Himsworth, 1972). Generally, however, criminal jurisdiction became the preserve of the ordinary courts (Anyangwe 1998, 52–53).

68 Usually by doing no more than removing race as a condition for determining jurisdiction.

and development faded into disenchantment, the dualist court structures of the past began to appear in a more favourable light.

In Africa, there are no clear data showing the degree of access to state courts. Nonetheless, it seems fairly obvious that most people are excluded by reasons of finance, geography and a sense of alienation caused by linguistic and cultural factors (Stevens 2001, 1–10). Thus, the poorer and more marginalised members of the population suffer a pernicious form of indirect discrimination, making nonsense of any official claim to fair trial.

The financial barrier is clear, and certain states have sought to remedy the problem by providing legal aid, small claims courts and various diversion techniques, such as mediation and arbitration. Of these, legal aid is the most important, and for criminal defences it is considered a basic human right.[69] A recent South African study has shown, however, that legal aid is eaten up by criminal defences, and, because men are more likely to be the accused, they benefit most. In consequence, the needs of women are neglected. They have no means of suing for divorce and the payment of maintenance, which are matters of particular concern to women (Allen 1995, 147–148).

The geographic distribution of courts is notoriously skewed in favour of areas where wealth and power are concentrated. For those living in rural areas and the sprawling settlements of urban Africa, the provision of courts is glaringly inadequate (Abel 1979, 196–198).

Africa is a continent with an estimated 1,500 to 2000 indigenous languages. Given such diversity, most governments have opted for English, French or Portuguese as official languages, although only a handful of their citizens enjoy full proficiency. It follows that most litigants experience a language barrier in court proceedings.

For criminal proceedings, the ICCPR requires the free provision of interpreters, if accused persons 'cannot understand or speak the language used in court'.[70] There is no similar provision for civil proceedings, and – curiously – no provisions for interpreters whatever in the African Charter. Data are not available

---

69 Article 14(3)(d) of the ICCPR, General Assembly resolution 2200A (XXI) (1966) and para 8 of the ACHPR Dakar Declaration (1999). See, also Udombana 2006, 307, 323.

70 Article 14(3)(f). Paragraph 40 of the UNHRC General Comment No 32 states that: '*This right arises at all stages of the oral proceedings. It applies to aliens as well as to nationals. However, accused persons whose mother tongue differs from the official court language are, in principle, not entitled to the free assistance of an interpreter if they know the official language sufficiently to defend themselves effectively.*'

on the number (and effectiveness) of interpreters actually provided by African states.

Cultural barriers are obviously very difficult to measure, but it nonetheless seems clear that the combination of foreign languages, laws and procedures makes the formal justice system not only inaccessible but also intimidating and even counterproductive: if the outcome of a case does not measure up to a litigant's expectations, the legitimacy of the system correspondingly suffers.

7. CONCLUSION – AND THE RIGHT TO CULTURE

Although the formal judicial system in Africa is quite incapable of meeting legal needs, it attracts by far the greatest attention, and indeed financial support. By comparison, little thought is given to the traditional courts, largely because they do not enjoy the prestige of the formal sector, but also because they are considered unable to comply with fundamental human rights.

The latter criticism overlooks the fact that formal courts are equally serious offenders. The delays in hearing cases, the conditions of detention (both pre- and post-trial), the competence, independence and partiality of the judiciary are only some of the areas in which formal courts are found wanting (Udombana 2006,300; Stevens 2001, 6; Odoki 1994). Another point frequently overlooked is the fact that proceedings in Western style courts may well offend African views of fairness,[71] and, in certain respects, traditional courts may come closer to realising human rights than formal state courts.[72]

Even if we accept the fact that traditional courts do offend human rights, the gravity of these violations must be weighed against their potential for realising second- and third-generation rights. The second-generation right – access to justice – has already been discussed above. A right straddling both first and second generations is culture.[73]

71 Thus, few question the acceleration of the judicial process in formal courts (through such devices as the evidentiary rule of relevance) in order to save time and costs. These practices would offend customary ideas of *audi alteram partem*, which require courts to devote as much time as is needed to reach a settlement satisfactory to both the parties and the community. In fact, the very measure of an effective court is the length of time it is prepared to spend delving into details (Bennett 2006, 164–165).

72 Strengths that were apparent even to the colonial authorities (Hailey 1945, 302).

73 As a first-generation right, culture is the equivalent of a freedom of expression: UN Committee on Economic, Social and Cultural Rights General Comment No 21 (2009) (Donders 2002, 149–162).

In terms of Article 27 of the ICCPR[74] and Article 17(2) of the African Charter,[75] individuals are the main beneficiaries of this right. Groups benefit from the growing catalogue of rights protecting indigenous peoples,[76] notably those contained in the 2007 General Assembly Declaration on the Rights of Indigenous Peoples.[77] The right to culture imposes, by implication, several duties on the state. First, it must tolerate different cultural practices. Hence, although the customs and habits of a group may seem unusual and even threatening to the wider society, the state must permit divergence from the norm.[78] Secondly, the state is obliged to preserve the existence and identity of the group: it may not compel its citizens to assimilate to a national norm. Thirdly, the state may not to discriminate against any particular cultural group.[79]

Finally, the state must allow the group to foster its separate identity through means such as speaking its own language, worshipping according to certain religious tenets or organising itself according to its own distinctive system of personal law. A group may therefore require the state to respect its unique institutions, including those designed to resolve disputes (Himonga and Manjoo 2009, 310). In fact, the latter may be considered critical to the way in which a group concretises its law and ultimately its identity.

If these considerations fail to weigh sufficiently heavily against the right to fair trial, it should also be remembered that, in the conflict between culture and rights, the two sides should not be regarded as static opposites (Shweder et al. 2002, 11–12). Instead, they are both evolving and are both engaged in a dialogic relationship. Individuals, as the bearers of culture and rights, deploy both sets of norms in their everyday lives.[80] Hence, not only is culture a dynamic force that is constantly adjusting to the broad outlines of human rights,[81] but the codes of

74 In this provision, the identity of the right-bearer is ambiguous: '*In those States in which ethnic, religious or linguistic minorities exist, persons belonging to such minorities shall not be denied the right, in community with the other members of their group to enjoy their own culture, to profess and practise their own religion, or to use their own language.*' In 1992, this article was supplemented by a General Assembly Declaration 47/135 on the Rights of Persons Belonging to National or Ethnic, Religious and Linguistic Minorities.

75 '*Every individual may freely, take part in the cultural life of his community.*'

76 In Africa, however, the ILO Convention No 169 on Indigenous and Tribal Peoples (1989) arts 4, 13 and 23 is of little importance, because it has been ratified by only one African state (Central African Republic).

77 UN Res 61/295 (2007).

78 Article 1 of the UNESCO Universal Declaration on Cultural Diversity 2 November (2001). See, also, *West Virginia State Board of Education v Barnette* 319 US 624 (1943) at 642.

79 Thus minority protection includes a rule of equal treatment (Thornberry 1992, 317).

80 Abdullahi An-Na'im (2000) and other scholars have demonstrated we have moved beyond a view that human rights are simply a product of the West.

81 This process takes on a number of forms with differing effects, thereby resulting in what Sally Engle Merry has termed the 'vernacularisation' of human rights (Merry 2006).

human rights are also being interpreted and applied, and thereby adapting to new cultural situations (Englund 2006).[82]

Even more important is the need to remember that the traditional courts' failure to comply with certain human rights is no reason for states and NGOs to refuse to work with them. Once it is appreciated that traditional courts play a key role in hearing disputes, the very reason for engagement is their non-observance of human rights.[83] It must, however, be accepted that engagement will prompt only gradual change, since well-established cultural traditions are inevitably resistant to outside intervention. Nonetheless, given a voice in the outcome and process, individuals and communities often embrace the chance to adapt to new challenges.

BIBLIOGRAPHY

Abdullahi, A.N. (2000)
Islam and Human Rights: Beyond the universality debate: religion and the universality of human rights, 94 American Society of International Law, Proceedings of the Annual Meeting.

Abel, R. (1973)
A comparative theory of dispute institutions in society, *Law & Society Review* 8 (2): 217–347.

Abel, R. (1979)
Western Courts in Non-Western Settings: Patterns of Court Use in Colonial and Neo-Colonial Africa, in: Burman, S.B. and Harrell-Bond, B. (eds.) *The Imposition of Law,* New York: Academic Press, pp. 167–200.

Abel, R. (1981)
Conservative conflict and the reproduction of capitalism: the role of informal justice, *International Journal of Sociology of Law* 9 (3): 245–267.

Allen, J. (1995)
Focusing legal aid on criminal defence marginalises women's legal service needs, *South African Journal on Human Rights* 11 (1): 143–149.

Allott, A. (1965)
Towards the unification of laws in Africa, *International and Comparative Law Quarterly* 14 (2): 366–389.

Anyangwe, C. (1998)
The whittling away of African indigenous legal and judicial system, *Zambia Law Journal*, special edition, 46–67.

Ashworth, A. (2002)
Responsibilities, rights and restorative justice, *British Journal of Criminology,* 42 (3): 578–595.

82 A valuable recent contribution to this literature is Jensen and Jefferson (2009).

83 What is more, the co-dependency of state and chieftaincy (which is explored by van Rouveroy van Nieuwaal, 1992) would suggest the wisdom of engaging with both.

Ashworth, A. (2006)
Principles of Criminal Law, 5th ed., Oxford: Oxford University Press.
Baderin, M. (2005)
Recent developments in the African regional human rights system, *Human Rights Law Review* 5 (1): 117–149.
Baker, B. (2008)
Multi-Choice Policing in Africa, Uppsala: Nordiska Afrikainstitutet.
Bennett, T. (1985)
Application of Customary Law in Southern Africa, the conflict of personal laws, Cape Town: Juta and Co.
Bennett, T. (1995)
Human Rights and African Customary Law, Cape Town: Juta and Co.
Bennett, T. (2004)
Customary Law in South Africa, Cape Town: Juta and Co.
Bennett, T. (2006)
Traditional Courts and Fundamental Rights, in: Hinz, M. and Patemann, H. (eds.) *The Shade of New Leaves: governance in traditional authority; a Southern African perspective,* Berlin: LIT Verlag, pp. 157–166.
Bittner, E. and Platt, A. (1972)
The Right of the State to Punish, in: Gerber, R.J. and McAnany, P.D. (eds.) *Contemporary Punishment: views, explanations, and justifications,* Notre Dame: University of Notre Dame, pp. 24–30.
Bohannan, P. (1957)
Justice and Judgment among the Tiv, Oxford: Oxford University Press.
Bohannan, P. (ed.) (1967)
Law and Warfare: studies in the anthropology of conflict, New York: Natural History Press.
Brooke, N.J. (1954)
The changing character of customary courts, *Journal of African Administration* 6 (2): 67–73.
Burchell, J. (2006)
Principles of Criminal Law (revised 3 ed.), Cape Town: Juta and Co.
Burman, S. (1979)
Use and abuse of the “modern” versus “traditional” law dichotomy in South Africa, *Verfassung und Recht in Übersee* 12 (2): 129–141.
Comaroff, J. and Roberts, S. (1981)
Rules and Processes, The Cultural Logic of Dispute in an African Context, Chicago and London: Chicago University Press.
Cotran, E. (1965)
Integration of courts and application of customary law in Tanganyika, *East African Law Journal* 1: 108–123.
Daly, K. (2002)
Restorative justice: the real story, *Punishment and Society* 4: 55–79.
Donders, Y. (2002)
Towards a Right to Cultural Identity?, Antwerp: Intersentia.

Elias, T.O. (1956)
Nature of African Customary Law, Manchester: Manchester University Press.
Englund, H. (2006)
Prisoners of Freedom: Human Rights and the African Poor, Berkeley and Los Angeles: California University Press.
Epstein, A.L. (1951)
Some aspects of the conflict of law and urban courts in Northern Rhodesia, *Rhodes-Livingstone Journal*, 12: 28–40.
Epstein, A.L. (1969)
Injury and Liability in African Customary law in Zambia, in: Gluckman, M. (ed.) *Ideas and Procedures in African Customary Law*, Oxford University Press, Oxford.
Fallers, L.A. (1969)
Law without Precedent, Chicago: Chicago University Press.
Fitzpatrick, P. (1985)
Is it simple to be a Marxist in legal anthropology?, *Modern Law Review* 48 (4): 472–485.
Francioni, F. (2007)
The Right of Access to Justice under Customary International Law, in: Francioni, F. (ed.) *Access to Justice as a Human Right*, New York: Oxford University Press, 1–56.
Galanter, M. (2005)
Access to Justice as a Moving Frontier, in: Bass, J., Bogart, W.A. and Zemans, F. (eds.) *Access to Justice for a New Century, the Way Forward*, Toronto: Irwin Law, pp. 147–161.
Gluckman, M. (1967)
Judicial Process among the Barotse of Northern Rhodesia (2nd ed.), Manchester: Manchester University Press.
Gluckman, M. (1972)
The Ideas in Barotse Jurisprudence, reprint Manchester: Manchester University Press.
Griffiths, A. (1997)
In the Shadow of Marriage, Chicago: Chicago University Press.
Gulliver, P.H. (1963)
Social Control in an African Society: a study of the Arusha, London: Routledge and Kegan Paul.
Gulliver, P.H. (1973)
Negotiations as a mode of dispute settlement: towards a general model, *Law and Society Review* 7 (4): 667–692.
Gulliver, P.H. (1979)
Disputes and Negotiations: a cross-cultural perspective, New York: Academic Press.
Hailey, L. (1945)
An African Survey: A Study of Problems Arising in Africa South of the Sahara, Oxford: Oxford University Press.
Hamnett, I. (ed.) (1977)
Social Anthropology and Law, New York: Academic Press.
Himonga, C. and Manjoo, R. (2009)
The challenges of formalisation, regulation, and reform of traditional courts in South Africa, *Malawi Law Journal* 3 (2): 157–181.

Himsworth, C.M.G. (1972)
The Botswana Customary Law Act, 1969, *Journal of African Law* 16 (1): 4–18.
Hinz, M.O. (2010)
Justice for Justice and Justice for Peace: Legal Anthropological Observations on Traditional and Informal Justice Systems, in: Hinz, M. and Mapaure, C. (eds.) *In Search of Justice and Peace – Traditional and Informal Justice Systems in Africa*, Windhoek: Namibia Scientific Society, University of Namibia, pp. 3–24.
Holleman, J.F. (1974)
Issues in African Law, The Hague: Mouton.
Holleman, J.F. (1979)
Law and anthropology: a necessary partnership for the study of legal change in plural systems, *Journal of African Law* 23(2): 117–130.
Jensen, S. and Jefferson, A. (eds.) (2009)
State Violence and Human Rights: State Officials in the South, Routledge-Cavendish.
Koch, K.F. (1979)
Access to Justice: Anthropological Perspective, in: Cappelletti, M. (ed.) *Access to Justice* vol. 4, Sijthoff and Noordhoff, 1–218.
Koch, K.F., Sodergren, J.A. and Cambell, S. (1976)
Political and psychological correlates of conflict management: a cross-cultural study, *Law and Society Review* 10 (3): 443–466.
Koyana, D. and Bekker, J. (1998)
Judicial Process in the Customary Courts of Southern Africa, University of the Transkei.
Meron, T. (1989)
Human Rights and Humanitarian Norms as Customary Law, Oxford: Clarendon Press.
Merry, S.E. (1979)
Going to court: strategies of dispute management in an American urban neighbourhood, *Law and Society Review* 13(4): 891–925.
Merry, S.E. (2006)
Human Rights and Gender Violence – translating international law into local justice, Chicago: University of Chicago Press.
Morris, H.F. and Read, J.S. (1972)
Indirect Rule and the Search for Justice; essays in East African legal history, Oxford: Clarendon Press.
Moult, K. (2004)
Justice Served? Exploring informal justice mechanisms to address violence against women, University of Cape Town.
Myburgh, A. (ed.) (1980)
Indigenous Criminal Law in Bophuthatswana, University of South Africa.
Myburgh, A.C. and Prinsloo, M.W. (1985)
Indigenous Public Law in KwaNdebele, Pretoria: Van Schaik.
Myburgh, A.C. (1985)
Papers on Indigenous Law in Southern Africa, Pretoria: Van Schaik.
Udombana, N.J. (2006)
The African Commission on Human and Peoples' Rights and the development of fair trial norms in Africa, *African Human Rights Law Journal* 6(2): 299–332.

Nwogugu, E.I. (1976)
Abolition of customary courts – the Nigerian experiment, *Journal of African Law* 20(1): 1–19.

Odoki, B.J. (1994)
Reducing delay in the administration of justice: the case of Uganda, *Criminal Law Forum* 5(1): 57–89.

Opoku, K. (1974)
Traditional law under French colonial rule, *Verfassung und Recht in Übersee* 9(2): 139–153.

Pauwels, J.M. (1973)
La réforme du droit civil au Zaïre, comment concilier tradition et développement?, *Journal of African Law* 17(2): 216–226.

Prinsloo, M.W. (1983)
Inheemse Publiekreg in Lebowa, Pretoria: Van Schaik.

Roberts, S. and Palmer, M. (eds.) (2005)
Dispute Processes: ADR and the primary forms of decision-making, Cambridge: Cambridge University Press.

Roberts, S. (1979a)
Order and Dispute: an introduction to legal anthropology, New York: Penguin.

Roberts, S. (1979b)
Tradition and change at Mochudi: competing jurisdictions in Botswana, *African Law Studies* 17: 37–51.

Robinson, R.E. (1949)
The administration of African customary law, *Journal of African Administration* 1(4): 158–176.

Schärf, W. and Nina, D. (eds.) (2001)
Other Law: non-state ordering in South Africa, Cape Town: Juta and Co.

Schärf, W., Banda, C., Rontsch, R., Kaunda, D. and Shapiro, R. (2002)
Access to Justice for the Poor of Malawi? An Appraisal of Access to Justice Provided to the Poor of Malawi by the Lower Subordinate Courts and the Customary Justice Forums, Governance and Social Development Resource Centre, AusAID.

Seagle, W. (1941)
The Quest for Law, New York: Knopf.

Service, E. (1975)
Origins of the State and Civilization, New York: WW Norton.

Schwikkard, P.J. (1999)
Presumption of Innocence, Cape Town: Juta and Co.

Shweder, R., Minow, M. and Markus, H. (eds.) (2002)
Engaging Cultural Differences: the multicultural challenge in liberal democracies, New York: Russell Sage Foundation.

Spalding, F., Hoover, E. and Piper, J. (1970)
"One nation, one judiciary": the lower courts of Zambia, *Zambia Law Journal* 2(1&2): 1–289.

Stevens, J. (2001)
Access to justice in sub-Saharan Africa. The role of traditional and informal systems, Penal Reform International.

Thornberry, P. (1992)
International Law and the Rights of Minorities, Oxford: Clarendon Press.
Treschel, S. (2005)
Human Rights in Criminal Proceedings, Oxford: Oxford University Press.
UNDP (2005)
Programming for Justice: Access for All, a Practitioner's Guide to a Human Rights Approach to Access for Justice, Bangkok.
Van Niekerk, B. (1981)
Principles of the Indigenous Law of Procedure and Evidence as Exhibited in Tswana Law, in: Sanders, Anton J.G.M. (ed.) *Southern Africa in Need of Law Reform,* Durban: Butterworths, pp. 130–140.
Van Niekerk, G. (1986)
Comparative Study of the Application of Indigenous Law in the Administration of Criminal Justice in Southern Africa (unpublished LLM Thesis), University of SA.
Van Rouveroy Van Nieuwaal, E. (1987)
Chiefs and African states: some introductory notes and an extensive bibliography on African chieftaincy, *Journal of Legal Pluralism and Unofficial Law* 25/26.
Van Rouveroy Van Nieuwaal, E. (1992)
The Togolese Chiefs – Caught between Scylla and Charybdis, *Journal of Legal Pluralism and Unofficial Law* 32: 19–46.
Walker, D. (ed.) (1980)
The Oxford Companion to Law, Oxford: Oxford University Press.
Weber, M. (translated by A.R. Mendelson & Talcott Parsons) (1947)
The Theory of Social and Economic Organization, New York: Free press.
Wojkowska, E. (2006)
Doing Justice: how informal justice systems can contribute, UN Development Programme Oslo Governance Centre Report.

CHAPTER III

COURTS AND THE APPLICATION OF CUSTOMARY LAW IN MALAWI: TOWARDS THE REINTRODUCTION OF LOCAL COURTS

Kenan Tilombe MANDA

1. INTRODUCTION

This chapter discusses some of the challenges that arise when courts in the formal justice system apply customary law. After a short description of the history of Malawi's now defunct traditional courts, it describes the structure of the courts in Malawi since 1994 and how the courts deal with matters of customary law. The chapter then turns to a discussion of the proposals of the Malawi Law Commission to reintroduce a system of local courts specifically dedicated to customary law cases. These proposals have subsequently been adopted by the Malawian Parliament.[1] This chapter critically interrogates important aspects of the adopted reform proposals and presents a nuanced view on the application of customary law in Malawi.

2. HISTORICAL BACKGROUND

During the single party regime of President Banda and his Malawi Congress Party, Malawi's court system was a so called dual system comprising courts established under the Judiciary and headed by the Supreme Court of Malawi as well as traditional courts headed by the National Traditional Court of Appeal. The traditional courts fell under the executive arm of government and operated directly under the Ministry of Justice. Established in 1969, they had unlimited jurisdiction in matters to be determined according to customary law. The traditional courts were predicated on the old local courts that were introduced

1 The new Local Courts Act was passed in February 2011.

during the colonial era when the state administered customary law through District Commissioners with chiefs acting as advisors or assessors. After independence in 1964, the colonial local court system was replicated in the system of traditional courts with Resident Magistrates replacing the District Commissioners at regional and national levels.

Although originally established to have jurisdiction over customary law cases, traditional courts were soon given criminal jurisdiction over all cases including treason and murder.[2] Thus, they became a tool for silencing political opponents – real or perceived – to the one-party regime and committed many atrocities against Malawian citizens. The collaboration of the traditional courts with the single party state was made easier by the fact that they fell directly under the Ministry of Justice and would take instructions from the state machinery to ensure that certain people were convicted. Indeed, there were instances where people were acquitted in the High Court or a magistrate court falling under the Judiciary, only to be re-tried and convicted in a traditional court. The case in point is commonly known as the *Chilobwe* murders case, which involved a number of mysterious killings in a township called *Chilobwe* in Blantyre, the commercial capital of Malawi. Following a police investigation, a number of people were arrested as suspects in this case and taken before the Resident Magistrate Court which acquitted them because of a lack of evidence. However, the suspects were subsequently taken before a traditional court and convicted. One of the evidentiary principles in these Banda era traditional courts was that 'there is no smoke without fire'. In other words, if a person is said to have done something then he or she must have done the thing complained of. In effect, the courts believed that no one could lay a false charge against another person. Thus, falsely accused opponents of the political regime were convicted of crimes they did not commit.

Because of their role as instruments of oppression during the Banda era, the traditional courts were *effectively* abolished when the single party regime came to an end in 1994. Chapter IX of the new Constitution of the Republic of Malawi gave the courts under the Judiciary the specific mandate to have jurisdiction over all matters judicial in nature. The Constitution also gave the Judiciary the authority to determine whether a matter is within its competence or not.[3] In addition to these extensive powers, the Constitution ensured that there would be no other courts of superior or concurrent jurisdiction with the Supreme Court of Appeal and the High Court.[4] The remaining traditional court structures were absorbed in the High Court structures, through a process termed 'integration.'

---

2 The extension of the jurisdiction of the traditional courts to cover capital offences was made under General Notice 31 of 1969.

3 Section 103(2) of the Constitution of the Republic of Malawi.

4 Section 103(3) of the Constitution of the Republic of Malawi.

This process involved a series of meetings between officers from the Ministry of Justice and the Judiciary to look at ways to integrate those traditional courts that were not abolished by the Constitution into the Judiciary.

The Constitution prohibited the continued existence of the National Traditional Court of Appeal and the Regional Traditional Courts, which had concurrent jurisdiction with the Supreme Court of Appeal and the High Court respectively. However, the drafters of the Constitution saved pending legal actions that were before the District Traditional Appeal Court, the District Traditional Courts, and Grade A and B Courts, which were operating at the local level. For these traditional courts, the Constitution provided that they were to have the same jurisdiction, powers and procedures as before 1994, subject to an amendment or repeal of such powers by an Act of Parliament. Although there has not been an Act of Parliament repealing the powers of these supposedly saved courts, they have not been operational since 1994 because all their members of staff and their infrastructure have been integrated into the Magistrate Courts.

The integration process has been criticised for lacking a legislative mandate especially when the Judiciary appointed traditional court chairmen as magistrates, while the Constitution in fact 'saved' their traditional courts. The process has also been criticised for not taking into account the budgetary consequences of integration. It was not followed by an increase in the budget of the Judiciary so as to accommodate the additional personnel and infrastructure. While all members of staff from the traditional courts were introduced on the pay roll of the Judiciary, most of the infrastructure that was transferred from the traditional courts to the Judiciary fell in a state of disrepair as a result of inadequate funding.

In addition, specific legal questions around the 'saved' traditional courts remained. The Constitution in Section 204(1) gave the Registrar of the High Court the power to give directions to 'saved' traditional courts in terms of pending legal actions. At the same time, it could be argued that the 'saved' courts were still under the Ministry of Justice because prior to 1994 the decisions of these courts were subject to review and confirmation by the Chief Traditional Courts Commissioner, which was a position within the Ministry of Justice. According to the Constitution these procedures were still valid. Thus, although traditional courts were *effectively* abolished because they were no longer in operation, there were a number of questions in relation to their status in the judicial system.

With the traditional courts no longer functioning, the application of customary law fell on judicial officers who had no training in customary law. The definition of law that most judicial officers are accustomed to is limited to law that is contained in the statutes that are passed by Parliament or on the delegated authority of Parliament. Such a positivist approach to the law stems from legal training in which customary law receives no or very little attention. The introduction of statutory law and common law in countries like Malawi happened under the paradigm of bringing civilisation while in fact achieving colonial domination (Chanock 1985). In this context, customary law was regarded as backward and inferior to written law or common law. To what extent these views have permeated the minds of post-colonial jurists is a factor that needs further interrogation as it affects their perceptions of customary law as law in its own right.

Customary law goes beyond the realms of a positivist approach because it is unwritten, flexible and sometimes delves into areas of the metaphysical. It is not only about norms but extends to institutions which exist within African communities, including gods and ancestors. An understanding of law as that which is laid down by the sovereign or the state creates a conflict of perception: when looking at customary law most jurists conceive it within the confines of a state-centred conception of law. However, law is a contested concept which requires further interrogation and an understanding of the power dynamics that lie behind a specific conceptualisation.

3. THE STRUCTURE OF THE MALAWI COURT SYSTEM SINCE 1994

The current operating structure of the courts in Malawi is provided for in the Constitution, which establishes the Supreme Court of Appeal and the High Court as the two superior courts. While the Constitution does not specifically establish a Constitutional Court, a Constitutional Court is constituted on an ad hoc basis by judges of the Supreme Court or the High Court, whenever the Chief Justice certifies a matter to be a constitutional one, and refers it in first instance to the High Court or on appeal to the Supreme Court. Below the High Court the Constitution has established subordinate courts, which are presided over by professional as well as lay magistrates. These are established under Section 110 of the Constitution. The professional magistrates are those who are legally qualified and the courts in which they sit are called Resident Magistrate Courts. These courts function on three levels: Chief Resident Magistrate, Principal Resident Magistrate and Senior Resident Magistrate. These levels of professional magistrates are purely administrative since they all have the same jurisdiction. This is not the case with the lay magistrates who are divided into First Grade, Second Grade and Third Grade Magistrate Courts. There used to be Fourth Grade Magistrate Courts as well. They were created during the above mentioned process of integration to accommodate traditional court chairmen but have since been phased out. Only very few erstwhile traditional court chairmen remain in the Judiciary today. Most have died or retired. A fair number of them retired because they were illiterate and could therefore not maintain a record of proceedings as magistrates. In the traditional courts the records were maintained by a clerk of the court who would have undergone basic legal training. Some of the current lay magistrates were administrators or clerks of the court, either in the Judiciary or in the now defunct traditional courts, before they took a one year training course in basic law and became a lay magistrate.

In addition to the Magistrate Courts, the Constitution of 1994 established the Industrial Relations Court which has original jurisdiction over labour issues and employment related matters. There are ongoing discussions as to whether the Industrial Relations Court should be elevated to the same position as the High Court or whether there should be a Labour Division of the High Court, similar to the existing Commercial Division, which has been given original jurisdiction over all matters that are deemed to be commercial in nature.

Finally, the Constitution states that Parliament may establish traditional or local Courts, which shall be presided over by lay persons or chiefs. Because of the chequered past of traditional courts in Malawi, the Constitution has limited the jurisdiction of such courts as may be established by Parliament, exclusively to civil cases in customary law and such minor common law and statutory offences as may be prescribed by an Act of Parliament.[5] In 2004, consultations by the Malawi Law Commission brought to light that the abolishment of the traditional courts system had created a gap in the delivery of primary justice, especially where the application of customary law was concerned. It was noted that the Magistrate Courts were not as adept in dealing with customary law issues as the traditional courts had been. The Malawi Law Commission subsequently presented a proposal to reintroduce a system of local courts specifically dedicated to the application of customary law[6], which has since been adopted by Parliament. Before discussing the details of the adopted reform proposals, the application of customary law by the formal courts will be further discussed in the section below.

4. THE APPLICATION OF CUSTOMARY LAW

4.1. PROBLEMS IN THE MAGISTRATE COURTS

As indicated above, Magistrate Courts are regarded as less adept in dealing with customary law issues than the abolished traditional courts. Firstly, Magistrate Courts seem to display a lack of understanding or appreciation of customs and

5 Section 110(3) of the Constitution.

6 Malawi Law Commission Report on the Review of the Traditional Courts Acts, 2007.

customary practices. At times, customary law operates within a spiritual realm that is not easily understood by people who have a scientific approach to life and are trained in modern law. In fact, because there are no scientific explanations as to why some cultural norms are practiced, they are often misunderstood and dismissed as backward practices which are to be abolished or discouraged through the use of law, in particular the repugnancy clause.

Thus, magistrates seem to emphasize the application of human rights and common law, which they find to be in contrast with customary law. In fact, with the advent of the Constitution customary laws and practices were subject to scrutiny and were being measured against the Constitution. Those laws or practices that were deemed repugnant to the Constitution had to be changed, which increased the dynamics of customary laws and practices that are in themselves already flexible and constantly changing. This becomes an additional challenge in deciding which customary laws and practices are in effect.

A good example in this regard is the practice that exists in the patrilineal societies in the northern part of Malawi, where according to custom, custody of children is awarded to the father as long as he has paid *lobola* (bride price). This practice has now been superseded by requirements of the Convention of the Rights of the Child, which provides that the primary consideration for granting custody should be the best interest of the child. Although magistrates do not have jurisdiction to make orders of custody, a number of such orders have been made because magistrates do have jurisdiction over the dissolution of customary law marriages. Moreover, a course in Child Justice is an important part of the training of lay magistrates and the Convention of the Rights of the Child has been given great prominence in that course.

Witchcraft is another interesting example. The Witchcraft Act makes it an offence for anyone to profess that he or she is a practicing witch or wizard. Thus, modern law seeks to deny the existence of witchcraft. However, in the context of Malawian society, witchcraft cannot simply be dismissed by stating that it is merely pretence. There have been various reports of children being taught witchcraft and narrating their experiences. In other words, witchcraft is actually part and parcel of the way of life in Malawi and those who do not believe in its existence are probably a minority.

In addition to a lack of appreciation and understanding of customs and customary practices, there seems to be a problem of misrepresentation and distortion of customary law in the Magistrate Courts. The nature of customary law in Malawi, being diverse, unwritten, flexible and changing in response to new conditions and attitudes makes it prone to being misrepresented and distorted. Magistrate Courts have national jurisdiction and a magistrate's posting to a specific court does not depend on whether the person is familiar with the customs of the area where his or her court is situated. Thus, a magistrate is left to his or her own devices in terms of finding out what the applicable customary law of the area is. Some of these efforts include consulting local chiefs or elders and in some instances fellow magistrates and members of staff. Almost all of these consultations are done out of court and do therefore not form part of the court record. The fact that these consultations are done out of court makes it impossible for the parties to challenge the veracity of the information which the magistrate obtained.

According to the law, Magistrate Courts faced with questions of customary law must invite witnesses to testify as to what the applicable customary law is. The introduction of assessors, who would sit with magistrates on customary law related matters, has also been proposed. However, if a magistrate is not well versed in customary law, it is doubtful whether he or she will be in a position to effectively determine whether the witness or assessor is indeed an expert in the customary law before the court. Apart from that, the criteria for identifying experts may also be problematic. In most cases it probably would require an interview process to select an expert but who is to conduct the interviews? Some would argue that chiefs, as custodians of customary law, should be called upon as witnesses or should at least be in a position to inform the court as to who best to use as an expert witness.[7]

Customary law is sometimes surrounded by secrecy, especially where it is practiced by secret societies and is premised on spiritual beliefs. As an outsider one is not allowed to become privy to these customs unless one is initiated. This brings into question how a particular custom can be proved before a court of law. Even where the court manages to find experts to come and prove a custom, there would be questions as to the level of their expertise, since members of secret societies would in most cases not want to disclose their status in an open forum like a courtroom.

With modernity affecting all African societies, the purity of customary law also becomes an issue. The closer rural areas are to urban centres, the more customary law gets infused with aspects of modernity which exacerbates the problem of misinterpretation of customs and practices. The way around this problem might be to place the courts in the rural areas that are less 'tainted' by aspects of modernity and let them only have the jurisdiction to apply customary laws of those areas. This is what has been proposed by the Malawi Law Commission but

7 Some chiefs, while being custodians of customary law, may themselves not be well versed in customary law and rely on advisers to tell them what a particular customary law entails.

since the new Local Courts have not yet become operational this way to resolve the issue remains untested.

The problem of misconstruction or misinterpretation of customary law in the Magistrate Courts is further aggravated by the fact that judicial officers have not had any orientation into customary law except in the context of family law. In fact, the training programme for professional and lay magistrates does not include training in matters of customary law. Customary law in Malawi is so diverse that it is difficult to determine which customary law should be taught to magistrates. Ideally, the orientation of judicial officers towards customary law should be approached from an epistemological perspective.

If modernity is emphasized in the orientation of the courts then the local or traditional is relegated to the realm of the 'other' which leads to the use of labels such as 'archaic' and 'irrelevant' and reinforces the dominance of the modern. Clearly, the concept of justice that is applied to the traditional will then also be a modern one. However, one could question whether applying a modern concept of justice helps to restore the balance in a local community after a crime has been committed. There is in fact a difference between a crime and a wrong, which are the terminologies used in the modern and traditional justice systems, respectively. Customary law aims to address a wrong within a community, which in turn is understood to include God(s), ancestors as well as the living. Communities comprise of every part of nature, in other words, all living things together with gods and ancestors hold the fabric of society together. When a wrong happens it disturbs the social order of the community and customary law is aimed at restoring this order. Thus, traditional justice is restorative justice, geared towards restoring the balance in local communities. Ideally, the application of customary law within the context of the Malawi court system is premised on an understanding of these kinds of fundamental characteristics of customary law.

4.2. DEVELOPING CUSTOMARY LAW JURISPRUDENCE

Most of the courts in Malawi, especially the Magistrate Courts, do not seem to have an epistemological approach when it comes to applying customary law. Their understanding of customary law is limited to what they have read from the cases that have been decided by the High Court or the Supreme Court and what they have been told about customary law. The result has been that Magistrate Courts in Malawi have developed a hybrid law, which combines notions of customary law and common law. The problem with this is that it is subjective i.e. it depends on the magistrate's own understanding of what the applicable common law is and what the customary law of the area is. This is especially pertinent in view of the fact that only those notions of customary law which the magistrate feels do not run contrary to the norms of common law are retained to form part of the hybrid law. Clearly, we cannot maintain that Magistrate Courts are applying customary law when they are in fact developing hybrid law using their coercive power. In other words, people are forced to accept the hybrid law because the court has said so and not necessarily because it is what they perceive to be their custom. This is a source of conflict, especially since the Magistrate Courts are not courts of record and hence not binding. A decision just binds the parties before the court and not necessarily society at large, which in itself is also problematic as far as the development of customary law jurisprudence is concerned.

This is not to say that customary law cannot be changed or cannot be brought in line with human rights standards. Indeed it must be acknowledged that customary law is flexible enough to be adapted to the changing times. However, if customary law is made to look more and more like common law or indeed statutory law, then it loses its identity and can no longer be called customary law. Therefore, the implications of the trend to develop hybrid law are far reaching: we simply cannot talk about developing customary law jurisprudence without actually applying customary law. Thus, the decisions of the Magistrate Courts, which are developing hybrid law, may not be the best source of customary law jurisprudence.

In the High Court, customary law must be proved as a matter of evidence. This is in accordance with the provisions of Section 64 of the Courts Act,[8] which states that customary law should be treated as a question of fact to be determined by calling experts or persons whom the court deems to be well acquainted with such customary law. One could ask the question on what basis is the Courts Act treating customary law as fact and not law. It could even be argued that this is a clear demonstration of the fact that statutory law regards customary law as inferior which in turn is reflected in the actions of judicial officers as they apply the Courts Act. Be that as it may, this provision of the Courts Act clearly needs to be interrogated. If customary law is treated as fact, would a person be allowed to bring an appeal as a matter of fact and not law? And in terms of developing customary law jurisprudence are we developing jurisprudence on matters of fact?

Mwaungulu, J in *Likaku v Likaku*[9] observed that custom is not generally a matter of public renown and that not even judges are capable of knowing all or a substantial part of it. Mwaungulu, J went on to hold that matters of customary

8 Chapter 3:02 of the Laws of Malawi.
9 High Court of Malawi, Principal Registry Matrimonial Cause No. 10 of 1999.

law are and should be a matter of inquiry and that this is the only way of ensuring that customary law is not misrepresented. In my view, such inquiry needs to be extensive because preventing misrepresentation of customary law requires more than just a basic understanding of what the customary practice is. Indeed it requires a deeper interrogation of how customary law came to be, which in turn requires pedagogy and re-examination of the various epistemologies, the concept of knowledge and the question of what law is. This is especially true when it comes to the application of the repugnancy clause which is essentially a creature of statutory and common law.

It has to be understood that common law was a local concept that was (inter) nationalised through the process of colonialization which in itself was a violent process that did not allow for dialogue. In the context of Africa, statutory and common law were initially restricted to the localities where the colonialists had settled and spread through nations as they were colonised and the natives became 'civilised.' Thus, the 'local' law of the colonialists was nationalised and internationalised. It was applied to all tribes and nations without any interrogation or appreciation of what the 'other' law was and what role it played in regulating people's behaviour. Furthermore, the spread of this settlers' law came with the force of the gun or some other coercive power. There was little space for dialogue. Nowadays, the colonialists' laws are still being reinforced into the minds of modern jurists without much space for dialogue. Statutory and common law are taught in law schools where customary law does not receive the same kind of attention. Given this situation, we, modern day judges, may have to ask ourselves: From what position do we declare a custom repugnant? Is it from a position of dominance which we inherited from the colonial era because we are still using the laws that were used to dominate other cultures without getting a full appreciation of what these cultures and their customary laws entail? And, is not the requirement to 'prove' customary law within the courts, in itself, an admission of ignorance on our part of what these laws entail? How can we, judges, in our ignorant state declare customary laws repugnant? Are we not just perpetuating the 'civilisation missions' of the colonialists? Do we really appreciate what role the spiritual realm plays in the development of customary law or do we, like the colonialists, just dismiss what we have no appreciation of because it cannot be proved by modern day science?

The first step in the application of customary law should be to realise that customary law is law and should be placed on the same footing as any other law. In fact, Section 26 of the Constitution makes provision for the right to participate in cultural practices, while Section 200 recognises customary law as a source of law in Malawi. Thus, one would expect the High Court to recognise customary laws as law and not require that they be proved as fact through an evidentiary hearing as is currently required by an Act of Parliament. Because such evidentiary hearings do not interrogate what the definition of law or the concept of justice is one has to question from whose perspective customary law and traditional justice are being defined. After all, these concepts are not a given; they are contested terms, just like the notions of legality and illegality. But how does a court begin to create space for dialogue between the dominant statutory and common law and what is perceived as the 'other', i.e. customary law? Currently the examination of customary law in the courts is certainly predicated on measuring it against the formal structures and principles of statutory and common law, which are purported to be universal concepts aligned with modern reality.

Despite the Courts Act which states that customary law should be treated as a question of fact, there have been times when the High Court has taken judicial notice of customary law on appeal.[10] There are also instances where the High Court has awarded guardianship or custody of children, after a divorce, following principles of customary law, subject of course to the best interests of the child. This has happened in cases where the parties would have been married under the Marriage Act.[11] On the other hand, the High Court seems to have no hesitation to declare a customary law repugnant if it is deemed to offend the principles of equity or fairness, despite the fact that in most of these cases the parties themselves would have voluntarily elected to govern their relationship in accordance with the supposedly inequitable or unfair custom. It is important to note that in such instances customary law is required to conform to the received laws and it is from the point of view of these laws that customary law is evaluated. Can this be deemed to be an objective evaluation?

If we are to develop customary law jurisprudence, the courts must start by evaluating customary laws on their own merits. In my view, such an exercise cannot be accomplished by simply calling expert witnesses to come and prove a particular customary law. It requires anthropological study and analysis. Only through an anthropological analysis can the court begin to appreciate what customary law entails. Another prerequisite is to raise the courts' awareness of the fact that Malawi does not have a single but a plural system of law. In other words, semi-autonomous social fields which have rule-making capacities and the means to induce or coerce compliance coexist. In theory, these social fields are set within a larger social medium which can and does affect it and invade it sometimes at the invitation of the persons inside it and sometimes at its own instance (Moore 1978). In the case of customary law, however, it seems that the

10 For example in *Chitema v Lupanda* 2 A.L.R. Mal. 162; this decision was in contrast to an earlier High Court decision in the case of *Mwale v Kaliu* 1 A.L.R. Mal. 213, which held that the court cannot take judicial notice of customary law and that the same must be proved in evidence.

11 A case in point is *Kamcaca v Nkhota* (No. 2) 4 A.L.R. Mal. 518.

invasions of the larger social medium are not by invitation, but rather through dominance of the received, or as some have aptly put it, 'imposed' law. The 'imposed' law is often used to propagate views of modernity which are based on Western ideologies and this becomes a source of tension.

In most cases where customary law is contrary to written law, the written law will be given prominence[12], regardless of the fact that the parties, who are appearing before the court, may have regulated their conduct in accordance with customary law. Even where the parties want the court to give effect to customary law, the court will give effect to the written law. This has been the situation with matters involving chieftaincy. According to custom these matters are dealt with by the Paramount Chief, who is supposed to be the final arbiter, yet the High Court has been assuming jurisdiction over such matters because the Constitution grants it unlimited jurisdiction over any matter. There have also been cases related to the use of land, where the High Court, while recognising the existence of customary law in terms of land use, has used the principles of equity to grant a person the right of usage even though under customary law they would have been precluded from doing so. The case of *Dorothy Tambala v Wilfred Kachere*[13] is an example which involved a piece of land that was given to the respondent's grandfather by virtue of marriage into a particular village. Upon the death of his wife, the grandfather was forced to go back to his home village under a custom called *kusudzula* (which can be likened to the termination of a marriage). The effect of this custom was that the grandfather ceased to have any claims to land usage within the village he was married into. In this particular instance, however, the court ordered that the respondent was entitled to an equal share of the land by virtue of the fact that he was related to the appellant through marriage and also by virtue of having stayed in the village for quite some time. The appellant happened to be related to the respondent's dead grandfather's wife. While this is indeed a fair decision, the court never examined the significance of the *kusudzula* custom and why the community which practiced it felt the need to carry it out. In other words, the question why this custom was in existence and whether it had any spiritual significance in terms of 'spiritual cleansing' – which is often the case behind these customs – was never interrogated. This lack of interrogation of particular customs and their inter-linkages with the spiritual realm poses a challenge and creates a limitation in terms of how fully a particular custom can be appreciated.

All in all, the application of customary law in Malawi leaves much to be desired. It can be argued that access to justice is very limited for people who want to live

12 As was clearly demonstrated by Chimasula, AJ (as he then was) in *Zinga v Zinga* [1994] MLR 405.

13 Civil Case No. 21 of 2006 decided in the Principal Registry of the High Court.

in accordance with their customs. In fact, the lives of the majority of Malawians are regulated by customary law and yet there is no forum where they can have their matters effectively adjudicated using customary law as the primary law. There are simply not enough Magistrate Courts in the rural areas and where these courts are in existence they are applying hybrid rather than customary law. Furthermore, while the High Court, has tried to apply customary law by having it proved, access to the High Court is problematic for most Malawians due to the high costs involved as well as the complicated procedures for filing cases with the court. Thus, the Malawi Law Commission has recommended the reintroduction of a system of courts which will be dealing with customary law cases at the first instance and which will operate at the local level. These proposals will be discussed in more detail in the section below. The main question in the context of what was discussed above is whether these new courts will be applying customary law as propagated by local communities without reference to the notions of justice dictated by Western ideologies or whether notions derived from statutory and common law will be taken into account and if so, how?

5. THE RECOMMENDATIONS OF THE MALAWI LAW COMMISSION

Although the sentiments regarding the application of customary law by the formal courts undoubtedly played a role, the main consideration of the Law Commission for proposing the introduction of new local courts, was the existing lack of access to justice at the grassroots level and the wish to provide litigants with access to courts that are relatively cheap and uncomplicated in terms of court procedures. In this regard, the Law Commission took note of the research findings of Scharf et al. (2002) who found that most of the poor in Malawi have problems accessing the Magistrate Courts. They also found that in the absence of formal courts matters are being taken to chiefs and village headmen. These matters include those relating to bride price, divorce, small theft, issues of chieftaincy, customary land, wife snatching, destruction of crops, inheritance, witchcraft, elopement, adultery and cases of fighting where blood is not spilt, thus making up around 80 percent of cases in rural communities.

The overall objective of the reintroduction of local courts at grassroots level is to improve good governance in Malawi, which is one of the pillars of the Poverty Reduction Strategy that the country has adopted as a tool for development.[14] In terms of the structure of the Judiciary, the new courts will be subordinate to the

14 The ones in the recent past being the Malawi Poverty Reduction Strategy Paper and the Malawi Development and Growth Strategy.

High Court and operate at a level below the lay magistrate courts.[15] The presiding officers of the new courts will be lay persons rather than chiefs who already fall under the executive branch of government which would undermine their judicial independence. Initiatives under the primary justice programme have recognised the informal role that chiefs play in resolving disputes within their local communities. The new local courts are not meant to replace the adjudicating authority that chiefs have by virtue of their position. Instead, the introduction of the new local courts is aimed at formalising and recognising the role that customary law plays in regulating the behaviour of people at grassroots level. At the same time, it is hoped that Malawi can begin to develop customary law jurisprudence, which, as was noted above, is not highly developed at the moment.

5.1. THE STRUCTURE AND POSITIONING OF THE NEW LOCAL COURTS

The Law Commission has recommended that the new courts are to be called Local Courts and that they will have original jurisdiction over customary law matters.[16] They are to be the lowest cadre of courts within the judicial structure of Malawi with an appellate structure at the district level, from where appeals will lie with the High Court and eventually with the Supreme Court. The positioning of these new courts under the lay magistrates courts seems to be a reflection of the significance that is placed on customary law within the justice system. It resembles the set up during the colonial era when customary justice systems were assimilated into the colonial state's justice structures, the only difference being that the aim of controlling the rural population has been replaced by notions of access to justice.

With the Local Courts positioned at the bottom of the system how do we safeguard the quality of justice? It is quite clear that courts at the lower levels of the judicial echelon have problems when it comes to funding and resources. The lack of resources has in most cases affected their quality of work which in turn affects the quality of justice. To really appreciate the quality of justice that is being delivered at the different levels of the judicial system in Malawi, one would need an analysis that falls far outside the scope of this chapter. What is important here is to highlight the quality of justice as an area of concern. The positioning of the new Local Courts might also affect the perceptions that judicial officers in the courts above them will have about these courts. This is especially critical for courts that will hear appeals from the new Local Courts.

15 See Malawi Law Commission Report on the Review of the Traditional Courts Acts, 2007.
16 The Malawi Law Commission Report on the Review of the Traditional Courts Acts, 2007.

The Law Commission has recommended that the Local Courts must keep records of their proceedings and provide reasons for their decisions. In combination with the recommended establishment of a District Local Court of Appeal, which will also be a court of record, this is intended to assist the development of customary law jurisprudence in Malawi. These recommendations imply that the High Court would have to take judicial notice of the customary law that would have been applied at first instance and on appeal by the District Local Court of Appeal. However, in dealing with those appeals will judicial officers, who have a bias towards written law, give due respect to the decisions that are made in the lower courts based on unwritten and flexible customary laws? Or would the tendency be to ensure that the decisions of the local courts conform to the decisions made in the higher courts and to the written law or indeed to a 'modern kind of thinking' as to what law is supposed to be? It remains to be seen from whose perspective customary law jurisprudence will be developed. Suffice to say that these questions are closely related to the problems with the application of customary law and the development of hybrid law as discussed in the section above.

5.2. PRESIDING OFFICERS AND ASSESSORS

The Law Commission proposed that the new Local Courts are to be presided over by lay persons who will be employed on the basis that they possess sufficient knowledge of the local customs of the area in which the court is to be situated so as to be considered experts in its customary law. They will bear the title of Chairperson. The Law Commission also proposed that chairpersons would have to be literate and have at least a secondary school qualification so as to be able to maintain a record of their cases. The Law Commission did not resolve the issue of how to select chairpersons but opted to treat this as an administrative matter for the Registrar of the High Court to resolve. During the one party regime, traditional court chairmen were selected through an electoral process, whereby names of possible candidates would be proposed and members of the community would vote for the person whom they felt was most suitable for the job. It remains to be seen whether the Registrar will adopt a similar process for the selection of local court chairpersons. One outstanding issue is the role of the chiefs in the selection process. It is difficult to see how the Registrar would be in a position to determine whether a candidate has sufficient knowledge of the customs of a particular local area without the involvement of the chief. In my view, the chief who is the custodian of the local customs would have to be involved in the selection of the local court chairperson. This can, however, bring the objectivity of the candidate into question, especially when the candidate is viewed as being the 'Kings man'. The same problem arises in the selection of assessors.

The Law Commission has recommended that the Local Courts at all levels of their proposed hierarchy will sit with assessors who will act as an extra source of customary law should the chairperson need their advice during proceedings. The function of these assessors is mainly to give advice in all civil matters involving customary law. Therefore, assessors will have to be well versed in the customary law of the area in which the court is located. It is also envisaged that the assessors will be monitoring the sale of property seized pursuant to court orders in order to ensure transparency and accountability in conducting such sales.

5.3. JURISDICTION

The Law Commission has recommended that the new courts should have only local jurisdiction, i.e. jurisdiction restricted to the area in which the court is located. Furthermore, the Law Commission proposed that matters of inheritance and land disputes be excluded from the jurisdiction of the Local Courts. Matters of inheritance were found to be volatile and complex and closely related to the phenomenon of property grabbing which has been criminalised in Malawi and is considered a serious offence. However, if inheritance matters are governed by custom is it appropriate to exclude them from the jurisdiction of the new courts? Does this not reflect a lack of appreciation of the reasoning behind customary practices related to inheritance? Where should the level of intervention be? Is a law that reintroduces Local Courts the best way to engage with customary law in matters of inheritance? Or should there be dialogue in order to develop an appreciation of what the various customary laws entail and the reason why they were introduced and are being practiced? I believe these are pertinent questions that need to be asked before the new courts become operational.

The exclusion of land disputes from the jurisdiction of the new Local Courts seems to be appropriate given the fact that Government has adopted a Land Policy which recommends the establishment of Customary Land Tribunals under the Land Act. In addition, Parliament has extended the jurisdiction of Magistrate Courts to include disputes involving customary land, which jurisdiction had hitherto been restricted to the High Court. The reasons that were cited for this decision revolved around the difficulties that parties involved in land disputes have to access the High Court. Some High Court judges have observed that land disputes under customary law are too complex to be left in the hands of magistrates, especially in view of the fact that magistrates do not have jurisdiction to grant injunctions to stop usage of a piece of land.

This is perhaps a reflection of the difficulties that are arising especially in areas where most of the customary land was sold by chiefs to estate owners. It must be noted that in Malawi it is a matter of law that customary land is not owned by anyone. It is held in trust by the chief for the benefit of the community. Against this background, one has to ask whether title to customary land really passed to current estate owners, whose title dates back to the days of colonialism. In other word, were chiefs in a position to sell customary land to settlers? These questions need further interrogation most notably in land disputes between local communities and owners of large estates. Should these matters come before the High Court, the question which title would be recognised would have important implications for the application of customary law and the development of customary law jurisprudence. The question of precedence of title can in my view not be left to the customary land tribunals or local courts.

Another jurisdiction related matter concerns the custody of children. The Law Commission recommended that the Local Courts should have jurisdiction to distribute matrimonial property following the dissolution of a marriage celebrated in accordance with customary law. However, the Commission felt that it would not be appropriate for these courts to handle matters related to the custody of children because customary law predetermines these matters without taking into account the best interests of the child as provided for in the Convention on the Rights of the Child. This is clearly an area where human rights have been given prominence over customary law. It reflects a perception that customary law is unfair and therefore not fit to govern these matters.

An alternative approach would have been to make a distinction between custody and guardianship: custody can be awarded to one parent in terms of the customary law under which the parties celebrated their marriage while guardianship is awarded to the other parent if that is in the best interest of the child at that point in time. It is important to acknowledge that what is in the best interest of the child may very well change over time. Thus, a degree of flexibility is needed. Guardianship might have to change if a child attains a certain age, depending on gender as well. This kind of reasoning takes account of the main point of the Convention on the Rights of the Child which is that prominence must be given to the best interest of the child. At the same time, it creates a space for dialogue by taking customary law into account. Simply removing custody matters from the jurisdiction of the Local Courts closes the space for dialogue and gives rise to complications, for instance, when it comes to claiming chieftaincy. If a woman is granted custody of children of a patrilineal marriage, then these children cannot claim the chieftaincy of their father. Thus, by giving prominence to human rights over customary law we are also affecting matters that are clearly within the realm of custom and tradition. When deciding to exclude custody matters from the jurisdiction of the Local Courts, these issues must be interrogated, especially in view of the fact that these reforms are intended to assist in the development of customary law jurisprudence.

Finally, in terms of criminal jurisdiction, the Law Commission recommended to restrict the jurisdiction of the new Local Courts to minor statutory offences, whose sentences are not likely to exceed twelve months imprisonment. The Commission recommended that, while the Local Courts would be able to sentence a person to up to twelve months imprisonment, these sentencing powers should be considered reserve powers. Where a local court would impose a term of imprisonment, it would immediately have to be converted to community service. Only in very exceptional circumstances would a local court be allowed to impose imprisonment and it would then be required to justify the sentence.

The Commission recommended that matters of witchcraft be excluded from the jurisdiction of the Local Courts because it would otherwise lead to victimisation of innocent people and unnecessary encroachment on people's rights. It must be noted that chiefs sometimes 'try' people accused of practicing witchcraft. There have been numerous reports of people who are deemed to be witches and who die as a result of cleansing rituals performed by witchdoctors who are invited by the chief to perform such rituals. Similar problems could arise in the context of the new Local Courts which is the reason to exclude witchcraft cases from their jurisdiction.

However, this argument is problematic because it assumes that victimisation of innocent people and unnecessary encroachment on their rights does not take place within the 'formal' justice system. In reality, suspects are being convicted in the Magistrate Courts for practicing witchcraft on the basis of mere assertions. The court does not stop to interrogate why such assertions are made and in most cases will not have a full appreciation of the case because it is not likely to delve into the spiritual realm. For instance, the court will not call a witchdoctor as a witness although he or she can be considered an expert in matters of witchcraft, because doing so will be forcing the person to commit an offence under the Witchcraft Act. Calling such expert witnesses would, however, give the court an opportunity to appreciate the spiritual elements of the case and it could well be that with such expertise a person wrongly accused of practicing witchcraft could be exonerated in a Magistrate Court.

6. CONCLUSION

The extension of the jurisdiction of magistrate courts to matters involving customary land already showed Parliament's concern about the lack of access to justice. Parliament has now gone a step further and passed the Local Courts bill, thus approving the establishment of Local Courts dedicated to customary law cases. All that remains now is for Government to implement the legislation and bring the new courts into operation.

One challenge that will have to be overcome is funding and resources for the new Local Courts. The Judiciary in Malawi currently struggles to get the funding it needs for its operations and the new courts could easily become an extra burden on an already overstretched budget. Indeed, this could be a major impediment to the establishment of Local Courts in Malawi.

Overall, the reintroduction of local courts into the judicial echelons is a welcome development but it remains to be seen whether the new courts will apply customary law as it is propagated within the various local communities or whether they will take principles from statutory and common law into account and if so, how. While these reforms are a step towards the development of customary law jurisprudence, they could prove a failure if customary law is not given a space for dialogue. It must be appreciated that there is a conflict of perceptions and perspectives between statutory and common law and customary law that cannot simply be denied; it needs to be addressed through dialogue. We, as jurists, need to be aware that what we have come to view as law is mainly the will of the politically dominant, which in most cases tries to suppress other forms of social regulation for its own benefit.

BIBLIOGRAPHY

Chanock, M. (1985)
Law, Custom and Social Order: The Colonial Experience in Malawi and Zambia, Cambridge: Cambridge University Press.

Moore, S.F. (1978)
Law and Social Change: The Semi-autonomous Social Field as an Appropriate Subject of Study, in: Moore, S.F. (ed.) *Law as Process: An Anthropological Approach*, Abingdon: Routledge, pp. 54–59.

Scharf, W., Banda, C., Roentsch, R., Kaunda, D. and Shapiro, R. (2002)
Access to Justice for the Poor of Malawi? An Appraisal of Access to Justice Provided to the Poor of Malawi by the Lower Subordinate Courts and the Customary Justice Forums, Report prepared for the UK Department of International Development – DfID, accessible at www.gsdrc.org/go/display/document/legacyid/1293 [accessed on 27 May 2011].

CHAPTER IV

POWERS, RIGHTS AND CITIZENSHIP: THE 'RETURN' OF THE TRADITIONAL AUTHORITIES IN MOZAMBIQUE*

Maria Paula G. MENESES

1. INTRODUCTION

There is a growing interest in Mozambique concerning traditional authorities and their relation to the State. Neither unique nor exclusive to Mozambique, this situation remains a central area of political debate throughout the African continent. The question does not centre upon discerning the existence of a politically determined 'authority' that presides over ethnic groups, but rather about its space and its social construction, as well as its future participation in local politics.

Research carried out in Mozambique reveals important contradiction in the discourse and practices on the political opening towards other political forces in the country, including traditional authorities, rising questions on potential human rights abuses (Meneses 2006, 2007). In the case of traditional authorities and their role in local administration and governance in Mozambique, it is important to first understand the nature of their power and space to rule and to interrogate if their power constitutes a challenging opposition to that of the modern State. I use the tools of ethnography to analyse the politics towards local, community (including traditional) authorities in Mozambique, and to understand the dynamics associated with them. This chapter will first discuss certain concepts that are essential to understanding the Mozambican context; it will then analyse how the implementation of the modern colonial State impacted upon the socio-political complex that later on became captured under the stereotype of traditional authority; and, finally, based upon this analysis, it will

* This chapter is based on fieldwork that was conducted between 1998 and 2008. I would like to thank everyone who made this research possible, as well as the insights of several colleagues in discussing this material with me. I am grateful to FCT, whose grant PTDC/AFR/103057/2008 – FCOMP-01–0124-FEDER-008664 funded part of this research.

broaden the discussion on the predicaments and options that these authorities posed to the Mozambican State after independence, especially regarding conflict resolution.[1] The multiple meanings associated with the category of 'traditional' will help explore how the boundaries between powers and institutions were (and still are) conceived and continuously redefined by colonial authorities, anthropologists, local chiefs and local elites, as well as by contemporary State authorities. The different discourses about authority and legitimacy will help us identify points of support and reference that have maintained and justified the diversity of situations that are present today.

This article seeks to contribute to the current debates surrounding questions of power and politics of belonging, including citizenship. The ongoing debates about the intricate web of institutions involved in social regulation highlight their importance. These instances, which are carriers of distinct journeys and historical densities, have produced a complex relationship with the formal structures of the State. While such an analysis is useful for Mozambique, it draws from and is applicable to other situations both in Africa and in other regions of the globe. Such an analysis also provides a way of understanding the underlying culture wars being waged to redefine current forms of belonging in multi-ethnic states.

The insights provided by a combination of historical and cultural analysis are key in clarifying the rationales that have been used for constructing the figure of 'traditional authority' as a homogeneous group, in opposition to the State, and producing them as suspects who quite often are seen as perpetrators of human rights abuses. As in other contexts, this research contributes to the study of the responsibility of social research about stories that, although silenced or ignored, must be revisited and (re)questioned.

2. TRADITION, BETWEEN THE PAST AND THE FUTURE

In recent decades, the awareness of indigenous peoples and traditional authorities has reached global dimensions. In African contexts, the concept of traditional power is associated with the notion of endogenous legitimacy, which, despite superficially suggesting a return to the local, are in fact discourses about global access. In other words, a web of histories and contextual situations suggest an alternative cosmopolitan perspective about the world (Simone 2001, 25; Mbembe 2002, 7).[2]

---

1 Mozambique obtained its independence in June 1975.

2 In their effort to transcend the dominant cosmopolitan perspective, alternative concepts of cosmopolitanism share characteristics that appear to be contradictory (cosmopolitism and

Several studies on traditional authorities in Mozambique have privileged rural contexts as space of analysis (Harrison 1998; Gave, Soft and Dove 2003; Gonçalves 2005; Kyed and Buur 2006). The justification for this approach seems to be based upon the assumption that the more remote an area is, the less 'contaminated' it would be and the forms of local power therefore more authentic. This position is supported by the modern/traditional dichotomy, one of the key dichotomies upon which the contemporary State is constructed. The dichotomy modern/traditional translates into a geography of political differences that is defined by a territorial detachment, where traditional becomes associated with rural contexts as spaces where pre-colonial power structures endured. However, no tradition can consider itself the correct image of a previous practice since traditions are created and recreated by the very modern historical processes. The legitimacy of the traditional authority is guaranteed by those that do not govern according to norms of the formal modern State, whose authority is defined according to socially sanctioned structures.

This analytical approach has its roots in the colonial administration, a political exercise that introduced critical distortions in local power structures (Meneses 2010). The modern colonial administration in Mozambique gradually imposed a singular vision of history that did not consider other knowledge systems as equal and relegated them into a place of inferiority by granting science and the modern bureaucracy the power to explain and organize the world (Meneses 2007). This colonial intervention brought new conflicts between different experiences, forms of knowledge and cultures. The modern Western thought, which is based on hierarchies and dichotomies, established an 'abyssal' fracture that divided the world in two: the metropolitan, civilized world and the colonial world (Santos 2007, 45–46). Such a division assumed that the realities that occurred in the colonies did not include the norms and knowledge that were used in the 'old', metropolitan world. At the roots of this world was the 'universal' principle establishing that the forms of knowledge in the colonial space did not have any use for the civilized world. The colonial zone was rapidly transformed into the expression of local, traditional knowledge, the metonymy of the traditional authorities.

The African political authorities, homogeneously categorized and neglected in formal law, took upon different forms of social regulation that existed beyond official colonial law and, exiled from the formal justice system, came to be

patriotism, cosmopolitism and ethnic group, etc.) in their search for counter-hegemonic solutions in ways of being in the world. These alternative conceptions mobilize different collective actors (not always mutually intelligible), vocabularies and resources in their search for better ways to articulate their struggles in global networks. See, for example, Bhabha, 1996; Appiah 1998; Diouf 2000; Werbner 2002 or Santos 2006, regarding this last perspective.

described as the expression of 'traditional law'. The social dynamics that constituted the complex system of 'traditional law' were generated by an overlap of various epistemological, cultural, social, political, national, transnational and experiential dimensions that compels an analysis that articulates these various dimensions in action.

Contemporary African societies rest upon regimes of development that were constructed by various colonial regimes. Some of the newly independent regimes inherited the colonial propensity to exercise power through a severe exercise of economical and administrative unification. In name of the national unity, these governments sought to transform the presence of the multiple cultural regimes into a historical sequence of events and policies. Such is the case of Mozambique, where the current State is essentially a heterogeneous system of knowledge and normative processes (Meneses 2006, 2007). It is therefore important to study the design of present institutions to improve social intervention and identify situations where people still have no access to justice, becoming extremely vulnerable to political violence and human rights abuses.

It is important to understand the political and social dynamics when evaluating the ruptures and continuities between the colonial administration and the independent Mozambican State and to propose a more complex interpretation of that which is otherwise regarded as 'post-colonial'. The relationships between colonial authority and other references of political power were never symmetrical since they were marked by unequal power relations. At the same time, they indicate the presence of dialogues, mutual interferences and appropriations that mark and structure contemporary Mozambique. This point is extremely important for the study of the multiple forms of power that exist in the social fabric of contemporary urban contexts. Research carried out in several Mozambican urban spaces reveals the interference of the colonial policies in current political cultures, generating new hybrid forms in contacts, confrontations, fissions, and fusions taking place among the diverse political cultures (Santos and Meneses 2006; Meneses and Santos 2009). The political mutations that Mozambique has experienced throughout the last century – colonialism, socialism, and neo-liberalism – are reflected in the State's current regulations and action of political administration. The heterogeneity of the Mozambican State, as analysed by Santos (2003, 63), elapses from the action of different forms of social regulation resulting in a situation of legal pluralism.[3]

The concepts present throughout this article – tradition, ethnicity, colonialism, and the modern State – require an historical criticism to contextualize the contours they have acquired in Mozambique. A refined analysis of the

[3] It echoes, politically, in Article 4 of the Mozambican Constitution of 2004.

metamorphosis of 'traditional authorities' stimulates a conscious reading of existing relationships between the distinct forces and actors involved in local governance, by examining them as a specific feature of colonial political culture's violent intervention. The multiple forms upon which contemporary political cultures have laid their foundations (both during the colonial period and after independence) should be analysed in a manner that will help (re)learn and recognize which functions introduced by the colonial State remain active in contemporary Mozambique.

The effort to build an administrative structure that ideologically justified the exogenous, Portuguese administrative intervention in Mozambique was a distinctive tendency of the colonial period. The relatively recent construct of the figure of traditional authority[4] symbolizes the emerging interest, from the African side of society, to confront the presence of the European colonizer, a fact often used to legitimize and reinforce the power of the colonial state as a superior form of social organization (Scott, 1998). Ethnicity, traditional law and traditional authorities came to signify the disappearance of 'pristine' elements of pre-colonial Africa. Recognizing the different power relations between the colonizer and the colonized, any analysis of the dynamics of contact between the two will detect sequences of influence and interaction; that is, the appearance of new cultural moments.[5] In an attempt to bypass the simplistic nature of binary categories, Cooper (1996, xii) entices a complex reading of this colonial contact, which resulted in a vast contact zone, or space of intelligibility, ambiguity and interaction between colonizers and colonized. This contact zone, full of moments of resistance and of adaptation to the colonial interventions,[6] has given opportunity to the emergence of new forms of authority and representation.

---

4 The creation of this socio-political figure came from an ethnographic perspective that privileged the study of tribal 'habits and traditional customs' and were defined by linguistic and cultural patterns. Based upon their studies repetitive behavioural patterns and thought processes, these authors tried to delineate the several cultural systems characterized for future comparison with Western systems. This knowledge would aide in improving the relations between the Portuguese colonial administration and African social groups.

5 In Mozambique, it is important to mention, for example, the presence, in the days of today, of traditional authorities in urban spaces, as is the case of the "*régulo*" Luís in the neighbourhood Manga-Loforte, in the city of Beira (Meneses et al. 2003), of the *régulo* Xavier Matola, in the city with the same name (Jossias, 2004), or from *régulos* in various localities in the city Angoche (Meneses and Santos 2009).

6 For example, there are endless studies indicating that African customary law was altered by the colonial contact. As a consequence, many researchers considered the customary law to be a complex colonial construction that augmented another version of the modernity (ex. Snyder 1981; Chanock 1998).

3. CIVILIZATION, CULTURE AND CITIZENSHIP IN THE COLONIAL CONTEXT

3.1. NATIONALITY AND CITIZENSHIP: TOUGHENING THE ABYSSAL LINE

The notion of nationality emerged in the European panorama by mid 19th century, and within half a century it became a strong and stable concept. From then on, it was strongly determined by private international law, defining the legal connection that connects an individual to the State. The central question that was then presented to jurists and parliament members was how to identify which criteria would help characterize this connection, and, from this point on, how it would be possible to define the union of nationals as subjects to the sovereignty of the State, transforming rights into an element of an individuals' social qualification (Mamdani 1996).

In the Portuguese case, the implementation of a modern colonial system at the end of the 19th century brought a radical change in the legal situation of the majority of those who inhabited the overseas colonial spaces in Africa through the racialization of citizenship. From then on one witnessed the dissociation between the native or the indigenous, (endowed with ethnic identity, and therefore guaranteed only private rights, specific to a given 'ethnic' group) and the citizen (privilege of the civilized, guaranteed by the colonial public right). An analysis of the racialized disassociation between citizen and native is central to understanding how colonial categories were established through a very necessary regime of rights and obligations.[7]

The demand for Portugal to transform itself into a modern colonial power escalated the direct intrusion of knowledge that was assumed to be superior because it was endowed with legal authority. This ideology was quickly set into power, reinforcing the notion that everything should be judged and validated according to the canons that emanated from continental Portugal. A native's transformation into civilized citizen required that he or she emulate the colonial society in his or her manner of thinking by using the metropolitan references, and avoiding any reflexive questioning about the ambiguous character of the colonial relation. Such a perspective necessitated categorizing the heterogeneity, giving rise to several forms of ethnic classifications that were imposed upon the colonized. These groups speedily proliferated over the social map of Mozambique. They started to be locally administered by entities that the colonial State recognized as their legitimate representatives: the traditional authorities. The

[7] This theme is discussed in fuller detail in Santos and Meneses, 2006.

process of (re)creating these traditional authorities helped detach the citizen and the native subject (national) of the colonies. Despite minimal academic output that focuses on how the Portuguese colonial system was structured at the turn of the 20th century, this period is essential to understanding how a system of indirect rule through the natives was established, and also mirrors what was being experienced in the other neighbouring colonies.

In 1899, following the promulgation of the Portuguese Labour Law, the populations residing the colonies were formally divided in two classes: native and non-native or civilized. The non-native held the same rights of citizens residing in Portugal and lived according to the metropolitan laws, while the natives lived according local laws and where subjects to the distinct legal procedures in each colony (Penvenne 1995; Meneses 2007). The 'non-native' born in the colonies possessed all the privileges associated with Portuguese citizenship: would not have to request the ingression into statute of citizen, and, in being a descendant of colonists, was born a citizen.[8]

Upon the founding of the Republic in Portugal, the legislative system broadened the existing system of social hierarchy based upon racial differences with the formal establishment of an extremely restricted and profoundly hierarchical identity in which the culturally diverse 'other' became identified with a primitive.[9] The colonial discourses and the legislative practices dictated who was native[10] or non-native, a legal condition of which everyone had to abide by.

The power invested upon the traditional authorities, seen as expressions of other, local institutions, required a clear detachment of rights between natives (subjects) and citizens (colonizers). The identity of each was determined in official documents, the true *curricula vitae* of their holders: the native card for the black people, naturalized according to their affiliations on the ethnic map of Mozambique; and for the non-native, the passport or any other citizenship document that contained information about his/her origin – 'originary' of Mozambique (equivalent to 'second-class white' since they were born in Mozambique or in other colonial spaces) or European for the case of the Portuguese from the metropole.

---

8 The group of the colonizers was also itself fragmented between 'naturals' of Mozambique, those from other colonial spaces, as well as those who came from the metropole. These latter came to be defined, for a long time, as 'first class' Portuguese.

9 The reality of multiculturalism was one of central vectors for social hierarchization within the colonial space.

10 African Eurocentric culture is rarely assumed to be 'ethnic' and it is therefore difficult to acknowledge ethnicity within dominant Western culture. In the colonial context, the notion of native or indigenous is practically synonymous with black person or African.

The Estado Novo (from 1928 on) consolidated policies of segregation. This was inaugurated in the colonial space with the implementation of the first "*Estatuto do Indigenato*"[11] which designated the legal inferiority of the natives (now susceptible of being even submitted to a disciplinary and repressive regime) and consecrated his/her statute of non-citizen without compromise.

Until it was abolished in 1961, the ensuing versions of this Law always insisted upon radical definitions of the native, to whom the "*private customs of their respective societies*" applied. In this sense, the various versions of this Law repeatedly insisted upon the lawful definition of the native, "*black individuals or their descendants who, having been born or living habitually* [in the colonies], *still did not* [possess] *the demonstration and the required individual and social habits that were intrinsic for the application of the private and public rights of the Portuguese citizens*" (Article 2).

The "*assimilados*"[12] – a third category found in the colonial space – was also specified in these statutes, stipulating the conditions of access to the Portuguese citizenship in great. In terms of the Law of 1929, the '*assimilados*' were old natives who had acquired the Portuguese citizenship after proving to cumulatively satisfy the cultural requirements that marked a radical cut with their former ethnic identity: to speak correct Portuguese; to have good behaviour and to have acquired the education and the habits essential for the integral application of the private and public rights of the Portuguese citizens, among others (Article 56).

The Portuguese law applied strictly to defend the interests of colonist citizens. Only non-natives (acceding to State administration) could access formal courts to resolve their problems, or natives whenever there where conflicts that affected the condition of the colonist. This distinction comes with a simple explanation. As stated by Sampayo et Mello, "*the private indigenous law does not advantage for the colonizing State with the substitution of European law, in general absolutely inadaptable to the native institutions of the family, of property, of inheritance, etc., that is worth protecting*" (1910, 154). For this author, the use of colonial power to control criminal justice was bluntly justified because it would make "*evident that the Europeans could be the only ones to punish in order to show that they are the ones in charge*" (1910, 178).

In 1933, the enactment of the Organic Law of the Colonial Empire introduced the protection of the indigenous both as a duty of the colonial administrative authorities and as a duty of the colonists. Together, they "*should watch for the*

11 The first set of law for the native. The first version, "*Criminal, Civil, and Political Statute of the Natives of Angola and Mozambique*", was approved by Decree No. 12.533, of 23 October 1926.

12 Those who had assimilated the key elements of Portuguese civilized culture.

conservation and development of the populations" (preamble to the Chapter VII), by reinforcing previous stipulations. Conservation and development, two seemingly contradictory principles, were given emphasis in this context, translated into the consecration of a perennial state of civilization framed by a model of colonial development. These lawful procedures symbolized Portugal's artefact power to create the category of natives, legally consecrating the rupture between citizens and indigenous, each group served by distinct normative systems. It was precisely this assumption of Portuguese colonial policy that Santos (2007, 4) recognizes to be the structural factor of the abyssal thought, "*the impossibility of the co-presence of both sides of the line*". In other words, the systems of social regulation for the use of the natives in Mozambique veered towards a peripheral geopolitical location conducive to processes of scientific and political neglect, separating the conflicts and the instances that mediated them from contemporaneity.

3.2. HIGHLIGHTS OF COLONIAL ADMINISTRATIVE REFORMS

According to the colonial policies that were implemented within Portuguese colonial territories in Africa, the modern judiciary system was established as one of the main vectors of the colonial intervention, rearranging the space of Portuguese Africa as preceding modern legal knowledge. Previous legal systems were now presented as inferior in terms of the knowledge and expertise that they contained. The next stage of this reasoning legitimized the 'obvious' primitiveness and backwardness of the structures and forms of political organization of 'ethnic' groups, a key element used to justify the need to introduce new, more progressive (in Western terms) spaces for political organization, justifying the colonial mission and the implementation of modern colonial administration. However, if the primacy of Western law, the foundation of colonial social hierarchy, separated inhabitants into citizens and indigenous, it was necessary to ensure the presence of legal bodies that were responsible for managing private conflicts between those who were classified as indigenous. Based on other colonial experiences according to such reasoning, Portugal subsequently introduced the system of indirect rule, where the figure of the traditional authority emerged as paramount. Many representatives of these traditional authorities were recruited from local ruling families,[13] a fact that facilitated the management of these populations while simultaneously guaranteeing the presence of figures endowed with local legitimacy. This would gradually facilitate the comparison between the modern

13 When considered necessary to prosecute its policy, the Portuguese colonial regime supported local rules that designated chiefs through succession and, consenting to the existence of a private, consuetudinary law to resolve the problems of local societies.

exercise of power assumed by the colonial State and local administration, now assigned to the traditional authorities. The figure of the traditional authority – consolidated in the figure of the *régulo* – was hereditary and often based their legitimacy through local pre-colonial lineages, which were not always real (Gonçalves Cota 1944). Indeed, should these local authorities ever oppose colonial authorities, they would be replaced by a more reasonable, humble personages (Meneses et al. 2003, Meneses 2006). Similarly, other local positions, often with religious connotations, continued to exist. However, their political importance diminished gradually, whenever they were not directly associated with traditional authorities (i.e., when their role was not administratively recognized).

In 1929, with the approval of the Overseas Administrative Reform,[14] the legal application of indirect rule in the colonial management of Mozambique came into force: the colonial State would recognize only one *régulo* per subdivision of each traditional territorial unit.[15] The *régulos* became part of the colonial system: they managed tax collection from the native population, workforce recruitment of natives, and resolved the conflicts and other problems that affected the population under their jurisdiction. The monopoly of the power that the Portuguese administration granted to the *régulo* was a new reality in Mozambique. In previous eras, the administrative and political authority was characterized by interdependence shared among several leaders of a given region, in various forms and hierarchies.[16]

In this new administrative system, the colonial Government created numerous incentives, including the use of badges, to entice the allegiance of several *régulos*.[17] In constant reconstruction, the significance of local traditional authority evolved and acquired new forms to appeal to the colonial

14 Decree No. 23.229 of 15 November 1929. Soon thereafter, a series of reforms would be added into the Colonial Act, which was integrated in the Portuguese Constitution. The Organic Law of the Portuguese Colonial Empire was enacted in 1933 with a series of administrative reforms that reinforced these administrative devices. For instance, the Overseas Administrative Reform of 1933 attributed the task of tax collection to the leading traditional authorities, whose role was recognized *de jure* as "*civil administration assistant in the colonies*".

15 There were two kinds of organization units that composed territorial structures during the colonial era: councils and circumscriptions. In predominantly in urban areas, councils reigned under the State law as citizens under the mandated of civil authorities. In rural areas, the basic administrative unit was the circumscription (today district), which was directed by an administrator and subdivided into several units of chieftainship, headed by *régulos*.

16 E.g. titles such as *hosi*, *hombe*, *mfumu*, *mambo*, *mwene*, *nyakwawa*, *samasuwa*, *sheiks*, *xhés*, traditional healers, counsellors, religious leaders, etc. are actually attributed to different positions in local power structures and varied according to local languages and to local memories and historical experiences.

17 See, for example, the Circular No. 2469/B/2 of the Central Division of the Native Affairs, of 25 June 1952, regarding uniform plans for traditional authorities.

administration and to local populations, as well (Geffray 1991; Meneses et al. 2003; Dinerman 2004).

Gradually, these traditional titles were losing their meaning as both the *régulos* and their assistants were increasingly perceived to be effective elements of the colonial State. Despite their affiliation with the colonial administration, however, the double role of the *régulos* should not be underestimated. These authorities did impose programs to improve living conditions for their populations from their privileged positions, sometimes deciding to directly confront the colonial system, or the escape to neighbouring countries (Bonate 2007).

This brief review supports the ideas advanced by those who have investigated other African contexts: without the presence of these authorities, it would not have been possible to implement the modern State in Africa (Mamdani 1996, 67; Oomen 2005). This indirect form of public administration would profoundly impact social relations within spaces where colonial relations were imposed. Despite being punished by the colonial State, institutions of traditional power were complex political actors that simultaneously acted as an important factor in terms of cohesion and the (re) construction of identities.

In 1961, the dual legal system present in the Portuguese colonies – for the citizens and for the natives – came to an abrupt end as a response to the nationalist struggles for liberation in Angola, Guinea-Bissau and Mozambique. Cunningly, the decree that abolished the Statute justified the enduring presence of a double political legality – the citizen and the subject – as a space of multicultural celebration that was confirmed by the diversity of peoples composing the normative imperial spaces. All inhabitants of the "*territory of the Portuguese empire*" became officially citizens of a "*multiracial society*", the fruit of "*wise and opportune union between respect for local customs and the purpose of assimilation*".[18] Prejudices, however, continued to significantly influence colonial policy, reaffirming inequality between the colonizers and the colonized – as several decrees and laws continue to reveal.

This brief review exhibits the ambiguities and complexities associated with the notion of tradition. The historical context of its introduction remains central to understanding contemporary social dynamics and policy, particularly the role that traditional authority came to assume. It was the axis for the (re) constitution of identity upon which several actors, forms of legitimization and (re) productions of power were articulated and discussed (West and Kloeck-Jenson 1999; Santos 2003). Yet, tradition was not a mere byproduct of colonial intervention. As in a game of mirrors, tradition, was continuously (re)interpreted, (re)formulated and (re)built – as either subjects or citizens.

---

18 See Decree No. 43.893, of 6 September 1961.

4. OLD AND NEW ACTORS IN THE POLITICAL FABRIC OF INDEPENDENT MOZAMBIQUE

Since its independence, Mozambique has passed through complex political processes that have resulted in significant changes, including the question of traditional authorities. These political transformations contributed to the evolution and convolution in the political arenas.

The historical analysis helped uncover the multiple meanings associated with traditional authority. One commonality shared among them has been how these authorities continued to maintain an important profile in local administration, especially in mediating conflicts and day-to-day problems. The person holding the title of traditional authority is normally presented as being the one to coordinate group activities, to maintain group unanimity and to reach agreements among his counsellors (Meneses et al. 2003; Dava, Macia and Dove 2003; Gonçalves 2005). The prolonged existence of these authorities and their political notoriety are explained by the popularity their political intervention gained for them in their areas of jurisdiction.

The political context in newly independent Mozambique was instigated by political emancipation, and demanded a new approach to this form of citizenship. It was imperative to overcome the hierarchical categorization of difference, namely, the notion of first- and second-class citizens, the legacy of colonization. Despite significant changes in policies with the recognition of multiculturalism taking place in several African countries, the Mozambican case merits a more detailed analysis. For the majority of Mozambicans the colonial period was characterized by a form of citizenship based on ethnic belonging (i.e., a form of collective identity). In reaction, the dominant political project of an independent Mozambique, defended by *Frelimo*,[19] required the legal equality shared by all the citizens, independently (and fundamentally without relation) from their ethnic roots. "*Kill the tribe to build the nation*" – a popular phrase from the revolutionary period – reflected this objective, i.e., the emergence of a national identity without an ethnic past. Nevertheless, the struggle for nationalism had also been a cultural struggle for the recognition of the social mosaic that Mozambique represented, crucially influencing debates around the legitimacy of traditional authorities as forms of political representation in independent Mozambique. These debates remerged strongly by mid 1990s and led to the constitutional preservation of these authorities in the political scene in 2004.[20] However, the legal documents,

19 *Frelimo* (Mozambican Liberation Front) has been the political force in power since the national independence, both during the single party system and after the introduction of the multiparty system in 1992.

20 Article 118 from the Constitution of 2004: "*The State recognizes and values Traditional Authority that have been formally recognized by the population and according to the customary*

far from replacing the structures that came from the colonial era, reflect an attempt to construct new sites of local power, which generated new instances and actors that gradually traditionalized and increased the heterogeneity local political structures.

4.1. AMPLIFYING THE PLURAL NETWORK OF JUSTICES

In Mozambique, the independence signified a break with the colonial past, including the interference in practices of power. The "*breaking-up of the State*", the "*creation of the New Man*" and the "*destruction of traditional ideas and obscure practices*" were some of the ideological principles that guided these transformations, including the construction of an alternative policy based on public power (Meneses 2007, 2008b). *Frelimo* sought actively to put an end to traditional systems for local administration because they were perceived to be a feudal remnant, incompatible with the country's public, popular power. The abolishment of the traditional authorities was a core piece of the central political administration, only to come to an end when the country was shaken by violent conflicts (beginnings of the decade of 1990).[21] In 1975, a document from the Council of Ministers stated: "[the] *destruction of past structures is neither a secondary task, nor an ideological luxury. It is a condition for the triumph of the Revolution*" (*Frelimo* 1976). Following this approach, *Frelimo* banished the religious and traditional authorities during the first years of the Mozambican revolution.[22] Local elites and power structures associated with the colonial administration were stigmatized, and the multiple practices conceived to be associated with the traditional realm[23] were banished from the public sphere, a fact that also occurred in some neighbouring countries.

---

law", as it is also the State's responsibility to fit the participation of the traditional authorities "*into the economic, social and cultural life of the country according to the law*". It is also worth mentioning that the constitution never defines 'traditional authority'.

21 Despite the existing connection between the colonial administration and traditional authorities, there are endless and widely known examples of the double role played by chiefs who used their positions of privilege to access the State and to secure better living conditions for their populations. Correspondingly, many supported the fight for national liberation, having been, however, very modestly compensated by *Frelimo* after independence (Geffray 1991; Meneses et al. 2003, 2006; Bonate 2007).

22 Decree No. 6/78, of 22 April 1978, banished traditional authorities as members of local, State administration. The hostilities directed towards traditional authorities stood still during the period of transition to independence.

23 The practices associated with traditional healers, the ceremonies to request rain and rituals to control the agricultural pests were also considered secretive and were therefore strongly discouraged (Meneses et al. 2003; Meneses 2008b).

Grupos Dinamizadores[24] were created during the transition period to fill the void of power generated with the abolition of traditional authorities. This form of grassroots popular organization would emerge in public institutions, in factories and in companies, in schools and residential neighbourhoods, but never knew a formal legal structure.[25] These groups were considered the seeds of the new grassroots popular power. Becoming member of a *grupo dinamizador* was blocked to whomever was considered associated with the previous colonial administration, thus excluding the *régulos* from the possibility of participating in these new structures.

The *grupos dinamizadores* performed multiple functions, taking over functions that were previously carried out by the traditional authorities: management of social questions, conflict mediation, maintaining law and order, administration and regulation. Strongly politicized and connected to the *Frelimo* organizations,[26] the *grupos dinamizadores* were expected to introduce the 'new' political priorities of the new government to all of the Mozambican citizens.

The Third *Frelimo* Congress, in 1977, came to symbolize the transformation of a revolutionary movement into a political party. As such, it also defined the orientation of territorial administration and the kind of role a single party would come to play in State administration. One of the referential elements was the recognition, at the Congress, of the urge to fight the enduring remnants of colonial mentalities, determining the "*need to completely destroy the colonial-capitalist apparatus of the State* [...] *accelerating the creation of new organs of state Power at the levels of district and locality*" (*Frelimo* 1977). In practical terms, it meant the reinforcement of the State policy aimed at actively eliminating the presence traditional authorities from the political-administrative map.

But the State's attempt to penetrate at local levels encountered countless obstacles. *Frelimo* sought to construct a popular State that would 'break away' from the State apparatus inherited from colonialism. This political project entailed in *Frelimo*'s transformation into a single State-party. In reality this meant a system of public administration, where the secretary of the party was simultaneously a government staff member. In 1979,[27] *Frelimo* decided to realign the *grupos*

24 Dynamizing groups.

25 In the early years, a *grupo dinamizador* consisted of eight to ten people selected in public meetings, where participants would discuss the competences of the candidates and raise their arms to vote democratically. Candidates would be refused if they were discovered to be associated with practices described as reactionary. Each *Group* was led by a secretary and a secretary's assistant. Groups of popular vigilance were also created to support the work of the *grupos dinamizadores*.

26 As the Mozambican Woman Organization (*OMM*), production councils (later transformed into unions), etc.

27 These decisions were taken during the first national meeting on cities and communal neighbourhoods (s/a 1979).

dinamizadores in a manner that would reinforce the State-party's presence at the local level. Despite *Frelimo*'s decision to separate the base party units and the functions of *grupos dinamizadores* (s/a, 1979), *Frelimo* reinforced the indiscriminate interactions between the party units and the *grupos*, expression of a grassroots organization.

During the first years of independence, the government's policy towards local power was heavily influenced by a modernist agenda that ignored many of the local cultural traditions. Coaxed into a project of radical modernization, *Frelimo* tried to create an entirely new hierarchy of secretaries and administrative staff members elected through diverse processes. Almost inevitable, the most educated revolutionary cadres in the country convened for *Frelimo*'s project to extend the modern State throughout the country, including the most remote rural spaces. In other words, it advocated that all Mozambican citizens were free and equal before the law of the modern State.[28] Their power emerged from a form of knowledge that denigrated the traditionalism of local chiefs and the secretiveness of the traditional cultures (Geffray 1991; Santos 2003; Meneses 2006, 2007). As a result of this homogenizing policy, many of the cadres could not answer and did not respond to many of the questions that, in socio-legal terms, local populations posed.

This political approach had profound effects throughout the country, as the customary law would be transformed into a symbol of traditional African society to be overcome in order to reach the standards for development that First World countries established. The recognition of ethno-cultural differences was considered an ill-advised political decision.[29] Independence corresponded to the introduction of new local actors in both urban and rural environments: initially the *grupos dinamizadores* and subsequently neighbourhood or village secretaries. In addition to these new local actors, the aforementioned political structures also began playing important roles in local administration, increasing the complex nature of the heterogeneous Mozambican State.

Although the State sought actively to relegate traditional authorities into a secondary plan, they did not disappear from the public sphere. In fact, their activity and public political intervention continued have a strong imprint in both

---

28 According to *Frelimo*, the State would be democratic, united ad non-racist during the period of 'socialist revolution', which would stimulate the development of a single national culture and of an economic base that guaranteed an improved standard of living for everybody.

29 The absence of a deep reflection on the country's actual cultural diversity created a feeling that colonialism had kept people in ignorance, superstition and fear. This helped create a single, homogenous national culture during the first years of independence. This culture would later impact diverse groups of Mozambicans and be verified by their assertion to the right to education and science.

rural and urban environments. Several studies conducted in Mozambique suggest that traditional hierarchies began to be integrated into the institutions of local power (Geffray 1991; Meneses et al. 2003; Dinerman 2004).

Frelimo's 'anti-obscurantist' crusade added new critical discourses to the cultural sphere and revived the colonial legacy as a form of vengeance: traditional leaders would compare *Frelimo*'s concessions to those of the Portuguese, furtively criticizing many of the options taken. Many of the *régulos* would assess *Frelimo*'s proposals with suspicion, gradually untying their links with the State national project. The resort to a traditional criticism was not the fruit of a simple opposition between immutable traditional communities and a modernizing State. It was a critical and historically rooted criticism against the authoritative implementation of a centrally produced and deeply flawed policy and, while not a rejection of modernization *per se*, it was the rejection of a certain – failed and coercive – modernization that attempted to affirm local control over the populations through a processes of centralization.

Towards the end of the 1970s, local actors began to re-examine the Mozambican political context with a deep reflection on 'Mozambicanness' and the meaning of citizenship based upon the notion of local authority, and its sources of legitimacy. Locally, the figures of the secretary and of the 'former' *régulos* gradually gained legitimacy based on their political action, as many came to be (again) recognized as authorities. The central concern, according to those who appealed to local authorities to resolve their problems, was the efficacy of this source of authority. The coherence and power of tradition, norms, customs and ethnic identity lies in how they inform peoples of their identity and on the manners in which they should act based upon their conscience and these points of reference. As discourses, however, the traditions, customs and ethnicities are continuously reinterpreted and reconstructed like regulated improvisations and, as such, their legitimacy is subjected to permanent evaluation. Throughout the 1980s, the policy of *Frelimo* did not want to accept the country's ethno-cultural diversity and therefore it came to unintentionally reproduce the dichotomy of the colonial era: the 'other cultures' of the natives, which were considered inferior and archaic by the colonial State, (re)emerged in political discourses as a symbol of incapacity of the State to face the present challenges. The adjective 'traditional' increasingly came to actively characterize and reaffirm the demand for autonomy, self-representation and self-preservation. In debates, traditional was used to symbolize 'our, local culture', whereas the modern State was being perceived to be the alterity, as the undying remnants of the dichotomy established between citizenship and subalternity.

4.2. THE RETURN OF 'OLD' ACTORS

The modern Mozambican State's failure to recognize the objectives and projects of local communities contributed to an armed conflict that spanned for over a decade.[30] As the war spread in the mid-80s, *Renamo* seriously began to question *Frelimo*'s contention that traditional authorities were obscurantist institutions, vestiges of a feudal past. Despite the subalternization, the *régulos* endured in colonial times and their depreciation after independence. Traditional authorities kept a strong presence in the political fabric because of their proximity to the populations they administered. As the war was coming to an end, it was not easy for traditional authorities to decide upon which position to take in relation to the parties' involved in the conflict. By then, *Frelimo* government's attitude towards them had become rather ambiguous.

As research shows, in several cases the *régulos* assumed a rather dubious attitude towards the conflict, so that the conflict would not come to deeply affect a given area (Meneses et al. 2003). Nevertheless, many authorities throughout vast regions of North-Central Mozambique began to support *Renamo* (Geffray 1991). *Renamo* supported itself through old institutions as it gradually reintroduced the chiefs as agents of local power in areas under its control (Meneses et al. 2003; Gonçalves 2005). These authorities played a fundamental role in mobilizing youth to join in the ranks of *Renamo*'s guerrilla armies. Local taxes were reintroduced in the areas under *Renamo*'s control.[31] Local authorities also had the responsibility to resolve local social problems and conflicts (including land tenure issues), from which *Renamo* normally abstained from intervening in. With the spread of war, there was also growing tension from within *Frelimo* over its policy of open hostility towards traditional authorities at this time. In the early 1990s, the government sponsored a series of studies to better understand the country's question of traditional power (O'Laughlin 1992; Lundin and Machava 1995–1998).

In 1992, *Frelimo* and *Renamo* signed the peace agreements, which was decisive for social and political stability. One of Renamo demands during negotiations was the constitutional, effective recognition of traditional authorities (conceived of here as only the *régulos* and their subordinates). Until quite recently, this remained one of Renamo's banners of struggle. However, increasingly aware of these authorities' power, *Frelimo's* presidential candidate, Joaquim Chissano,

---

30 *Renamo* (National Resistance of Mozambique) was inevitable in this context. *Renamo* was founded towards the 1970s and it transformed itself from movement of resistance into a political party once peace was established. It became one of the main political forces in Mozambique with the introduction of the multiparty system.

31 Namely, a sustenance tax, which permitted *Renamo* to maintain its military force.

openly defended traditional authorities during the first multiparty elections in 1996.[32]

During the electoral process, *Frelimo* and *Renamo* began to seek more support from and with traditional authorities. Both political parties and the traditional authorities understood administrative control as a means of exercising political control. The major Mozambican parties – *Renamo* and *Frelimo* – perceived and continue to perceive traditional authorities to be an extension of the State and a way to increase their administrative competency and their presence at the local level.[33]

In an attempt to challenge the policies proposed by *Frelimo*, *Renamo* gradually introduced administrative politicized structures in rural and urban areas that virtually reproduced the *grupos dinamizadores* that had been developed after independence (Meneses and Santos 2009).

The process of opening a multiparty system is widely discussed as having contributed to the national democratic expansion at local levels by creating autocracies in 43 towns. This process of decentralization, however, brought several problems that not only conjugated into party conflicts, but also between several forms of political representation and legitimacy.

Confronted with the exuberance of structures of local power in 2000,[34] the Mozambican Council of Ministers published a decree that guaranteed the government's role nominating local administrators where it officially recognized the diversity of authorities throughout the country for first time. The government's structures, as stipulated by the decree, had the obligation to consult and cooperate with the 'community authorities' in the exercise of the local administration. This reference to communal authorities broadened the concept of leadership to include several social actors: "*traditional leaders, neighborhood or village secretaries and others leaders legitimized as such by their respective communities*" (Article 1). In its most restricted sense, this came down to grouping traditional authorities with religious leaders, the secretaries of *grupos dinamizadores*, notable local personalities, etc.

32 In 1994, the Law of municipalities (Law No. 3/94) explicitly recognized the African socio-cultural reality, including the traditional forms of governance for the first time.

33 This issue merits a more detailed analysis. Indeed, the combination that legally regulates the operation of local power structures, refer specifically to 'communal authorities' as an important part of this process. This includes references to specific laws regarding the correlation between the government (local state power) and these authorities (Law No. 8/2003, of 19 May – Law of the Local Organs of the State and its regulation – Decree No. 11/2005, of 10 June).

34 Decree No. 15/2000, of 20 June 2000 and the Diploma 107-A/2000, of 25 August 2000.

The ministerial diploma nº 80/2004 sought to clarify this definition, under which communal authority was designated as (Article 1) "*people who exercise a certain form of authority over a determined community or social group, such as traditional leaders, neighborhood or village secretaries and others leaders who have been legitimized by their respective community or social group*". Two central categories are clearly established – the "*traditional leaders*" and "*neighborhood or village secretaries*" – joined by "*other legitimized leaders who exercise some economic, social, religious or cultural role that has been accepted by the social group to which they belong*".

This legislation was produced by the central government that cunningly sought the covert integration of the wealth and power of local institutions into local systems of administration. *Frelimo* also sought to capitalize political space through this manoeuvre.

The process for recognizing community authorities is not free of risks and problems. The criteria for the precedence or hierarchization of authorities is established in article 10 of Decree No. 15/2000, leaving it to the communities to declare a representative to the administrative authorities according to their respective norms and principles.[35] The decree-law No. 80/2004 more accurately establishes the mechanisms for legitimization. The selection of traditional leaders must be validated "*according to the rules of their community*" (Article 8), whereas secretaries will be chosen (and thus legitimated) based on the "*criteria established by a respective local community or social group*" (Article 9). In other words, there is an element of difference in the selection process of these community authorities that includes direct legitimization (elections for secretaries) and other forms of selection that do not include forms of direct democracy. An elected leader is then formally recognized by a local-level representative of State administration.

The fundamental recognition of established *régulos* and their assistants (and in some cases even of secretaries) was validated in the rural areas where this decree was mainly applied. Only recently have other instances, such as traditional healers and religious leaders, been integrated in this complex structure and formally recognized by the Mozambican State as forms of local power. However, their dissatisfaction with such a delay has been quite obvious.[36] Present in the countryside and recognized by the social bases as noticeable entities, their critical voices are at times problematic but are nevertheless an important component in the deliberation of quarrelsome situations (involving issues as access to land, family disputes, and cases of witchcraft accusations, etc.).

35 Several legal documents on the matter refer to several levels of authority, although the first phase of the process only included the 'top' authorities (specifically referred to as "*first level authorities*"). The process for formally and legally recognizing the three-level communal structures is currently virtually accomplished.

36 These facts were repeatedly cited during interviews conducted during research.

The process for the formal recognition of communal authorities indicated that there were around 13,500 registered leaders in both urban and rural contexts already by 2003. Around 10.7% of these leaders were already formally recognized by the State.[37] An interesting trend emerged towards the end of 2006, when the process for the formal recognition of these authorities was more advanced. The total number of formally recognized traditional authorities reached 18,950 with a proportional growth in the number of leaders ranking below *régulo*[38] whereas the proportion of secretaries saw a significant reduction, representing 17.6% of all authorities. These numbers suggest that the implementation of the 'new' authorities did not compete with the authority of other actors, whose culturally and historically founded legitimacy remains important.[39]

The process for recognizing communal authorities has gradually been opening a space for the empowerment of the local communities, expanding the possibilities for action in the search of the solutions to their problems.

The introduction of autocratic elections in several Mozambican cities and towns occurred at a moment where, throughout the continent, the dominant paradigm was questioning State bankruptcy and appealing to the growing participation of the civil society through democratization and decentralization, presented as the solution to revert the situation. In urban spaces, the autocrats are perceived to be a space for civil society action. In the rural world, however, traditional authorities are experts, essentially an African variant of civil society. Their recognition does not only legitimize forms of popular governance, but challenges the oppressive centralist governance in place (Weimer 1986, 48–49). The complexity of the political structures and actors that are present in the urban space explains why struggles for the recognition of communal authorities have been so difficult; as they are reflected in complex institutional disputes around delimiting the jurisdictional spheres for each one of these actors and structures (Jossias 2004; Meneses and Santos 2009). For example, in urban areas, traditional authorities are seen mainly as instances of consultation,[40] contrasting with the neighbourhood secretaries that are an integral part of the administrative structure of the public authorities.

This short discussion highlights the implications associated with the (re)introduction of traditional authorities (seen here in their broader significance), over the decades following the triumph of the nationalist struggle. Throughout this time, the State gradually lost its political legitimacy, then it recuperated it

[37] The percentage of women is quite small among the recognized authorities.
[38] Lower level authorities, such as '*cabos de terra*', '*tinduna*', etc.
[39] This data was obtained from the Ministry of State Administration that supervises the process for recognizing these authorities.
[40] Interviews with *régulos* of the city of Matola and of the city of Beira, in 2005–2008.

and became a genuinely Mozambican State. This required the recuperation and the re-evaluation of practices that were previously considered to be traditional. In fact, these practices possess more popular legitimacy than the legal projects of the State and have persisted, in part, due to the vacancy of State power in several regions. The figure of 'community authority' is constructed in the ideological relations that relegate people into the expressions of local authority (*régulos* and their subordinates). At another level, it defines the difference between those who are seen as power (*régulos* in rural contexts), who do legitimate work, and the ones that 'support' the local administration (*régulos* in urban contexts).

The formal State recognition of communal authorities has been the reinvention of tradition, the creation of new actors, and the revival of beliefs and customs upon which several political leaders 'ground their Mozambicanness'. However, recognizing the presence of 'other' authorities beyond those formally established by the modern State is a challenge that simultaneously implies 1) other epistemic references beyond that of the techno-bureaucratic operation of the State (including the legitimacy through the ancestors, etc.) and 2) the denial of a single model of citizenship (through the hereditary recognition of privilege and plural notions of law and local administration).

5. CONTEMPORARY POLITICAL IMPLICATIONS OF LEGAL PLURALISM

The continuity of principles proposed by the modern State project to revolutionize the social structure of Mozambique resulted in a sequence of attempts to integrate the 'other' (mainly defined as the traditional space) into a centralized rationality that did not legally recognize differences that are the products of specific experiences whose memories have continued to persist over time.

Surpassing the colonial vision of the State as a "*space built by the European [whites]*" to regulate alterity (seen as synonymous with disorder), the analysis of the traditional authorities in its broader sense permits that they be visualized as references around which people (re)constitute their identity, and around which the political activities of multiple actors are articulated. In this context, the analysis of the colonial encounter helps discern how the existing forces built new spaces for action and new kinds of social organization in which the definitions of modern and traditional continuously acquire a new meaning in a constant tension between various social forces. As this research unveils, the tensions associated with the State conversion and the communities' counteractions seeking to find a space to participate in the administration of their regions according to their needs have come to produce various hybrid structures for social control – a history that deserves a detailed analysis of the modern (re)invention of traditional power.

From the perspective of local actors, the people legitimated leaderships that would call upon to resolve problems, whether this authority was part of the official State structure or from the realm of community structures. Beyond local State administration, appealing to traditional authorities depends on loyalty or confidence that is recognized within them, based on their knowledge and power to resolve problems and their protection group interest. This form of legitimacy is verified by those who appeal to these authorities with new conflicts and problems on a day-to-day basis and who can verify their ability to successfully address them.

It is evident from this evaluation that the current legal system in Mozambique extends well beyond formally established legal systems to respond to problems that are essential to communities. Upon trying to find solutions to their problems, these communities have developed alternative forms of governance and justice that challenge the construction of a democratic and plural legal system. As the situations discussed in this article reveal, the strength of answers that 'come from below' address the need for a legal system that the monolithic official justice cannot address.

Several processes of negotiation and appropriation on the meanings of justice have occurred among the multiple legal institutions, including moments where transformation has served the interests of communities. These processes have had a profound imprint in Mozambique. The presence of multiple institutions and forum shopping in conflict mediation is synonymous with an official legal system that is unjust and has rested upon continuous situations of abuse and judiciary corruption (Santos and Trindade 2003), a truly challenge to human rights. Indeed, in the still predominant representations of the local, legal systems remain linked to making particular groups of people susceptible to abuses that allow them to be treated with less than human respect and dignity.

The Mozambican State has come far, now contributing to the development of other justice systems by promoting legal reform. Despite this process, the State has attempted to invisibilize the diversity present at local level. Central in the discourses of several communal judges, secretaries, chiefs, and others leaders is not only a demand for recognition, since the recognition signifies their subordination to State structure, but their demand for dignity and respect. As observed, it is not so much a deliberate neglect of universal human rights declarations, but rather the insistence of the colonial rhetoric of localizing the 'other' legal systems that permit and justify the persistent invisibility of the heterogeneity of legal institutions, only recognized, by the State, as 'local' institutions of conflict mediation.

In short, defining the acceptance and legitimacy of local traditional structures is undeniably difficult. The legitimacy of local authorities implies they have been accepted by communities as having the right to govern and administrate justice, and that this compliance is more or less voluntary. Thus, it is fundamental to distinguish between political strategies that sought to create consensus and those that sought to obtain a sense of obedience. The former falls upon a question of legitimacy while the latter may result in acceptance or produce resistance to decisions. For the first option to be enduringly effective, power will have of be transformed into a legitimate form of authority. Otherwise, it could be transformed in an exercise of self-destruction.

The notion of a multicultural State, which suggests a homonymous compatibility between nation and State, is neither possible nor necessary. As the on-going political debates accentuate, the State is more and more as a political space disputed by several actors and forms of governance, marked by distinct histories and political trajectories. The fact that multiple legal structures function alongside the official justice does not signify the insignificance of its legal recognition. In fact, this situation reveals that a breach exists between reality and the established, official legal order, which is unable to answer all the citizens' demands. The fact that the people do not identify with the official justice indicates the need for deep legal reform that is also based in the true recognition of the right to diversity, where culture assumes a fundamental role in fighting for a justice system that reflects the unique histories and the distinct struggles of various communities. Such must also operate in dialogue with the conditions for emancipation proposed by the country. To be truly democratic, this reform will have to rest upon cross-cultural dialogues as a solution for the differences, pluralisms and the broader respect for human rights (Santos 2006, 39–42).

In the search for forms of justice based on their norms and principles, communities have been developing practices based on traditional cultural references, never once questioning their Mozambican identity. These traditions continue to be (re)worked according to contemporary demands, incorporating global human rights norms into their justice systems, which are constantly renewed (Meneses and Santos 2009).[41] In the ongoing debates, the right to culture as space of self-determination (re)emerges as a multicultural and democratic moment that demands greater participation by and representation of

41 One of the most problematic aspects of these justice systems comes from the continued presence of local administrations that reproduce the exclusion and to the subordination of women, which still persists (Arthur and Mejia 2006).

the communities in political matters that affect their lives.[42] Citizenship is more than a set of political rights guaranteed by the constitution; it also includes a set of economic, social and political relations between social groups and structures of power as well as between the position of the individual in the political space of citizenship. At the same time, it opens up a space for broader political involvement and participation, incorporating other material and metaphorical spaces that reflect other forms of knowledge and experiences.

BIBLIOGRAPHY

Appiah, K.A. (1998)
Cosmopolitan Patriots, in: Cheah, P. and Robbins, B. (orgs.) *Cosmopolitics*, Minneapolis: University of Minnesota Press, 91–116.

Arthur, M.J. and Mejia, M. (2006)
Instâncias Locais de Resolução de Conflitos e o Reforço dos Papéis de Género, *Outras Vozes*, 16, 1–8.

Baptista-Lundin, I. and Machava, F.J. (eds.) (1995–1998)
Autoridade e Poder Tradicional, Maputo: Ministério da Administração Estatal, 2 vol.

Bhabha, H.K. (1996)
Unsatisfied: notes on vernacular cosmopolitanism, in: Garcia-Morena, L. and Pfeifer, P.C. (eds.) *Text and Nation*, London: Camden House, 191–207.

Bonate, L. (2007)
Traditions and Transitions. Islam and Chiefship in Northern Mozambique (ca. 1850–1974), Cape Town: University of Cape Town, PhD Dissertation.

Chanock, M. (1998)
Law, Custom and Social Order: the colonial experience in Malawi and Zambia, Portsmouth, NH: Heinemann.

Cooper, F. (1996)
Decolonization and African Society: the labour question in French and British Africa, Cambridge: Cambridge University Press.

Dava, F., Macia, M. and Dove, R. (2003)
Reconhecimento e Legitimação das Autoridades Comunitárias à luz do Decreto 15/2000 (o caso do grupo etnolinguístico ndau), Maputo: ARPAC – Instituto de Investigação Sócio-cultural.

de Sousa Santos, B. (2003)
O Estado Heterogéneo e o Pluralismo Jurídico, in: de Sousa Santos, B. and Trindade, J.C. (eds.) *Conflito e Transformação Social: uma paisagem das justiças em Moçambique*, Porto: Afrontamento, vol. 1: 47–95.

de Sousa Santos, B. (2006)
The Rising of the Global Left: the World Social Forum and beyond, London: Zed Books.

42 I.e., mechanisms of participating 'from below' that permit 'informal' forms of administration and conflict resolution from within the confines of the modern State.

de Sousa Santos, B. (2007)
Beyond Abyssal Thinking: from global lines to ecologies of knowledges, *Review* XXX (1), 45–89.
de Sousa Santos, B. and Trindade, J.C. (eds.) (2003)
Conflito e Transformação Social: uma paisagem das justiças em Moçambique, Porto: Afrontamento, 2 vol.
de Sousa Santos, B. and Meneses, M.P. (2006)
Identidades, Colonizadores e Colonizados: Portugal e Moçambique, Relatório final do Projecto POCTI/41280/SOC/2001, Coimbra, Portugal.
Dinerman, A. (2004)
Processes of State Delegitimization in Post-independence Rural Mozambique: the case of Namapa district, Nampula Province, *Journal of Historical Sociology*, 17(2–3): 123–184.
Diouf, M. (2000)
The Senegalese Murid Trade Diaspora and the Making of a Vernacular Cosmopolitanism, *Public Culture*, 12(3): 679–702.
Frelimo (1976)
Documentos da 8ª Sessão do Comité Central, Maputo: Departamento de Informação e Propaganda.
Frelimo (1977)
O Partido e as Classes Trabalhadoras Moçambicanas na Edificação da Democracia Popular, Maputo: Departamento do Trabalho Ideológico.
Geffray, C. (1991)
A Causa das Armas em Moçambique, Porto: Afrontamento.
Gonçalves, E. (2005)
Finding the Chief: political decentralization and traditional authority in Mocumbi, southern Mozambique, *Africa Insight*, 35(3): 64–70.
Harrison, G. (1998)
Marketing Legitimacy in Rural Mozambique: the case of Mecufi, northern Mozambique, *Journal of Modern African Studies*, 36(4): 369–391.
Jossias, E. (2004)
Autoridades Locais em Moçambique: dinâmicas e processos de sua articulação. Paper presented at the VIII Luso-Afro-Brasilian Conference of Social Sciences, Coimbra.
Kyed, H.M. and Buur, L. (2006)
New Sites of Citizenship: recognition of traditional authority and group-based citizenship in Mozambique, *Journal of Southern African Studies*, 32(3): 563–581.
Mamdani, M. (1996)
Citizen and Subject: contemporary Africa and the legacy of late colonialism, Princeton: Princeton University Press.
Mbembe, A. (2002)
Les Nouveaux Africains: entre nativisme et cosmopolitanisme, *Esprit*, 10: 1–10.
Meneses, M.P., Fumo, J., Mbilana, G., Gomes, C. (2003)
As Autoridades Tradicionais no Contexto do Pluralismo Jurídico, in: Santos de Sousa, B. and Trindade, J.C. (eds.) *Conflito e Transformação Social: uma paisagem das justiças em Moçambique*, Porto: Afrontamento, vol. 2, 341–420.

Meneses, M.P. (2006)
Traditional Authorities in Mozambique: between legitimisation and legitimacy, in: Hinz, M. (ed.), *The Shade of New Leaves: governance in traditional authority – a Southern African perspective,* Berlin: Lit Verlag, 93–119.
Meneses, M.P. (2007)
Pluralism, Law and Citizenship in Mozambique: mapping the complexity, *Oficina do CES*, 291.
Meneses, M.P. (2008a)
Corpos de Violências, Linguagens de Resistência, *Revista Crítica de Ciências Sociais*, 80, 161–194.
Meneses, M.P. (2008b)
Maciane F. Zimba e Carolina J. Tamele: médicos tradicionais, dirigentes da AMETRAMO, in: Santos de Sousa, B. (ed.) *As Vozes do Mundo*, Porto: Afrontamento, 337–384.
Meneses, M.P. and Santos de Sousa, B. (2009)
The Rise of a Micro Dual State: the case of Angoche (Mozambique), *Africa Development*, XXXIV (3–4): 129–166.
Meneses, M.P. (2010)
Pluralismo jurídico e memórias plurais. Paper presented at the Conference on State and Non-State Public Safety and Justice Provision: The dynamics of legal pluralism in Mozambique, Maputo.
O'Laughlin, B. (1992)
A Base Social da Guerra em Moçambique, *Estudos Moçambicanos*, 10: 107–142.
Oomen, B. (2005)
Chiefs in South Africa: law, power and culture in the post-apartheid era, Oxford: James Currey.
Penvenne, J.M. (1995)
African Workers and Colonial Racism, Oxford: James Currey.
Ranger, T. (1996)
Postscript: Colonial and Postcolonial Identities, in: Werbner, R. and Ranger, T. (eds.) *Postcolonial Identities in Africa,* London: Zed Books, 271–281.
S/a (1979)
1ª Reunião Nacional sobre Cidades e Bairros Comunais, Maputo: Imprensa Nacional de Moçambique.
Sampayo and Mello, L. (1910)
Política Indígena, Porto: Magalhães e Moniz Lda.
Scott, J. (1998)
Seeing Like a State, New Haven: Yale University Press.
Simone, A.M. (2001)
On the Worlding of African cities, *African Studies Review*, 44(2): 15–43.
Snyder, F. (1981)
Colonialism and Legal Form: the creation of customary law in Senegal, *Journal of Legal Pluralism*, 19: 49–90.
Weimer, B. (1996)
Challenges for Democratization and Regional Development in Southern Africa: focus on Mozambique, *Regional Development Dialogue*, 24(1): 141–160.

West, H. and Kloeck-Jenson, S. (1999)
Betwixt and between: 'traditional authority' and democratic decentralization in post-war in post-war Mozambique, *African Affairs*, 98: 455–484.
Werbner, R. (2002)
Cosmopolitan Ethnicity, Entrepreneurship and the Nation: minority elites in Botswana, *Journal of Southern African Studies*, 28(4): 731–753.

CHAPTER V
TRADITIONAL JUSTICE AND HUMAN RIGHTS IN POST-WAR AFRICAN COUNTRIES: PROSPECTS AND CHALLENGES

Joe A.D. Alie

1. INTRODUCTION

The contemporary African political landscape has been inundated with deadly civil conflicts, which have had a telling effect on the development process and on the lives of ordinary people. Millions are displaced and thousands forced to seek refuge in neighbouring countries under very difficult conditions. Even more disturbing are the gross human rights violations, war crimes and crimes against humanity that characterise these wars. Young boys and girls are forced to take adult responsibilities at an early age, often as soldiers, and these are notorious for committing the worst atrocities. Rebel armies in northern Uganda, Liberia, Democratic Republic of the Congo (DRC), Liberia and Sierra Leone abducted children and, through coercion and indoctrination, turned them into effective and dastardly killing machines. Young girls and women were routinely violated and their dignity degraded. In these wars, it is often tricky to distinguish between a perpetrator and a victim and it is not uncommon for rebel fighters to commit serious acts of aggression against family or community members. The Rwandan genocide of 1994 vividly shows this disconcerting phenomenon. Despite the civil nature of the conflicts, the wars are heavily internationalised due to the selfish and competing interests of neighbouring and other rogue states. Clear examples are found in the DRC, Liberia and Sierra Leone wars. In the DRC, for instance, all of that country's neighbours have involved themselves somewhat in the conflict and this interest has been largely mercenary – to plunder the DRC's huge natural resources.

The reasons for Africa's wars are many and various. They range from innate ethnic and religious hatreds, which are often exploited by ambitious leaders to the absence of democracy. The direct and indirect costs of the wars are staggering (International Action Network on Small Arms, Oxfam and Saferworld 2007). It is understandable, therefore, why considerable efforts are being made to deal with past crimes and to establish the rule of law. These efforts have involved, for instance, the use of traditional justice mechanisms to complement formal state processes. This paper will look into the use of traditional justice mechanisms in Africa in general – with special attention for some aspects of traditional justice in Sierra Leone.

2. CONFRONTING THE JUSTICE CHALLENGE

Several travelling models of conflict resolution are currently employed in Africa to deal with the complex issues arising from these wars. They include truth commissions, special tribunals and courts, and power-sharing arrangements. The accountability instruments (truth commissions, special tribunals and courts) have different objectives and goals; nevertheless they all aim to seek justice not only for the survivors but for society at large. There are serious practical issues connected with justice for past crimes in a post-war situation, two of which are: (a) *the timing*. For example, which should come first – peace or justice? Or should the two be tried concurrently? And what are the dangers of pursuing both at the same time? (b) the *method of accountability*. How can one get the perpetrators of heinous crimes to account for their actions: by recourse to retributive or restorative justice or a combination of both? Will these actions stop impunity? Thus, although justice is an integral part of the conflict resolution and peacebuilding processes, it however, poses its own challenges, particularly from a human rights perspective (see points 4 and 5). What then is justice? Limitations of space and time do not permit a comprehensive review of this term and concept. However, a United Nations definition, which this writer finds acceptable, is:

> An ideal of accountability and fairness in the protection and vindication of rights and the prevention and punishment of wrongs. Justice implies regard for the rights of the accused, for the interests of victims and for the well-being of society at large. It is a concept rooted in all national cultures and traditions and, while its administration usually implies formal judicial mechanisms, traditional dispute resolution mechanisms are equally relevant. (United Nations 2004, 4)

This definition encompasses traditional justice as well.

It is common knowledge that although imported and more formal methods of justice seeking are widely used in post-war African countries, such as the International Criminal Tribunal for Rwanda in Arusha set up to try those accused of committing the genocide in that country in 1994, they have serious short-comings which tend to minimise their efficacy. These accountability mechanisms are not only very expensive to administer, but more importantly, are too time-consuming and quite detached from the majority of the people whose interests these courts are expected to seek. They are rooted in Western notions of justice, which are often at variance with African concepts of truth-seeking, accountability and reconciliation. Western justice systems have largely been shaped by the retributive paradigm and have accordingly "*influenced decisions to prosecute perpetrators of major war crimes and human rights abuses.*" (Harvey 2006, 4). The retributive paradigm may have its origins in the Nuremberg trials after World War II. This does not suggest, however, that retribution has no place in traditional justice systems.

Retribution may not always be suitable for post-war justice in Africa for several reasons. Firstly, it has the potential of further polarising the community instead of healing it. This is because in many post-war societies:

> Victims, perpetrators and survivors in general continue to live in the same communities. This continued coexistence, though possibly inevitable, may be marked by residual fears, animosities, and tension. In other words, post-conflict communal life is often driven by the legacies of violence. A central task of peacebuilding is to transform communal relations from a state of "negative peace" (usually defined as an absence of armed conflict) to one of "positive peace" (defined as a structural transformation towards a socio-political and economic system capable of fostering justice and ensuring a self-sustained peace). Such a transformation is beyond the scope of formal, retributive justice; rather, it requires a more holistic and locally-relevant approach that addresses a set of concerns, including accountability, truth-telling, reparation, and reconciliation. (Peace Building Initiative 2009)

Secondly, the formal justice systems in most post-war countries are generally weak and therefore incapable of comprehensively addressing all the wrongs committed during the conflicts. Huyse (2009, 105) put it this way:

> Following a civil war or genocide, a country lies in ruins. Judges have been assassinated or are themselves suspected of complicity. There is virtual absence of lawyers. Buildings are unusable. The wheels of the judicial machine are unable to turn or grind to a halt after a short time... Moreover, the judicial system is dependent for evidence on the cooperation of the army and police; however, the composition and culture of the security forces often continue to embody the spirit of the old regime. They may destroy or withhold documents, so that the possibility of some perpetrators being acquitted cannot be ruled out. That is shocking for the victims; it is better to have no prosecutions at all than an operation which merely inflicts new pain.

Thirdly, there are political risks. As Africa's civil wars involve the active participation of large numbers of young people, trying and eventually imprisoning these youths may adversely affect the post-recovery process (see for example: Buckley-Zistel 2005).

Fourthly, there is sometimes a practical problem. In the South African experience, apartheid, as Huyse (2009, 105) clearly points out, "*was not the responsibility of a specific number of individuals; an entire generation of men and women helped to sustain the system*". Thus, in cases such as this, "*it is physically impossible to bring all those who bear some guilt before the courts*". Not surprising, therefore, even key leaders of the African National Congress (ANC) which had been in the vanguard of the struggle against apartheid in South Africa, opted for some form of amnesty and reconciliation to promote healing in the post-apartheid era, although the United Nations had declared apartheid a crime against humanity.

3. IS TRADITIONAL JUSTICE THE ANSWER?

Traditional justice is nothing new and has been practised by communities the world over for centuries. While it has been studied extensively in legal anthropology, its study for purposes of justice sector reform and transitional justice is relatively new, especially in the African context. It began to gain currency in the aftermath of the bloody civil wars that have been the bane of the African continent in the last few decades.[1] Traditional justice has been defined in many ways and the term 'traditional' is often used interchangeably with the words 'customary', and 'informal'. Penal Reform International (2000) defines traditional justice systems as "*non-state justice systems which have existed, although not without change, since pre-colonial times and are generally found in rural areas*". In certain cases, however, like in Sierra Leone (which will be discussed in more detail later), some aspects of traditional justice are an integral part at a base level of the formal justice system.

In recent years, non-governmental organisations (NGOs), development agencies and others interested in transitional justice in Africa have shown an increasing interest in local or indigenous dispute resolution mechanisms as their potential for peace building becomes evident. This interest is the result of two inter-related factors: (a) the hybridization of various transitional justice mechanisms (such as prosecutions, truth commissions and local mechanisms) and (b) the growing sense of disenchantment with international judicial approaches to post-conflict justice.

1 A recent book on the subject is Huyse and Salter (2008).

Hoffman (2008, 130) is highly critical of some of these international approaches. This is her opinion on the Special Court for Sierra Leone:

> The top-level processes most visible in the international arena often put massive resources toward initiatives that impact very few people directly – witness the more than $300 million spent on the Special Court in Sierra Leone to try the nine men most responsible for fomenting the war there. When peace-building initiatives do focus more on directly reaching the individuals most affected by the war, they are often either short-term or are disconnected from the strategic processes or community infrastructure that would allow them to have deep and sustainable impact.

Orentlicher (2007, 18) poses a relevant question. "*Given the extraordinary range of national experiences and cultures, how could anyone imagine there to be a universally relevant formula for transitional justice*?" Theidon (2006, 436) is more empathic, arguing that transitional justice "*is not the monopoly of international tribunals or of states: communities also mobilize the ritual and symbolic elements of these transitional processes to deal with the deep cleavages left – or accentuated – by civil conflicts*". In any case, common sense dictates that those who have suffered the most during civil conflicts must also be at the forefront of the reconciliation or healing process. In other words, they must be active players and not passive onlookers of processes that would have deep repercussions on their lives. It is no accident, therefore, that post-war societies in Africa are revisiting their past to 'rediscover' their age-old methods of seeking justice and reconciliation.

There are several examples across Africa and their potential for healing fractured communities is now widely acknowledged. Two of the more popular ones include *mato oput* (practised among the Acholi in Northern Uganda) and the *gacaca* courts in Rwanda (which have, despite some institutional deficiencies, facilitated the trial of thousands of persons connected with the genocide of 1994).[2] The goals of these two accountability and reconciliation mechanisms are comparable to some of the objectives of contemporary truth and reconciliation commissions (TRCs) found in many developing countries emerging from deadly civil conflicts, although their processes are different. The commonalities between TRCs and traditional justice systems include: providing space for survivors to tell their stories, recognising and condemning wrongs done (without necessarily imposing punishment), and in certain cases, providing reparations.[3]

---

2 The *gacaca* courts cannot be called truly traditional, since they have been greatly modified while dealing with the genocide cases in Rwanda. Nevertheless, the courts still contain significant elements of traditional justice.

3 The *gacaca* courts (see note 3 above) have, however, imposed penalties due to the horrendous nature of the crimes they are dealing with.

Kofi Annan in the document quoted above (United Nations 2004, 12) has acknowledged this potential as well, submitting that:

> Due regard must be given to indigenous and informal traditions for administering justice or settling disputes, to help them to continue their often vital role and to do so in conformity with both international standards and local tradition. Where these are ignored or overridden, the result can be the exclusion of large sectors of society from accessible justice.

More recently, the significance of traditional justice was underscored in a preliminary pact signed by the Ugandan Government and rebels of the Lord's Resistance Army (LRA) in June 2007. Part of the accord read as follows:

> Traditional justice mechanisms, such as... mato oput... and others as practised in the communities affected by the conflict, shall be promoted, with necessary modifications, as a central part of the framework for accountability and reconciliation.[4]

Major international donor institutions like the World Bank are now intervening directly in conflict resolution mechanisms in Africa, partly due to the huge costs of these wars on the development process. Legal reforms undertaken by the World Bank focus on such key areas as court reforms, legal aid, information dissemination and education, alternative dispute resolution, public sector accountability and research. What is of particular relevance is that the Bank recognises:

> All justice reform interventions should attend to particularities of socio-legal context, should consider the specific justice needs of poor people, and should be planned not in isolation, but from a system-wide perspective. Legal services and legal aid interventions should confront the challenge of scale, should consider alternative methods of service delivery, and should in some cases take care to maintain at least partial independence from the state. The use of non-court dispute resolution mechanisms should be guided by the benefits achieved in cost, time, harmony, and fairness. Evaluations of access to justice programs should go beyond "head counts" to demonstrate impact – on users of justice services as well as on society at large – and to weigh opportunity cost (Maru 2009, iii).

While the World Bank's interventions in the realm of the rule of law focus on "*non-court dispute resolution mechanisms*" in general, the latter clearly comprise traditional justice mechanisms. Wojkowska's work *Doing Justice: How informal justice systems can contribute* (2006), which was a UNDP-funded project, supports this assertion. In any event, the high profile role that traditional justice

---

[4] Quoted in Huyse and Salter (2008, 1).

now seems to enjoy stems directly from the implementation of judicial reform programmes because traditional justice is considered a tool to increase access to justice for the poor.

4. CHARACTERISTICS

The Peace Building Initiative (2009)[5] outlines four main characteristics of traditional justice systems: (a) The use of local languages: the language(s) used in traditional justice systems is local and thus familiar to the average person, whereas the formal justice system generally uses the official language(s) of the state, which may be unfamiliar to many people living in rural communities. (b) Geographical proximity: institutions of the formal justice system are usually located in the capital city or regional capitals, and are thus geographically remote from people living in rural communities. Traditional/informal justice systems, on the other hand, are located in villages and are geographically easily accessible to people. (c) Cultural relevance: formal legal proceedings can be complicated and confusing, whereas traditional/informal ones are more familiar and easily understood; they have also a better chance to fit the priorities of the community and local implications of the conflict. Therefore, their verdicts may be better accepted. (d) Costliness: referring to the formal justice system can be costly and time-consuming because it often entails travelling long distances, paying transportation costs, and legal fees, all costs that are generally at the very least reduced with the traditional/informal justice; this system can also be more efficient as it is generally not bureaucratic.

To these may be added certain salient features: the problem is viewed as that of the whole community or group; an emphasis on reconciliation and restoring social harmony; traditional arbitrators are appointed from within the community on the basis of status or lineage; a high degree of public participation; customary law is merely one factor considered in reaching a compromise; the rules of evidence and procedure are flexible; there is no professional legal representation; the process is voluntary and the decision is based on agreement; an emphasis on restorative penalties; enforcement of decisions secured through social pressure; the decision is confirmed through rituals aiming at reintegration; and like cases need not be treated alike (Penal Reform International 2000, 22).

In addition, the African justice system is process-oriented, rather than rule-based. To this end, Elechi (2004, 8) states that premium is placed on the "*process of achieving peaceful resolutions of disputes rather than on adherence to rules as*

5 Peacebuilding Initiative is a project of the Program on Humanitarian Policy and Conflict Research (HPCR) at Harvard University, www.peacebuildinginitiative.org.

the basis of determining disputes". And as he succinctly puts it, "*a fair judgment must take into account a wider range of facts and interests, including that of the community, without necessarily compromising the facts of the matter in dispute and the rights of the litigants*" (idem, 18).

Rather than coerce, African indigenous justice systems encourage offenders to step forward and take full responsibility for their actions. Accounting for one's misdemeanours would result in some discomfort but "*not so harsh as to degenerate into further antagonism and animosity*" (Elechi 2004, 18). There are, however, several instances where harsher methods are used to get the offender to own up, if he or she becomes uncooperative. Here are some examples from Sierra Leone.

One of the most common disputes in rural communities is sexual offence and there are three broad categories: adultery (commonly called *woman palava* or *woman damage*), incest and bush defilement (having sexual intercourse in the bush). Adultery cases usually affect only the individuals concerned (that is, the husband, wife and the male adulterer) while incest affects the whole family. Bush defilement is perhaps the most serious one as it impinges on the entire community.

A case of adultery arises when a woman 'confesses' her lover to her husband, or when the latter suspects that a certain man is having an affair with his wife. He becomes very angry at his wife and the transgressor but despite his anger, he still has room in his heart for forgiveness. The procedure for settling the matter can be quite simple but in few cases, very complex, depending on the attitude of the offender. Usually, the husband informs his close relations about the wife's misdemeanour, who in turn approach the relatives of the other man to verify the truth. If the man owns up and answers in the affirmative, he is asked to pay a small fee and to beg for forgiveness. Generally the aggrieved husband accepts the compensation and that ends the matter. This is usually how such cases are settled even in the local courts. Thereafter, the husband and the other man could live happily in the community, as if nothing ever happened between them.

This example is important primarily because of its social value. It underscores the capacity of Sierra Leoneans to forgive and reconcile with one another. It also greatly reduces the incidence of divorce (resulting from infidelity) with huge implications for the well-being of the children, if any. This act of forgiveness is also based on the local belief that "*when a gun is fired, it is fired*"; there is no way one can retrieve the fired cartridge (no use crying over spilled milk). At best, one could prevent another occurrence. Put in another way, one has to look forward and not to groan on the past unnecessarily.

In situations where the accused or suspect denies the charge, a less humane method of extracting confession from him may be sought, such as swearing. The aggrieved husband informs the chiefs and elders (with some money) of his intention to swear the alleged wrongdoer on a very potent medicine. Thereafter, the suspect is invited for interrogation and if he continues to deny, permission is then given to the husband to pursue the matter further. The services of a diviner or medicine man from a distant community (to minimise the incidence of bribery) are then sought but before the swearing takes place, a village crier, in the dead of night, warns everyone in the community of the impending visit of the medicine man, the potency of his medicine and the possible repercussions of the swear not only on the alleged offender (who is not named) but on his whole family. This may be done for three days. Usually family pressure is put on the offender to admit his guilt. If he does, the matter will be settled with minimal expenses paid. However, if the suspect waits until the medicine man arrives (his arrival is again publicly announced) before he accepts responsibility for his action he will have to pay all the fees incurred and at the same time pay the husband for the *woman damage*.

One would argue, of course that these adultery cases tend to reinforce the belief that the woman is the personal property of the husband, which is not in conformity with human rights principles. Fortunately, incidences of *woman palava* are now becoming rare even in remote communities, as women become more aware of their rights. Moreover, the Gender Acts passed by the Sierra Leone Parliament in June 2007 now give women a much greater say in marriage affairs than had been the case before.[6]

A case of incest, if proven, is handled differently. It requires purification or cleansing of the man and the woman by a special priestess because incest is considered a taboo.[7] Among some communities (e.g. the Mende), a male dog is included in the purification process because it is believed that only dogs and other lower animals engage in sexual relations with their close relatives. If the sexual intercourse was done in the bush (an abomination which affects the whole community), the culprits and the bush in which the incident occurred are cleansed and the ancestors appeased (through the pouring of libation). The ancestors in turn will ensure that the bush continues to provide for the livelihood of the community. No compensation is paid to anybody for incest cases.

---

6 These are (a) The Domestic Violence Act, (b) The Devolution of Estates Act, and (c) Registration of Customary Marriage and Divorce Act. All three laws provide protection to women. For an interesting discussion on the background to and importance of these laws, see, for example Skoll Foundation, 'Implementing the Gender Acts in Sierra Leone', www.socialedge.org (accessed 10/10/10).

7 What constitutes incest varies from ethnic group to ethnic group. However, they all agree that a sexual relation with a sister or brother is incest.

Incidents of theft are settled by shaming the thief and asking him to pay some costs. However, if he denies, some extreme forms of extracting justice may be resorted to, such as trial by ordeal. This can take many forms. For example, the suspect may be forced to drink some concoction and if he vomits, then his guilt is established. Sometimes, a red hot metal is put on his legs and if he feels nothing (that is, the hot iron does not burn him) then he is declared innocent of the charge. The reverse establishes guilt. In other instances, the accused may be asked to swear on a *sasa* (a kind of 'medicine' which has the potential of causing grievous bodily harm to the offender). The use of *sasa* is common among the Temne ethnic group in Sierra Leone.

Other communities also use potent 'medicines' to extract the truth or confession from accused persons. The Sherbro have the *pok*, on which persons suspected of crime and witnesses in court are sworn. If they swear falsely (being guilty of the offence they deny) or if they give false evidence, they could be affected by the *pok*. It could 'eat' their intestines or sexual organs or force their eyes out of the sockets. Such persons could die unless treated by the *pok*.[8]

These practices, especially the use of torture to extract justice, are a clear violation of the rights of the accused, who has little protection and in some instances no alternative method of seeking justice.

While retributive justice is applied to some very serious offences cited above, restorative justice is the norm particularly in post-war situations. Certain principles underlie indigenous justice practices and they include accountability for one's actions, followed by remorse, forgiveness and in some instances restoration of the dignity of the aggrieved person or party through the payment of reparations. Justice, peace and reconciliation are therefore inseparable. The ultimate goal is to rehabilitate both the injured person or party and the wrongdoer. It is justice that heals; thus justice is combined with reconciliation. An important element of traditional justice practices is their community-centred character. This can be illustrated by the following example from Sierra Leone.

During the armed conflict, the rebels routinely defiled sacred bushes, including secret society bushes and burial grounds. This unwarranted behaviour, according to the people's belief, not only angered the dead (ancestors), but could also lead to lower yields in their farms or even bring some misfortune to the community. In order to placate the ancestors, therefore, and make the land profitable again, the culprits and the defiled land were thoroughly cleansed in special ceremonies

[8] *Pok* is the equivalent of the *Sasa* among the Sherbro. *Sasa* and *Pok* are a type of talisman which the community believes, has the power to punish a wrong-doer. In my view, the power of these 'medicines' is more psychological than real.

administered by community elders and priests and priestesses. These cleansing ceremonies took place in many communities in southern Sierra Leone.

These practices recognise that although the human being is an individual, he/she is also a member of various groups and consequently:

> A conflict between two members of a community is regarded as a problem which afflicts the entire community. In order to restore harmony, therefore, there must be general satisfaction among the community at large, as well as the disputants, with the procedure and the outcome of the case. Public consensus is, moreover, necessary to ensure enforcement of the decision through social pressure. (PRI 2000, 26)

This is in sharp contrast to what obtains in Western societies, which are highly individualistic. Truth seeking and reconciliation sessions in African communities are generally held in public often with the active involvement of community members. This open, participatory and transparent system minimises the possibility of injustice.

Wojkowska (2006, 13) has proffered eight reasons why African communities prefer traditional justice to the formal courts system: mistrust of the law, fear, intimidation; lack of understanding – language issues, unfamiliarity of formal procedures and court atmosphere, low legal literacy; unequal power relations; physical and financial inaccessibility; formal systems are culturally 'uncomfortable' and lack legitimacy, since they can be complicit in conflict, past oppression and corruption; it usually takes a long time to process cases, involving high opportunity costs; and lastly going through the formal system may lead to more problems between the disputing parties.

In a similar vein, Chirayath, Sage and Woolcock (2005, v 5) are emphatic that imposing formal truth processes on communities without regard for their local mechanisms and legal systems may be both counterproductive and ineffectual for the following reasons:

(a) The failure to recognise different systems of understanding may in itself be discriminatory or exclusionary, and hence inequitable.
(b) There may be very good reasons why communities prefer indigenous conflict resolution methods and these must be recognised, understood and respected.
(c) There is ample evidence of the resilience of traditional justice mechanisms and attempting to stamp these out would be futile.
(d) Ignoring traditional systems and believing that top-down approaches will change practices at the local level has the tendency of reinforcing existing discriminatory practices of marginalised communities.

(e) Focusing purely on state regimes and access to formal systems in some ways assumes that such systems can be made accessible to all, while clearly even in the most developed countries this is not the case.[9]

5. THE HUMAN RIGHTS QUESTION

Although the United Nations gave international status to the concept of human rights through the Universal Declaration of Human Rights in December 1948, the human rights concept is as old as human civilisation and the notion was deeply ingrained in African cultural values long before the imposition of European colonial rule on the continent. The rights to life, food security and shelter were, for example, recognised in pre-colonial African political systems. However, Donnelly (1984) does not agree. He states, "*recognition of human rights simply was not the way of traditional Africa*" (at 308). Donnelly either displays his complete ignorance of pre-colonial Africa or he presents a rather jaundiced view of the pre-colonial African situation. He however concedes that even in cases where individuals had certain rights, these were subsumed in the rights of the community. This is correct because in African communities (unlike the West), the emphasis is on communal, not individual rights. Individuals enjoyed their rights within the framework of their group (Mwenda 2000). This is why, as has been stated before, the justice system takes cognisance of the collective interests and aspirations of the community. The communal concept of human rights has, for example, found expression in the African Charter on Human and People's Rights, which came into operation in October 1986.

Elechi (2004, 1) argues rather persuasively that African traditional justice systems took full cognisance of the human rights of both the victim and the offender. He says, "*the restoration of rights, dignity, interests and well-being of victims, offenders, and the entire community is the goal of African indigenous justice system*' and that '*opportunities for the achievement of justice are higher under the African indigenous justice system than with the African state criminal justice system, partly because, the empowerment of victims, offenders, and the community is the central principle of African justice*". He concludes,

> As a victim centred justice system, the first priority of African indigenous justice is the safety of victims. Assistance is given to victims to restore their injury, property lost, and their sense of security and dignity. Again, the victims' needs for information, validation, social support, vindication, are the starting points of African justice.

[9] Quoted in The Peace Building Initiative (2009).

Even though (a) human rights are not absent in African traditional justice it is important to acknowledge both its advantages and disadvantages. There are generally two opposing views regarding indigenous conflict resolution approaches. There are those who tend to glorify them and ignore or downplay their pitfalls. On the other hand, there are critics who see little value in the use of these informal methods and prefer more formal procedures that conform to international norms and practices. Be that as it may, traditional justice has certain merits: as indicated earlier, traditional justice is relatively cheap, affordable and culturally relevant; (b) low overhead operational costs; (c) with emphasis on reconciliation, traditional justice could avoid future conflicts (d) premium is put on community reintegration, healing, and the peaceful co-existence of survivors (perpetrators and victims) (e) justice, reconciliation and healing are all linked together and part of a whole (f) traditional law is not simply a set of rules exercising coercive power, but a system of thought by which certain forms of relations come to seem natural and taken for granted, modes of thought that are inscribed in institutions that exercise some coercion in support of their categories and theories of explanation (Engle 1988).

On the other hand, we can also identify some drawbacks: (a) the belief in the supernatural (God, priests and priestesses, ancestors, diviners and so on) is very strong among the communities and this faith greatly influences justice-seeking at the community level. It explains the use of rituals (for example, cleansing ceremonies), cursing and swearing in the justice procedure. However, cursing and swearing are completely at variance with modern legal systems, the rule of law and international norms and practices and they create the impression of backwardness. This has indeed posed a big dilemma for external actors, including non-governmental organisations and institutions interested in promoting traditional justice in Africa. (b) Miscarriage of justice by diviners is another problem although such abuses are not peculiar to traditional justice. (c) Traditional justice approaches seem ill equipped to deal with horrendous crimes; alleged perpetrators are denied due process and so there is injustice which further creates tension in the community and a potential source of instability. (d) These practices sustain existing power relationships and marginalise women and the youth. (e) There are geographical or territorial limitations. Traditional justice systems evolved to address the needs of specific communities within limited geographical boundaries. Thus, their application to other communities or groups may create serious problems. (f) A related issue is the fact that although many of Africa's contemporary wars are civil in nature, they are, as pointed out earlier, heavily internationalised, with many of the key actors often staying in foreign countries and directly or remotely controlling events in the warring territory. Traditional justice mechanisms lack the capacity to hold such actors and villains accountable for their actions. (g) Some of the truth-seeking mechanisms seem extremely harsh, but they are only utilised as a last option when the alleged perpetrator becomes uncooperative. It is common knowledge that societies the world over sometimes use severe measures to ascertain the truth from criminals. However, the use of extremely harsh interrogation techniques or invoking fear of the supernatural to extract information from an alleged offender may be bad for countries graduating from war to peace, for it further divides people and communities thereby making reconciliation hard to achieve. This is mainly because the alleged offenders often 'admit to their wrong-doing' not necessarily because they are convinced of their guilt, but out of fear of community sanctions and pressure that they may face from relatives and friends. The admission of guilt is therefore not a voluntary process; it is not 'coming from the heart' and therefore not genuine.

Let us have a closer look of some of the disadvantages with regards to the respect for human rights pointed out above. As mentioned, the traditional justice systems are highly patriarchal. This has its origins in pre-industrial societies, but as tradition continues to reinvent itself to address emerging issues, the gender bias in the organisation and operations of African traditional justice systems must be re-examined. In Mozambique, for instance, considerable use has been made of the *magamba* spirits in resolving conflicts and disputes arising from the long civil war. However, the *gamba* ceremony itself is gender biased. Igreja and Dias-Lambranca (2008) point out that:

> The women killed during the Mozambican civil war are unable to return as spirits to the realm of the living to claim justice. Only the spirits of men can do this. In this sense, although magamba spirits break with the silence of the past, structurally the justice they offer helps to reinforce patriarchal power in a country that is struggling for gender equality.

Similarly in Burundi the institution of *bashingantahe* is a largely male-dominated traditional justice system. The institution historically comprised "*men of integrity who are responsible for settling disputes at all levels, from the top of the hill to the level of the kings*". Although women now take the oath and are recognised as persons of integrity, they do not receive the rod of wisdom, only the men do (Naniwe-Kaburahe 2008).

The traditional justice system in Sierra Leone is equally patriarchal, but women have been involved somewhat in some of the processes. For example, "*women in communities conduct healing rituals for ex-child combatants. By ritually cleansing them of their past deeds... they enable the children to return and be accepted into a community*" (Anderlini, Conaway and Kays 2007).

The near exclusion of women is thus a major weakness of traditional justice systems in Africa. But we are also reminded that even in the formal justice systems all over the world, women are seriously under-represented (PRI 2000, 2).

In addition to its patriarchal character, it is suggested that the system is incapable of dealing with some of the disturbing aspects of Africa's newer wars, namely gross human rights violations and crimes against humanity. This is primarily because these crimes are too complex and particularly the latter, completely alien to most African communities. Moreover, their scope generally cuts across many geographical and political boundaries which makes it almost impossible for traditional justice systems to prosecute alleged offenders, even if they had the capacity to do so. From a human rights perspective and practical standpoint therefore, cases involving human rights violations, genocide and crimes against humanity should, in my view, be dealt with by the formal legal institutions and traditional justice systems would then play a complementary role in reconciliation and related matters.

6. THE SIERRA LEONE CONFLICT

Sierra Leone is a multi-cultural country comprising seventeen ethnic groups. Despite their cultural heterogeneity, these groups have certain commonalities, especially in the areas of justice seeking, dispute settlement and reconciliation. All the groups believe in the rule of law and justice as instruments for maintaining societal cohesion and harmony. Their accountability mechanisms include prosecution, arbitration and mediation. They also abhor impunity.

The country experienced an atrocious civil conflict from 1991–2002. An organisation calling itself the Revolutionary United Front (RUF) ignited an armed rebellion in Sierra Leone in March 1991. Although they enjoyed little public support, the RUF roamed the countryside terrorising the populace at will. Their trademark was crude amputations, rape and kidnapping of boys to use as child-soldiers and girls and women as sex-slaves. Sierra Leone was regarded as "*among one of the countries that has the world's worst records for recruiting child soldiers*" (Fofana 2004, 14). Many of these child-soldiers, according to Fofana, were less than fourteen years old; they were not only brave fighters but also remorseless killers. Based on their action and character, some were nicknamed 'Young Killer', 'Junior Blood' and 'Destroyer'. Other warring factions including Sierra Leone Army soldiers and members of the Civil Defences Forces also committed atrocities during the war. Human Rights Watch (2000) summed up the human costs of the war as follows:

> Sierra Leone's... conflict was characterized by unspeakable brutality. International war crimes of the worst type were routinely and systematically committed against Sierra Leoneans of all ages. The suffering inflicted upon the civilian population has been profound. While all sides committed human rights violations, rebel forces were responsible for the overwhelming majority.

According to the Government of Sierra Leone Poverty Reduction Strategy Paper (2005), the conflict left a trail of human tragedy.

> An estimated 20,000 people were killed and thousands more injured or maimed. Over 2 million people were displaced (500,000 fled to neighbouring countries). There was a mass exodus of skilled professionals, to Freetown and out of the country, leaving most of the country drained of skilled manpower. The damage extended to significant loss of property and the abduction of women and children for sex, labour and combat. Most of the country's social, economic and physical infrastructure was destroyed. Local community social and productive infrastructure such as markets, stores, rice mills, and community service buildings were completely vandalised. At the height of the civil conflict, there was almost a complete breakdown of civil and political authority in the country, giving rise to tremendous human rights abuses. Mining and agricultural activities, the lifeline of the country, were essentially brought to a halt. Farms were rampaged or abandoned while the livestock population was almost entirely wiped out.

The reasons why the country imploded into violence were captured in the Sierra Leone Truth and Reconciliation Commission report (2004 Vol. 1, 10):

> While there were many factors, both internal and external, that explain the cause of the civil war, the Commission came to the conclusion that it was years of bad governance, endemic corruption and the denial of basic human rights that created the deplorable conditions that made the war inevitable. Successive regimes became increasingly impervious to the wishes and needs of the majority. Instead of implementing positive and progressive policies, each regime perpetuated the ills and self-serving machinations left behind by its predecessor. By the start of the conflict, the nation had been stripped of its dignity. Institutional collapse reduced the vast majority of people into a state of deprivation. Government accountability was non-existent. Political expression and dissent had been crushed. Democracy and the rule of law were dead. By 1991, Sierra Leone was a deeply divided society and full of the potential for violence. It required only the slightest spark for this violence to be ignited. The Commission traced the roots of these lapses through the post independence period and into the colonial period.

Many writers are of the view that the internationalisation of the war and its prolongation were due in large measure, to the illegal exploitation and sale of the country's diamonds (Perez-Katz 2002, 1; Hirsch 2001). This is not quite correct.[10]

---

[10] More informed writings on the relationship between the Sierra Leone conflict and diamonds include Smillie, Gberie and Hazelton (2000), OTI, USAID (2000) and United Nations (2000).

While it is true that proceeds from the illegal diamond trade by the RUF prolonged the war, it is rather simplistic to assert that the entire conflict revolved around control of diamonds. Gberie (2005, 8) describes the RUF rebellion as a case of organised mass delinquency aimed mainly at criminal exploitation, not social protest.[11]

The Sierra Leone civil conflict, like many other wars in contemporary Africa, was heavily internationalised and it involved many actors who were engaged in the fighting as well as in the peace process. Some of the stakeholders instrumental in the transition from war to peace were the Economic Community of West African States (ECOWAS), whose peace-keeping troops, labelled the Economic Community of West African States Monitoring Group (ECOMOG), had been engaged in Sierra Leone since the start of the conflict although on a low key until 1997, the United Nations, some Western and African countries, and the government and people of Sierra Leone. Three peace agreements were signed before the war could end in January 2002. This was due largely to serious violations of the agreements particularly by the RUF. The first agreement, signed in November 1996, saw the deployment of UN peace monitors, the United Nations Observer Mission in Sierra Leone (UNOMSIL).

The most comprehensive of these accords was the Lomé Peace Agreement signed by the Government of Sierra Leone and the RUF in the presence of international observers, on 7 July 1999.[12] It granted, among other things, blanket amnesty which became a very contentious issue, especially for human rights organisations. The UN added a caveat to the agreement indicating that the amnesty did not apply to war crimes, genocide and crimes against humanity.[13] The UN subsequently established a peacekeeping mission in Sierra Leone (UNAMSIL), which then replaced ECOMOG.

7. JUSTICE AND RECONCILIATION FROM BELOW

Truth, responsibility and reconciliation were carried out at two levels, following the end of the conflict – one formal and the other informal. Two institutions – the Truth and Reconciliation Commission and Special Court for Sierra Leone, administered restorative and retributive justice, respectively.[14] In addition to

11 For a concise analysis of the background to the Sierra Leone civil war see, for example Alie (2008).

12 Peace Agreement between the Government of Sierra Leone and the Revolutionary United Front of Sierra Leone, 7 July 1999. Available at www.sierra-leone.org/lomeaccord.html (accessed 13/06/07).

13 For full discussion, see Hayner (2007).

14 For an analysis of the work of these two institutions see, for example, Hayner (2007).

these official institutions, justice and reconciliation have also been practiced from below.

7.1. REINTEGRATION AND RECONCILIATION OF EX-COMBATANTS

Several actors were involved in justice seeking and reconciliation from below. They included priests and priestesses, diviners and community elders who used rituals like cleansing ceremonies, mediation and arbitration. In these processes, justice was interlinked with reconciliation. In parts of the Northern Province, for example, community elders 'purified' child soldiers before they were reintegrated into their communities. Similar ceremonies took place in some southern and eastern towns. These ceremonies were not directly linked to the official peacebuilding programmes carried out by the government and international agencies. Some of the ceremonies received active support from local as well as international NGOs. Caritas, an international NGO working in the northern region, for instance, supported the community elders in the reintegration of the child soldiers.

The return of former combatants, especially RUF fighters, created some tension and unease in some communities. These ex-combatants were expected to show remorse for their actions and ask for forgiveness not just from community members, but also from their victims before their reintegration into the communities. The reconciliation process worked like this. When a former RUF fighter or a 'sobel'[15] asked for forgiveness from the victim and if the latter agreed (usually community pressure would bear on the victim to accept), both of them were required to demonstrate publicly that the matter was finally settled. They showed this by their willingness to allow an elderly woman (who was one of the mediators) to rub their chests with some wet mud and close to their hearts. They then embraced each other and drank water from the same cup. This was an indication that 'their hearts are cold again' and both parties now wanted to live happily as before. An intervention of the ancestors was invoked by the wet mud, which had been mixed on the floor (because these ancestors live below the ground). The climax of the reconciliation was merry-making, which reinforced that the parties were no longer enemies. One does not usually party with an enemy This form of reconciliation was prevalent in the southern half of the country and particularly among the Mende.

[15] 'Sobel' was a term coined during the civil conflict to refer to a regular soldier who was collaborating with the rebels. It means 'soldier-cum-rebel'.

The act of prostration was another reconciliation mechanism used to reintegrate some former combatants into their localities. The offender prostrated before the aggrieved person who then touched his or her head. Prostration demonstrated three key things: first, it was an acknowledgement by the offender that he/she had done wrong; second, it showed readiness to show remorse and third, willingness on the part of the aggrieved person or victim to forgive and reconcile. The TRC also used this reconciliation method.

Generally, before the reconciliation ceremonies began, the elders invoked the ancestors into their midst by pouring libation on the ground to appease the ancestors. Sierra Leoneans, like most other Africans, have an organic connection with the soil. Land has both economic and religious importance. It is the basis of sustenance and a source of economic security. Furthermore, land acts as a link between past, present and future generations. As such, land must be treated with respect and reverence. This is why anti-social behaviour like sexual intercourse in the bush is expressly forbidden.

7.2. COMMUNITY RECONCILIATION

A Sierra Leonean human rights organisation, Forum of Conscience, in conjunction with a United States-based foundation, Catalyst for Peace, has taken community reconciliation one-step further. It has rekindled an indigenous reconciliation and peace consolidation process known as *Fambul Tok* (Krio for 'Family Talk'). Families and groups meet to discuss and resolve problems, using the age-old traditions of confession, apology and forgiveness.

The programme works at the village level to help communities organise ceremonies that include truth-telling bonfires and traditional cleansing ceremonies. *Fambul Tok* is rooted in the understanding that reconciliation is a process and not a one-time event, and works with communities on a long-term basis. It ensures full community engagement – through initial consultations to determine whether people are ready to reconcile, and subsequently through community-led preparations and outreach for *Fambul Tok* ceremonies.

Following the ceremonies, *Fambul Tok* works with the communities to organise activities to support and sustain the reconciliation process. These have included radio-listening clubs, soccer matches and village-initiated community farms – projects through which newly reconciled individuals come together for the good of the community.

This community-healing process of reconciliation and forgiveness attempts to address the roots of conflict at the local level, and restore dignity to the lives of those who suffered most directly from violence. The work helps war-affected individuals reflect on the past and move forward in ways that avert the renewal of aggressions. By grounding reconciliation in indigenous practices, *Fambul Tok* helps create healthy communities capable of building new foundations of peace. It has succeeded in mending many broken relationships, especially between former combatants and their host communities (Hoffman 2008).

Importance of the chief in the dispensation of traditional justice

Paramount Chiefs and the lower chiefs have all been involved in settling some war-related conflicts, even though they are prevented by law from settling cases. Before 1963, Paramount Chiefs (who are the principal political leaders of their chiefdoms) adjudicated in certain kinds of cases. However, this judicial function was removed from them and vested in the Chiefdom Administration Court Chairmen, by the Local Courts Act of 1963. These Court Chairmen operate in the provincial areas and in all the 149 chiefdoms in Sierra Leone. They adjudicate mostly customary civil cases. Tribal Headmen perform a similar function in Freetown (Sierra Leone's capital) and other major towns. The court chairmen are assisted by a panel of elders and other local functionaries. They hold office at the pleasure of the Minister of Local Government and receive some instruction from a Customary Law Officer, who is a trained lawyer. Persons who are not satisfied with the decisions of the Chiefdom Administration Courts may seek redress in the Magistrate's Court.

Although Paramount Chiefs are legally barred from presiding over court cases, many people still recognise their authority and do bring their problems to them. There is hardly any Paramount Chief that does not have a *barray* (a large, open building) in his/her compound. The *barray* is not only a meeting place for elders to discuss important matters affecting the chiefdom; it is also an informal court house where community people meet with their chief to settle, mediate, restore fractured relations and reconcile with one another (sub-chiefs perform similar roles in the villages). Alterman, Binienda, Rodella and Varzi (2002, 23–24) point out that:

> The chief often fulfils the role of a judge in the customary law setting. While customary law is most institutionalised in the form of local courts, the public tends to consider the chief's audience the initial formal forum of customary law adjudication. Even where local courts are accessible and operational, the people turn to the chief in their disputes when their informal mediations or arbitrations in auxiliary social groups fail.

Manning (2009, 19) concludes:

> Chieftaincy remains the most important system of authority across rural Sierra Leone… Chieftaincy helps to keep the peace and mobilize collective action, and

provides systems for decision-making and the resolution of disputes that are familiar and accessible to average community members.

The TRC also involved these traditional rulers in its truth-seeking and reconciliation sessions. Although the Commission did not encourage local rituals of cursing, it did, in concert with these local leaders, establish monuments or memorials, particularly at mass grave sites, and supported indigenous reconciliation ceremonies such as pouring of libations and cleansing rituals. These ceremonies have contributed somewhat to building the peace in Sierra Leone.

The Sierra Leone Government's new Justice Sector Reform Strategy now recognises the important role chiefs and other community dignitaries can play in delivering justice at the local level. To this end, the strategy calls, among other things, for the training of chiefs and other local actors on basic concepts of human rights, jurisdiction, basic record keeping and so on.[16] When implemented, this strategy will be a major step forward in integrating human rights concepts into the traditional justice system.

7.3. PHILOSOPHICAL EXPRESSIONS THAT ARE GERMANE TO THE RECONCILIATION PROCESS

Sierra Leoneans have a forgiving spirit and this has been made possible or easier through some expressions. A common saying in most Sierra Leonean communities is "*There is no bush to throw away a bad child*". This thinking, for example, made it possible for former child combatants to be accepted back into their communities, after the elders had performed purification or cleansing rites.

"*Let us simply drink the water and not look at the bottom*". In other words, if we think too much of all the wrongs that the combatants did to us, we will never forgive and reconcile with them. Put differently, 'let bygones be bygones'.

"*Fambul tik kin ben, but ii nor de broke*" (A family tree may bend, but it will never break). This powerful Krio expression is relevant when one considers that during the war it was not uncommon for close relatives to be on the opposite side of the fighting forces. For instance, a young man could be with the RUF while his brother was a member of the Civil Defence Forces. After the war, these relatives had to reconcile with one another. They could not stop being relatives because they were in opposite camps. Their blood relation was much stronger than anything else was.

16 Government of Sierra Leone, Justice Sector Reform and Investment Plan: 2008–2010, Freetown, March 2008.

8. CONCLUSION: THE FUTURE OF TRADITIONAL JUSTICE

Sierra Leone operates a dual legal system – English common law and indigenous (customary or traditional law).[17] Traditional justice has a lot of potential for reconciling and rebuilding fractured communities in Sierra Leone and also in addressing justice-related issues especially in the hinterland. For many rural residents traditional justice is the only form of justice they see. Wojkowska (2006, 12) puts it this way: "*In Sierra Leone, approximately 85 per cent of the population falls under the jurisdiction of customary law, defined under the (1991) Constitution as 'the rules of law, which, by custom, are applicable to particular communities in Sierra Leone*'".

However, as indicated above, traditional justice has certain pitfalls which must be addressed if it is to continue playing a pivotal role in the lives of the majority of Sierra Leoneans in the 21st century. For example, traditional justice must adopt more humane methods and procedures. There is a need as such, to reconsider its reliance on the supernatural and the use of harsh methods to extract the truth. The attempt by the Government of Sierra Leone to expose chiefs and other local dispensers of traditional justice to human rights concepts is one way of addressing some of these drawbacks. Dale (2008, 2) supports this strategy. She states that:

> Justice reform efforts that work primarily with formal justice systems may, in leaving out the customary systems used by the majority of citizens, miss an opportunity to improve an aspect of the sector that is most relevant to a wide swath of the population. A comprehensive approach to justice reform requires understanding of and engagement with customary systems.

In addition, a radical rethinking in the field of jurisprudence is required if traditional justice is to be given the importance it deserves in the overall justice systems of African countries. It is true that traditional justice has certain inadequacies, especially when it comes to addressing questions relating to human rights. But it is equally important to note that even the formal courts systems, be they tribunals or criminal courts, have serious shortcomings as well. Thus, a mix of best local practices and more formal Western-type institutions stands a better chance of addressing the intricate issues of justice, forgiveness, reconciliation and peace building in post-war societies in Africa, including Sierra Leone. Put differently, international tribunals and the national courts can address grave human rights violations and crimes against humanity (although it is impossible for these justice systems to treat all the dreadful crimes) while the traditional

[17] For an analysis of the courts system in Sierra Leone, see, for example, Thompson (2002).

justice system concentrates on dealing with the less severe cases especially between community residents. The two forms of justice should complement one another. Lacey (2005, A1) aptly puts it this way: "*The International Criminal Court at the Hague represents one way of holding those who commit atrocities responsible for their crimes. The raw eggs, twigs and livestock that the Acholi people of northern Uganda use in their traditional reconciliation ceremonies represent another*".

BIBLIOGRAPHY

Alie, J.A.D. (2008)
Reconciliation and traditional justice: tradition-based practices of the Kpaa Mende in Sierra Leone, in: Huyse, L. and Salter, M. (eds.) *Traditional Justice and Reconciliation after Violent Conflict: Learning from African Experiences,* Stockholm: International IDEA, 123–146.

Alterman, O., Binienda, A., Rodella, S. and Varzi, K. (2002)
The Law People See: The Status of Dispute Resolution in the Provinces of Sierra Leone in 2002, Freetown: A National Forum for Human Rights Publication.

Anderlini, S.N., Conaway C.P. and Kays L. (2007)
Transitional Justice and Reconciliation. Inclusive Society, Sustainable Peace: A Toolkit for Advocacy, The Institute for Inclusive Society, 1–15, www.huntalternatives.org.

Buckley-Zistel, S. (2005)
The Truth Heals? Gacaca Jurisdiction and the Consolidation of Peace in Rwanda, *Die Friedens Worte* 80 (1–2): 113–120.

Chirayath, L., Sage, C. and Woolcock, M. (2005)
Customary Law and Policy Reform: Engaging with the Plurality of Justice Systems (Prepared as background paper for the World Development Report 2006: Equity and Development).

Dale, P. (2008)
Access to Justice in Sierra Leone: A Review of the Literature, Washington, DC: The World Bank.

Donnelly, J. (1984)
Cultural Relativism and Universal Human Rights, *Human Rights Quarterly*, 6 (4): 400–419.

Elechi, O. (2004)
Human Rights and the African Indigenous Justice System (A Paper Presentation at the 18th International Conference of the International Society for the Reform of Criminal Law, August 8–12, 2004, Montreal, Quebec, Canada).

Engle, M.S. (1988)
Legal Pluralism, *Law and Society Review* 22 (5): 869–896.

Fofana, L. (2004)
Sierra Leone: Captured Soldiers Handed over to UNICEF, at www.oneworld.org. Cited in: Sandabo and Teferi, *Child Soldiers, Rehabilitation and Social Reintegration in Liberia,* Uppsala: Life and Peace Institute.

Gberie, L. (2005)
A Dirty War in West Africa: The RUF and the Destruction of Sierra Leone, London: Hurst and Company.
Government of Sierra Leone (2008)
Justice Sector Reform and Investment Plan: 2008–2010, Freetown.
Government of Sierra Leone (2005)
Poverty Reduction Strategy Paper: A National Programme for Food Security, Job Creation and Good Governance, 2005–2007, Freetown.
Harvey, B. (2006)
Breaking Eggs/Re-Building Societies: Traditional Justice as a Tool for Transitional Justice in Northern Uganda (Law 372, Public Policy and Dispute Resolution). Submitted to Professor Maureen Maloney, Barbara Harvey, 13 April 2006, cfcj-fcjc.org.
Hayner, P. (2007)
Negotiating Peace in Sierra Leone: Confronting the Justice Challenge, Geneva: Centre for Humanitarian Dialogue and International Centre for Transitional Justice.
Hirsch, J.L. (2001)
Sierra Leone Diamonds and the Struggle for Democracy, London: Lynne Rienner.
Hoffman, E. (2008)
Reconciliation in Sierra Leone: Local Processes Yield Global Lessons, *The Fletcher Forum of World Affairs*, 32(2): 129–141.
Human Rights Watch (2000)
Letter to Mr Modibo Sidibe, Minister of Foreign Affairs of the Republic of Mali and Chairperson of the Joint Implementation Committee (of the Lomé Peace Agreement), Africa Division (23 January 2000).
Huyse, L. and Salter, M. (eds.) (2008)
Traditional Justice and Reconciliation after Violent Conflict: Learning from African Experiences, Stockholm: International IDEA.
Huyse, L. (2009)
All Things Pass, Except the Past, Brussels: AWEPA.
IANSA, Oxfam and Saferworld (2007)
Africa's Missing Billions: International Arms Flows and the Cost of Conflict, Briefing Paper 107, www.oxfam.org.
Igreja, V. and Dias-Lambranca, B. (2008)
Restorative justice and the role of *magamba* spirits in post-civil war Gorongosa, central Mozambique, in: Huyse, L. and Salter, M. (eds.) *Traditional Justice and Reconciliation After Violent Conflict*, Stockholm: International IDEA, 61–83.
Lacey, M. (2005)
Victims of Uganda Atrocities Choose a Path of Forgiveness, *The New York Times* (18 April 2005) A.1 (cited in 'Breaking Eggs/Re-Building Societies: Traditional Justice as a Tool for Transitional Justice in Northern Uganda' (Law 372, Public Policy and Dispute Resolution). Submitted to Professor Maureen Maloney, Barbara Harvey, 13 April 2006, cfcj-fcjc.org/clearinghouse/drpapers/2006-dra/Harvey.pdf (accessed 10/10/10).

Lomé Peace Agreement (1999)
Peace Agreement between the Government of Sierra Leone and the Revolutionary United Front of Sierra Leone, 7 July 1999, available at www.sierra-leone.org/lomeaccord.html.

Manning, R.E. (2009)
The Landscape of Local Authority in Sierra Leone: How "Traditional" and "Modern" Justice Systems Interact, Justice & Development working paper series, volume 1, issue 1, Washington, DC: The World Bank.

Maru, V. (2009)
Access to Justice and Legal Empowerment: A Review of World Bank Practice, justice and development working papers, Washington, DC: The World Bank.

Maru, V. (2006)
Between Law and Society: Paralegals and the Provision of Justice Services in Sierra Leone and Worldwide, *The Yale Journal of International Law*, 31: 427–476.

Mwenda, K. (2000)
Deconstructing the concept of human rights in Africa: Africa Economic Analysis, September 9, 2000, www.afbis.com.

Naniwe-Kaburahe, A. (2008)
The institution of *bashingantahe* in Burundi, in: Huyse, L. and Salter, M. (eds.), *Traditional Justice and Reconciliation After Violent Conflict*, Stockholm: International IDEA, 149–180.

Niobe, T. (2002)
In Pursuit of Justice: a report on the Judiciary in Sierra Leone, Commonwealth Human Rights Initiative and Sierra Leone Bar Association.

Orentlicher, D. (2007)
Setting Accounts Revisited, Reconciling Global Norms, *International Journal of Transitional Justice*, 1: 10–22.

Organisation of African Unity (1981)
African Charter on Human and People's Rights, Addis Ababa.

Office of Transition Initiatives, USAID (2000)
Diamonds and armed conflict in Sierra Leone: Proposal for the implementation of a new diamond policy and operations, August 2000.

Peace Building Initiative (2009)
Traditional & Informal Justice & Peacebuilding Processes, www.peacebuildinginitiative.org (accessed 20/6/10).

Penal Reform International (PRI) 2000
Access to Justice in sub-Saharan Africa: the role of traditional and informal justice systems, London, www.gsdrc.org (accessed 20/6/10).

Perez-Katz, A.M. (2002)
The Role of Conflict Diamonds in Fueling Wars in Africa: The Case of Sierra Leone, *International Affairs Review*, XI, (1), 160–75.

Skoll Foundation (2010)
Implementing the Gender Acts in Sierra Leone, www.socialedge.org.

Smillie, I., Gberie, L. and Hazelton, R. (2000)
The Heart of the Matter: Sierra Leone, Diamonds and Human Security, Report for Partnership Canada.

Talley-Kalokohg, N. (2008)
Peace in Pieces: The Failure of Peace Agreements in Rwanda and Sierra Leone, *Swords and Ploughshares, The Official Journal of International Affairs at the School of International Service*, Spring 2008, 1–15.
Theidon, K. (2006)
The Micropolitics of Reconciliation in Postwar Peru, *Journal of Conflict Resolution* 50 (3): 433–457.
Thompson, N. (2002)
In Pursuit of Justice: a report on the Judiciary in Sierra Leone, Commonwealth Human Rights Initiative and Sierra Leone Bar Association.
Truth and Reconciliation Commission (Sierra Leone) (2004)
Witness to Truth: Report of the Sierra Leone Truth and Reconciliation Commission, Vol. 1.
United Nations Security Council (23 August 2004)
The Rule of Law and Transitional Justice in Conflict and Post-Conflict Societies, S/2004/616, www.undp.org.
United Nations (2000)
Report of the Panel of Experts Appointed Pursuant to the UN Security Council Resolution 1306 in Relation to Sierra Leone, The United Nations, December 2000.
Wojkowska, E. (2006)
Doing justice: how informal justice systems can contribute, accessible at www.undp.org/oslocentre/docs07/DoingJusticeEwaWojkowska130307.pdf.

CHAPTER VI

REINVENTING AND VALIDATING THE COSMOLOGY AND ONTOLOGY OF RESTORATIVE JUSTICE: HERMENEUTICS OF THE TRADITIONAL ACHOLI JUSTICE SYSTEM IN NORTHERN UGANDA

Daniel KOMAKECH

1. RATIONALE OF THE STUDY: CONTEXTUALIZING THE ASSUMPTIONS AND TRAITS OF JUSTICE IN TRANSITIONAL JUSTICE

1.1. INTRODUCTION

This chapter interrogates the dominant authority of the modernist retributive justice epistemology that has reified itself as a privileged mode of knowing and practice on justice. The purpose is to establish an open ended epistemology of a justice system that is not limited to retributive justice but hermeneutically takes cognizance of the presence of restorative justice as well.

At this rate, it is hoped that the critical exploration into the misconstrued assumption on what tradition in traditional justice is, and into the general emphasis on modernist retributive justice, will yield a productive unpacking of this trend and pave the way for a more enlightened perspective on this framework of thinking.

The aim of this chapter is to emancipate the traditional justice system from an assault by modernist justice discourse. The way in which Acholi[1] conceptualise their traditional justice will be used to adumbrate the argument. The objective is

[1] The Acholi are an ethnic group found in the northern part of Uganda.

to reconstruct the narrative around traditional justice systems and, specifically, restorative justice among the Acholi.

1.2. THE THESIS AND OUTLINE OF THE CHAPTER

The first thesis of this study is that an authentic vision of justice in a transitional society needs to understand the local resource capacity. Secondly, traditional justice should not be cast in terms of polar opposites, namely a preferred as opposed to an inferior narrative, but rather as a cooperative dialogue that seeks understanding. Thirdly, contextualizing the debate on the Acholi justice system will provide us with an appreciation of like cases elsewhere, even though we do not want to commit the mistake of thinking that its thought is necessarily universal to all African communities.

The first section of this chapter (point 2) looks into the debate on tradition and how it has been skewed by the privileging of the modernist epistemology of justice, especially in favour of a retributive system. The section also tries, through hermeneutics, to problematize this mode of knowing and privileging one type of justice.

The following section (point 3) typifies the Acholi system of justice to reconstruct the attitude towards restorative justice. The chapter thus journeys into the cosmology and ontology of the Acholi with Placide Tempels' *Bantu Philosophy* as the framework.

We then look into the Acholi concepts of human rights and duties (point 4) to end with an invitation to the International Criminal Court (ICC) to begin to engage in understanding the Acholi cosmovision if its operation is truly to benefit the people of Northern Uganda (point 5).

1.3. CENTRAL ARGUMENT

The chapter does not argue for a polar discourse that privileges traditional justice over modernist justice, but for an all-inclusive appreciation. The complementary role of traditional justice in general and restorative justice in particular should not only be recognized, but also accepted as an equal component in transitional justice policies. To be in a position to understand the emphasis of the traditional justice system[2] on restorative justice, one needs to understand that an offence is

2 The term 'traditional justice system' is used here to denote a comprehensive approach that spans from interpretation, identification, practices and the philosophy of traditional justice.

not to be seen or understood as a crime but, rather, as a wrong or sin that needs a moral and religious approach. The traditional system does not condone or encourage impunity, nor does it seek to punish.

It proactively engages with the issue, with a view to taking collective responsibility for the wrong committed and to restoring broken relationships through a strong moral sense of shame and remorse, as opposed to the approach taken by a system of courts and police. It therefore complements the school of thought that argues that peace building initiatives, and specifically justice systems, must have their roots in local societies and must depend on indigenous knowledge for success and sustainability. Consequently, the chapter argues that scholars in this field must engage in unscripted conversations rather than assuming peace and justice as a norm, thereby constructing solutions from without (Cubit 2010, 32).

This argument is not confined to a particular region nor is it confined to the (all too often) polarized debate between the West and Africa. It nonetheless challenges the modernist normative doctrinaire of justice by trying to introduce more emancipative discourses about justice and a nuanced interpretation derived from lived experiences. It holds that a third party intervention is unfortunate, because it supersedes a people's own discourses and practices of justice (ibid.).

1.4. METHODOLOGY

This is an inductive and analytic study seeking to establish the role of traditional justice in transitional justice based on a case study of the Acholi system. The study could not use a deductive method because that would mean prejudging the issue which, in turn, would fail to determine whether the justice discourse has been part of the problem.

The study is motivated by an emancipating, open-ended epistemology, that moves beyond a logocentric modernism into clarification of existence and critical hermeneutics. The study largely depends on secondary data and a few primary data of qualitative nature. It was felt that the matter under discussion was less familiar at an empirical plane and fieldwork would achieve very little. The theoretical framework of this chapter is the cosmology and ontology of the justice system in Acholi, using Placide Tempels' Bantu ontology to inform the discussion. Consequently, the observations and conclusions are unique to Acholi people, although they may have relevance to other situations.

To be able to present this position and to corroborate data, the paper was aided by a focus group discussion with specially selected respondents from Acholi who are not only advanced in age (over the age of fifty) but also the custodians of

Acholi tradition and culture. In addition interviews were carried out at individual level with Acholi sages, particularly those versed in the practice of anthropology, African philosophy and religion. The data from the respondents were organized around no particular guiding questions but were derived from a simple conversation that allowed unrestricted open-ended thought. A total of nine individual respondents were engaged, three of whom were females.

2. LIVE AND LET LIVE: A CRITIQUE OF DOMINANT MODERNIST JUSTICE IN TRANSITIONAL JUSTICE DISCOURSE

2.1. INTRODUCTION

The contestation apparent between the traditional justice system, which is largely restorative, and the modernist system, which is retributive, must not be viewed as an historical contest for dominance, but as an outcome of popularizing and privileging the modernist epistemology as a framework in conceptualizing and theorizing about justice in general and retributive justice in particular.

This section tries to pick up this discourse and takes the debate beyond an epistemological competition to a far richer experience that connects human beings in their diversity, namely to an open-ended epistemology that interprets justice, its application and its meaning. Consequently, the section is established on certain themes: first, the often misconstrued notion of tradition; second, the modernist epistemology and how it has informed the conception of justice; third, problematizing and challenging the dominant notion of the modernist epistemology in the context of ICC in northern Uganda.

2.2. THE MODERNIST CRITIQUE OF TRADITION

The notion of 'tradition' – which flies in the face of the modernist epistemology – was trivialized by the archetypical colonial anthropology of Levy-Bruhl (1966) and Levi-Strauss (1962) who demonized native practices and reinforced this with an epistemology that has been spiritedly defended.

In his work, *How Natives Think*, Levy-Bruhl (1966) categorizes African tradition as pre-logical, mystical and irrational. In other words, the modern mind is regulated by reason with organized conceptual mapping while the primitive mind is not. This discourse was more than a description; it fulfilled several functions in the context of the modernist and colonial superiority complex. In other words, meaning was used to maintain the image of a civilized colonial master and primitive Africa, and thereby to justify colonialism as a mode of social life.

This construction of so called 'tradition' and 'natives' in Levy-Bruhl's work (1966, 54) found precedents in Hegel (1966, 91–100), Kant and many others. In *The Philosophy of History*, for instance, Hegel had used modernist epistemology, and thus saw Africa as still locked in tradition, a land of childhood, outside self-conscious history, enveloped in the dark mantle of night. Africa had no history of its own to add to world history, no movement for development, nothing was to be found in harmony with the rest of humanity.

For his part, Kant's theory of *Sensus Communis* established the notion of individual aesthetic judgment, namely the individual hardly affords a judgment unless it is shared by a community of others. But under his qualifying term 'primitive isolates', certain societies, which were considered to be steeped deep in tradition, were exempt from these moral dialectics. In Africa, the narrative on tradition has met equal ridicule among its own academics. Senghor (1966, 17), in his *Negritude*, was trapped in this polar discourse and admitted that the 'negro is a man of nature', sensuous and responsive to the rhythms of his surroundings; although he did not lack reason, he displayed a different form of reason. Hountondji (1996, 60) did not mince his words, and simply said that tradition was a form of ethnography with traits as 'timeless codes of behaviour', or 'the African world view', and the 'myth of primitive unanimity'.

Appiah (1992, 26) lamented the so-called global African mentality (or world view) as simply nostalgic, romantic and lacking seriousness. He remarked that Africans have too many (different) problems to be distracted by a *bogus* basis for solidarity. In all these cases, tradition was considered to be outdated in the new economic, social and political conditions of an emerging so called 'intellectual' or 'fully industrialized modern world'. Instead of privatizing the mind, it was argued that tradition took us into collectivity and 'thinking at large'. Tradition therefore did not have the capacity for critical distance in thought and feeling.

These assumptions became key traits in the critique of tradition and subsequently of traditional justice. Let us now examine the modernist epistemology and its influence on tradition and traditional justice.

2.3. THE MODERNIST EPISTEMOLOGY AND RETRIBUTIVE JUSTICE

Descartes (1937), as the 'founder' of modern epistemology, established a framework within which to understand modernity and knowledge in general. Descartes proceeded to construct a system of knowledge by establishing criteria of truth that discarded perception as unreliable and instead admitted only deduction. In this 'Cartesian Doubt', Descartes sought for knowledge that would be incapable of being destroyed. He sought to construct an unshakable ground from which all other knowledge could be based.

This Cartesian method – *cogito ergo sum (I think, therefore I am)* – emphasizes that, what I thought I had seen with my eyes, I actually grasped solely with the faculty of judgment which is my mind (Descartes 1937). Hence, Descartes' characteristic of modernity was a quest for certainty, a clear delineation between subject and object, and a view of the world that was always forward-moving towards a unified system of knowledge.

With this foundation, the 19th century theory of science emphasized 'Cartesian Doubt'. To this end, scientists popularized the notion of self-correction that would gradually lead to truth. Laudan (1981) calls this the 'Self-Corrective Thesis'. Peirce (1974, 775) added that systematic, self-correcting scientific inquiry would lead to truth. In this case, modernist epistemology postulated that a subject or object of inquiry is separate from the world surrounding it (Pattie 1991, 61). In other words, the epistemology took, as the paradigm of knowledge, a clear, distinct, discursive and certain prepositional knowledge that is known to any one capable of average cognitive reasoning. For example; it should be clear that 1+1= 2, grass is green and metal expands once heated, no matter the time and space.

To Toulmin, modernity and modernist epistemology is unquestionably a 'good thing'. He hoped that, for the sake of the rest of humanity, the whole world would soon become 'as modern as us' (Toulmin 1992, 13).

The foundation of modernity therefore has been built on this epistemology, where reality is conceived within mechanical/social laws that are themselves universal. This knowledge paradigm builds a theoretical assumption that there must be one all-embracing, universal science concerning the nature of things, thereby constructing a vast system of indubitable and self-evident truths. This belief in an absolute natural order of society produces a perfectionist ideology and a pre-ordained harmony to which men are irresistibly driven for the pursuit of and attainment of the so-called collective purpose. Of necessity, the task is to destroy the expression of differences and to create an enduring universal view.

Consequently, the construction of a system of self-evident truths justified the creation of a 'technocracy' in the area of governance, namely, a system in which technically trained experts rule by virtue of their specialized knowledge and position in the dominant political and economic institutions, (Fischer 1990, 33; Hoffman 2001, 49).

What does this imply for the concept of 'justice'? Modernist epistemology considers justice as a matter of applying laws and rules. It created a so-called scientific definition of offences, from a legal standpoint, as law breaking, and not harm. Justice establishes whether the offender is outside the law, and therefore guilty and a 'criminal' – a word that is inherently negative, judgmental and non-restorative (Gorringe 1996, 266). In the phrase, *"Let the punishment fit the crime"*, Cavadino and Dignan (1997, 39) give us the heartbeat of the modernist notion of the proportionality of the penalty for a misdeed to the severity of the offence. While Kant, in *The Metaphysical Elements of Justice*, reinforces this conception, Martien adds that a judicial punishment can never be used merely as a means to promote some other good; instead, it must be imposed on the offender only on the ground that he has committed a crime (Martien 2005, 174). The offender will be subject to fixed penalties, without reference to the victim or restoring the relationship between the victim and offender. In other words, once guilt has been scientifically proven by lawful evidence, punishment has to be levied; a kind of *lex talionis* (law of retaliation) will be applied, as stated by Honderich (1969).

Accordingly, retributive justice favours the modernist epistemology, which is impersonal and centred on impersonal principles, transcending custom and history. In the same vein, its law assumes a central authority and 'legitimate' initiation of action by a 'neutral' court that becomes the centralized dispenser of justice. In general, retributive justice goes beyond morality and virtue and is conditioned by external legal mechanisms and control. It is unconcerned with wrong and remorse, concentrating instead on the crime and proof of guilt by courts of law. More importantly, it emphasizes the individual burden of guilt and a statist notion of crime.

This implies that the definition of crime has shifted from the victim to the state. The state somehow becomes a victim, and consequently pursues the case. Thus, the primary victim becomes suddenly a spectator in his or her own case, attending the state like an altar boy, who furnishes the priest with the incense for the Sunday ritual.

The engagement between the offender and the victim is not only minimized but is also discouraged through the formal court procedures. Hence, there is no dialogue; there is no inner search on the part of the offender, and no forgiveness on the part of the victim. This is partly because the victim is not in charge, and partly because there is no process of reconciliation.

This approach is entrenched and institutionalized in the International Covenant on Civil and Political Rights. Such institutionalization makes us think that it is a given, and in conformity with the values espoused by the global community.

However, the obsession with 'international standards' has a relentless ignorance and combative attitude towards alternative justice. In order to re-orient this attitude, so as to become more open-minded and to enter a cooperative dialogue, the subsequent section uses as an example the International Criminal Court's (ICC) operation in the northern part of Uganda, in particular among the Acholi who have been in the middle of a twenty-year civil war between the Lord's Resistance Army (LRA) and the government of Uganda.

2.4. THE ICC AND RETRIBUTIVE JUSTICE IN THE NORTHERN UGANDA ARMED CONFLICT

It was 29th July 2004 when, upon satisfactory evidence, the ICC Prosecutor qualified the situation of the crimes in northern Uganda as having reached the gravity threshold. In view of Uganda's referral to the ICC in December 2003[3] this meant that the crime level meted by the Lord's Resistance Army (LRA) was no longer a domestic issue but had reached an international plane and was likely to destabilize international peace. Supporting the operation of the ICC, a report entitled *Forgotten Voices*, based on a popular survey by the non-governmental organisation International Center for Transitional Justice and the Human Rights Centre of the University of California, Berkeley, gave a strong opinion in favour of retributive justice for crimes committed in Northern Uganda (Batard 2005, 21).

On 8th July 2005, an arrest warrant was issued by the Pre-trial chamber of the ICC for the five senior leaders of the Lord's Resistance Army (LRA) accused of crimes against humanity and war crimes.[4] The idea was that the indicted top LRA commanders would be brought to book for their crimes.

The ICC mandate provides for it to play the role of a supra-national jurisdiction for what is qualified as the 'most serious crimes'. The ICC was expected 'to put an end to impunity for the perpetrators of these crimes and thus to contribute to the prevention of such crimes'.[5] However, in order to contextualize this mandate

3 Coalition for the International Criminal Court, www.iccnow.org/?mod=northernuganda.
4 Www.icc.joselinevolquart2.
5 The Rome Statute of the International Criminal Court, http// www.icc-cpi.int.

and to establish the controversy, we need to situate the ICC operation in northern Uganda within the range of its international mandate.

Unlike the International Criminal Tribunal for Rwanda and the International Criminal Tribunal for Former Yugoslavia, the ICC recognizes national courts as retaining the primary criminal jurisdiction. Article 17 of the Rome Statute establishing the ICC provides that a case will be inadmissible before the ICC when it is being investigated or prosecuted by a state which has jurisdiction, unless the state is unwilling or genuinely unable to carry out the investigation or prosecution. At the same time, the prosecutor has a countervailing discretion under Article 53(2)(c) to consider that there is no sufficient basis for prosecution because it is not 'in the interests of justice', taking into account all the circumstances, including 'the interests of victims'.[6] Bartlet (2009, 46) defines these interests as providing 'a countervailing consideration where positive requirements of admissibility and jurisdiction are established'.

The notions of admissibility and consideration for the victims have helped the victims of northern Uganda to emphasize the local alternative justice system and challenge the ICC's operation. But why did they want to challenge the ICC?

The ICC ignored the historical context of the conflict as perceived by the people themselves, as well as the people's view on how best to end it. On the basis of interviews with NGOs and international bodies in northern Uganda, Volquartz (2005) argues that the ICC was in danger of perpetuating the war and pushing the LRA back into the bush, thereby provoking a continuation of the atrocities. Olyet[7] remarked that the only way to solve the problem was through forgiveness and reconciliation. The Anglican Bishop, Macleod Baker Ochola, reiterated this in his lament that '*this kind of approach is going to destroy all efforts for peace. People want this war to stop*' (Allen 2006, 85). The Acholi narrative of the conflict indicated that the armed conflict in the area was more complex, and should not be simplified into arrests and prosecutions. Instead, the conflict should be handled more openly in order to reconcile parties. The ICC method became not only inapplicable but also provocative. More importantly, the Northern Uganda conflict was specific, as perpetrators were in most cases also victims, and nobody knew with certainty what actually caused the conflict or whether it was right to attribute all the blame to one party.

The confrontation with the ICC is not a question of competition for dominance, but is rather about the notion and application of justice. Whereas the ICC looked

6 International Criminal Court, Interest of Justice, September 2007, www.iccnow.org/?mod=interestofjustice.

7 Vice Chairman of the Concerned Parents Association, a Ugandan NGO working on the reintegration of child ex-combatants.

at justice from a modernist epistemology, i.e. a legalistic, punitive dimension, the Acholi traditional system prefers the notion of 'wrong' to 'crime' and 'restoration' to 'retribution'. In their understanding of justice, the Acholi thought the ICC was expected to appreciate their perspective, and to be able to use – or at least integrate – it with the ICC perspective. The failure to meet this expectation came to be seen as increasingly antithetic to traditional values. It is thus clear that there was a gap between the ICC and the local population. The latter felt strongly that they were not consulted and that no time was allotted for their stories and experiences of the conflict. This meant that the ICC pursued a flawed and compromised system of justice that was at odds with local values and traditional practices. The so-called ICC 'justice' was therefore foreign and distant. Consequently, the credibility of the ICC was irrevocably lost.

The question that needs to be answered is what the very notion of justice is. The fact that this matter became hotly contested among the Acholi suggests that the ICC's idea of justice was not only a new phenomenon but also had little impact on the local population. The following section examines the traditional system of the Acholi, following their cosmology and ontology.

3. THE RESURGENCE OF THE TRADITIONAL JUSTICE SYSTEM IN NORTHERN UGANDA

3.1. THE NOTION OF TRADITION IN THE ACHOLI COMMUNITY

Although the rise of modernity and its epistemology constituted a severe assault on tradition, the notion of tradition did not simply disappear (Cianci and Eliot 2007, 5). To the contrary, tradition has been revived by popular will and fear of cultural decay (ibid.).

From the Latin word *'traditio'* – which actually has nothing to do with pre-logical or infancy or remoteness as Levy-Bruhl and Levi-Strauss would have us think – tradition simply means handing down or the delivery of a doctrine, a living reality and a link between the past and the future. On the basis of this, the Acholi emphasize their traditional justice as a process that has and should be handed down in order to link the past with the future.

Various surveys have been conducted to suggest that support for traditional justice is not clear and uniform in the larger Acholi community. Three subgroups can be distinguished among today's Acholi population: those who were in LRA captivity, those who were in Internally Displaced Persons' Camps (IDPs) and those who were scattered outside their birth place. Over the more than twenty years of civil war, Acholi cosmology has been variously understood and applied. This phenomenon makes it difficult to present a uniform understanding of the Acholi value systems, particularly with regard to justice and reconciliation. In a broad sense, they have readjusted to external realities, as we will see below. Moreover, since the advent of Christianity, some Acholi have an uneasy feeling that certain rituals, are 'satanic'. As a result, there has been a shift away from the mandatory performance of traditional rituals to respect for individual choices.

That means that we cannot claim a complete and conclusive understanding of the Acholi value system. Even so, this paper attempts to establish the values, particularly concerning justice and reconciliation, in an original form. It does not delve into the question whether this 'original' form is correct or not, because it is very difficult to establish an uncontested answer. Let us look into this matter in detail, in order to contextualize the inquiry and proceed to the Acholi system of restorative justice.

3.2. RECONSTRUCTING AND VALIDATING TRADITION: A HERMENEUTICS[8]

According to Walsh and Zema (1985, 165–166), hermeneutics as a concept comes from the Greek word *hermeneuein,* which means, to translate or interpret.[9] Currently, this concept has become a methodology of investigation and interpretation of human experiences. Bernstein (1978, 87) argued that, as a method, hermeneutics has no set of standards for proving the superiority of one paradigm over another and that knowledge or knowing cannot be detached from actual historical practices (Bernstein 1983, 67). Hence our theorizing and conceptualization cannot appeal to a permanent, temporal standard of rationality but must adopt a deep gaze at the historicity and situatedness of understanding and meaning.

Hermeneutics requires a decentred understanding of the social and natural world and an ability to see that world not as intrinsic but as 'out there'. One must be willing to subordinate one's personal desire to exploration of the world (Seidman and Wagner 1992, 349). This means that the correspondence between framework, understanding and reality must be conceived as a criterion for any

8 This discussion is largely summarised and picks out only a fraction of the whole corpus on hermeneutics since the purpose is not a sustained argument but to show to the reader the framework and the methodological orientation of this work.

9 This meaning grows from the Greek myth of a god called Hermes (or in Egyptian tradition the full name is Hermes Trismegistus) whose task was to carry message(s) between gods and between gods and man (Walsh and Zema 1985).

validity claim. Meaning, and thus knowledge, is therefore an interpretation that is always situated within a living tradition and our inescapable historicity, which is a particular 'horizon' of understanding based on culture and personal presuppositions.

So, hermeneutics is not only an epistemology (or simply a method to guide interpretation) but is also, and more importantly, a social ontology that discusses personhood, selfhood, cognition and consciousness as embedded in a social context or tradition. This means that our actions are, on many occasions, guided by interpretation. We must therefore be willing to take into account our own 'vision of things'. Accordingly, hermeneutics takes the full measure of our historical and cultural embeddedness, together with the inexorable limitations of human understanding.

When turning specifically to justice, the argument is that we cannot shape a human rights discourse by privileging a particular discursive rationality or social discourse. Rather, we should adopt an open-ended discourse on justice that allows for a dialogue, understanding and subsequent appreciation of differences and uniqueness.

3.3. ACHOLI COSMOLOGY AND ONTOLOGY: TEMPELS' FRAMEWORK

Within the context of Levy-Bruhl's (1966) and Levi-Strauss's work (1962), Tempels undertook missionary work in Congo. He introduced existentialism and hermeneutics, which increasingly questioned the rationalism, objectivism and scientism that had previously been taken for granted. Hence, Tempels' work – *Bantu Philosophy* (1959) – reconstructed the world around the natives' own vision, whatever it happened to be.

In his conception of ontology, Tempels gives us a dual meaning. Unlike the Western scholastic philosophy that sees ontology as, 'being as such', 'the reality that is', 'anything that exists', 'what is', the Bantu (African) understands being as that which has force. Being is force and force is being (Tempels 1959, 31).

Created beings in Africa are not complete in themselves, but are in a bond with one another, implying an intimate ontological relationship, whereby the one interacts with the other (ibid.). Here lies a unique principle: recognition of the intimate nature of things. At the same time, beings or forces are differentiated into species according to their vital power or their inherent vital rank (ibid.).

The notion of the vital power then brings in the idea of increasing the forces of the other or diminishing them (diminution of life or of a being). So, beings relate among themselves in accordance with their vital force, namely grouped in respect of their nature, of their intensity of life, by class, and of the precedence according to primogeniture (ibid.). The universe of beings or forces is therefore organically constructed in what can then be called an ontological hierarchy (ibid.).

In the ontological hierarchy, God is ranked highest because he is absolutely responsible for the establishment and enforcement of the vital force of other beings. He is the supreme, complete, perfect force, in and of himself. He has his existential cause within himself (ibid.). Second to him are the first fathers of men to whom he first communicated his vital force; third, the living dead who form a chain and exercise their vitalising influence on the living; next, the elders who reinforce the life of their people; after elders come the other human beings (men, women and children); and other lesser beings (animals, plants and inanimate beings).

Masolo's (1994, 49) notion of 'being as force' and 'force as being', tells us that matter and force merge into a unity in which force subordinates matter under its dynamism. This vital force is the invisible reality of everything that exists, but is supreme in a human being. It is therefore integrated into all aspects of human life, and the most fundamental base of reality.

Kagame also acknowledges this reality when he remarks that it reveals vitalistic concepts that have semi-consciousness at the basis of all beings' activity and that the whole ontological universe is filled with a hierarchy of vital forces (Diop 1981, 323). Various other African societies including Mali, Yoruba and the Asante acknowledge this. Mbiti also accepts this idea, that African people know that the universe has a power, a force in addition to the items in the ontological categories (Gyekye 1995, 73).

3.4. COSMOLOGY AND ONTOLOGY AMONG THE ACHOLI OF UGANDA[10]

In Acholi, ontology is not conceived in the transcendental aspect by separating it from its attribute, 'force'. Force, as rightly observed by Tempels, is a necessary element in being, and the concept 'force' is inseparable from the definition of being. Secondly, beings are bound together and preserve a bond with one

10 The subsequent verbatim in this section are the result of the focus group discussions and individual interviews.

another, an intimate ontological relationship. Thus, the Western concept of a being as 'being as such', namely beings entirely independent of one another, is foreign to Acholi thought.

It should be noted that, much as the Acholi look at beings as tightly knit one to another and thus in a cob-web of relationships, they are as well differentiated into species according to their importance, what Tempels calls, 'vital power'. Reflecting Tempels' ontological hierarchy the Acholi distinguish *Rubanga* (God), who is above all; below him we have *Kwaro* (the first fathers of the Acholi); *Jo muto* (the living dead); *Rwot* (Chief); *Ludito* (elders); *Coo* (men); *Mon* (women); *Lutino* (children) and the least forces like *Lee* (animals), *Yadi* (plants) and *Jammi ma pe kwo* (inanimate beings). It is important therefore, at this stage, to have a closer look at this ontological hierarchy and what each group signifies.

Above all other beings, is *Rubanga* (God), who has force in himself and increases force of other beings. The importance accorded to Him in Acholi becomes clear in names given to Him: *Lacwec* (Creator), *Rubanga Latwee (*Almighty God), *Langee jammi duc (*All-knowing), *Rwot pinaka naka* (Lord for all time and space). What we see here is *Rubanga* as the highest being or force. This is the Absolute Reality, the origin of all that was, is and will be; the Absolute ground, the Sole and the Explanation of the universe.

Next in the hierarchy are *Kwaro* (ancestors); the founders of the different clans, to whom God first communicated his vital force. They constitute the most important chain binding human beings (who are still living) to God, and so they occupy an exalted position in Acholi thought. In solving any social misunderstanding, an Acholi would say *kwaro wa pe mito ni wabed ki adega dega ikinwa* (Our ancestors do not want us to nurse hatred among ourselves). In case of a disaster, such as the infertility of women, famine, drought and war, Acholi people would fall back to the *kal abila* (ancestoral shrine) for revelation and insights of how best to tackle the problem. In a traditional marriage ceremony, familiarization and friendship making, you hear words like; *kwaro ni nga* (who is your ancestor)? Or *I a ki I kwaro mene (*from which ancestor do you descend)? A family or clan that belonged (in terms of genealogy) to one of the most important ancestors was given high social status and privileges.

The *Rwot* (chief) comes immediately after the ancestors because he is the overall administrator of the people, and carries out the policies that God, ancestors and the people command and want respectively. His significance is evident in, for example, the following saying: *Cam wa ki ipoto oto ducu pien rwot cwinye pe yom* (Our crops have all died because the chief is not happy).

The level of *Ludito* (elders) comes immediately after the chiefs. Its significance can be derived from sayings, such as: *Peko eni, wan lotino per watwero, ulwong ludongo gang* (This problem is beyond our capacity as youths, invite the elders); *Ladit ka pe, ci gang otur* (Without an elder, a home is dead/crumbled).

After the elders are the *Coo* (men) who are responsible for security and for the homesteads. *Gang man oto ba*, as women will lament, *coo pe*! (This home is dead, men are not there!) *Mwony opoto! Coo tye kwene?* (War has broken out, where are the men?) *Wilobo olanya*, as a widow cries for her dead husband, *anga co na kodi, tongo bota yen, pura poto*! (What a cruel world, who will sow for me the seeds in the garden, cut down trees/logs, dig the garden!)

Mon (Women) come slightly after the men, as the following sayings show: *Mego en acel* (a proverb meaning, a mother is available and always beside the child, no matter the situation), *Labongo mon, gang pe cung matir* (Without women, a home cannot stand).

Lutino (children) come last in the chain of human relationships, but are very important: *Nywal ber* (Giving birth is very important); *Lutino aye deyo* (Children are blessing); *Anga ber kato cene ni*? (Who is this, who is more important than money?).

Lee (Animals), *Yadi* (Plants), *Jammi ma pe kwo* (inanimate beings). This level of the other animate and inanimate beings form the last level in the chain of beings, with the following signification: *Lee gwoko paco* (Animals are very useful in a home); *Labongo yadi, cam pe* (Without plants, there is no food) *Jammi ma pe kwo ducu pi gi tek. Wamato pii, wayubu agulu dek ki lobo bene* (All inanimate beings are very important. We drink water and we make our cooking pots using clay).

From the above, we gain some access to the Acholi cosmology and its hierarchical character. The Supreme Being – *Rubanga* – is at the apex and our phenomenal *wilobo* (the world) is at the bottom. Meanings, therefore, within this broad comprehensive ontological pluralism, are categorical distinctions. All these entities are not on the same level but depend on their vital power.

3.5. THE ONTOLOGICAL HIERARCHY – RECONCILIATION AND RESTORATION IN ACHOLI

The ontological structuring in Acholi is thus very clear, and, in consequence, each and every being (especially humans) knows his or her specialized tasks and ought to perform them. Failure to live up to this expectation results in a rebuke, punishment or the wrath of God falling on oneself, family, clan and even the society. This is the reason why we gather near the fireplace: to teach the young and for elders to consider their or each other's strengths, weaknesses, opportunities and threats. Shrines are also constantly visited in order to hear, be advised and sustain good relationships with the living dead and especially with *Rubanga*.

Thus, actions that contribute to the stability and dynamics of this order are judged morally good, while those that create instability are seen as morally bad. Let us note here that, while the Acholi cosmology celebrates stability through the preservation of a network of social ties, the cosmology is not rigid and reactionary. The beings in this hierarchy interact and influence each other, either negatively or otherwise. Either way, this influence makes the ontological hierarchy dynamic and refurbishing.

It is also important to remind ourselves that human beings, as part of the hierarchy, come with their different experiences. Such a situation impacts dynamically on the cosmology, suggesting that it is a living organism, i.e. living as an experience, living as a collection of historical beings, but at the same time, re-living and perpetuating its identity.

It is this implicit philosophical core, namely, the ontological hierarchy of beings, that explains restorative justice among the Acholi people. The Acholi emphasis on restorative justice is meant to create a far reaching social contact that restores calm and brings the victim in a dialogue and conversation with the offender to make each regain his vital force and position in the ontological hierarchy.

In the interest of stability and restoring social peace with *Rubanga*, both victim and offender are given voice space to narrate their stories. By ensuring equal participation, the parties are helped to find meaningful co-authorship of the narratives. The purpose is to denounce an evil act without labelling anybody a criminal.

Instead, an interpretation of an offence as a *wrong* is within the frame of the cosmology and ontology. The offence is not simply committed against an individual but against the entire community of beings in the hierarchy, including the victim. As a result restoration and balance is needed in the ontological hierarchy. Thus, conflict is not between individuals, but is a phenomenon that engulfs the entire group. That means that responsibility for responding to a wrong is returned to the community. In this case, a wrong takes a social rather than an individual dimension, with the sole aim of holistic healing and reconnection in the ontological hierarchy.

The process starts with a voluntary admission of wrong doing, enforceable by the religious signification that even when you conceal, it shall be known through the intervention of God as the supreme being. This is an acceptance of responsibility and an indication of repentance and remorse before the community (Braithwaite 1989). This act of acknowledgement is meant to fast-track the society to recovery and forgiveness through the remaking of relationships and the restoration of the ontological balance (Latigo 2008, 107).

In a typical sense, therefore, Acholi view conflict and war, on the one hand, and aspirations for peace, on the other, in a comprehensive and holistic way. It follows that the African notion of peace is not limited to peace-keeping and peace-making but is rather peace-building through conflict prevention and transformation.

Consequently, conflict, violence and war are understood from breakage of the ontology, while peace means restoration of the hierarchy to normalcy. From this, such acts are no longer crimes but wrongs or sins, because one will have shattered the social, cultural and not simply the legal bond of the community. More importantly, they have offended God. Peace in Acholi, therefore, is a reconnection, what they call *Roco wat* (reconciliation), a healing process viewed as such, and not as retribution.

Far from being dislocated in a past that no longer exists, these practices have always been situated ontologically. According to Finnstrom these rich values are continually summoned to address problems – what he calls, 'present concerns' (2003, 299).

4. ACHOLI TRADITIONAL JUSTICE AND HUMAN RIGHTS[11]

4.1. ACHOLI UNDERSTANDING OF HUMAN RIGHTS

The Acholi recognise human dignity and rights, which can be seen in their word *dano* (a human person), implying dignity and *twero* (rights). The Universal Declaration of Human Rights proclaims the rights of mankind referring to the '*... recognition of the inherent dignity ... of all members of the human family*'.[12] However, this should not lead us to believe that all world communities understand human dignity in the same way. For the modernist, 'dignity' is

11 This part limits itself to the discursive frame of the Acholi justice and human rights without a concrete manifestation in the applications.

12 The Universal Declaration of Human Rights, 1948, preamble.

understood from the Kantian perspective, namely, from the ethics of the 'categorical imperative', where Kant declared that we ought never to treat man as a means but always as an end in himself.

This notion of dignity, however, places individuals within the frame of autonomous beings and isolates them from the community. Contrary to this, with the Acholi, human dignity ought to be respected within one's proper relationship with the society, both at the horizontal and vertical level. This is what the Acholi say: *Dano ka cel acel nongo woro ki ingo ma en otimo maber pi lwak* (Each individual gets respect and worth from one's good deeds towards the society).

Here, dignity is not private and individual, but public and collective. The human earns dignity if he or she has learned from and obeys the community. A non-social and atomised individual ought not to have dignity, but should be likened to an *opego* (pig) or a *latal* (sorcerer).

This in no way reduces the person to a thing, an object to use and to be used. Instead, the individual is inherently and intrinsically endowed with abilities by God through the first fathers and the living dead. Each individual is therefore an active being who contributes to and sustains society.

The human person is at the centre of all Acholi activity and thought, and, because of this, anything that tends to lower or misrepresent the human, is regarded as evil (*cilo*) or an act of evil (*tim cilo*), while that which furthers the wellbeing is good (*ber*) and correct (*atir dog myero*). Because of this fact acts such as murder, sorcery, jealousy, bewitching a young lady not to get pregnant and give birth, curse, disrespect and greed, are dangerous and evil, while child fertility, blessing, good health and good neighbourhood are admired and good.

Each person then must be respected, because by nature he or she is a contributor to the good life of the social whole. Without individuals, there is no such a thing as society. This means, therefore, that each person has reciprocal moral worth that should be respected by the others in order for the person to attain meaning in his or her existence, and further meaningful contribution to the social whole, hence human rights.

4.1.1. The Acholi concept of rights being natural and communal

God is the 'strong one' (*ladit*): he who possesses force in himself, and the source of the force of every creature. He is an absolute reality, the sum total of all, an infinite natural. If God created other beings, then other beings share God's characteristics, namely being eternal (in terms of possessing souls – especially human beings) and having rights that need to be respected and observed.

In view of this, we see a kind of basic declaration of equality and naturalness in the sense that all created beings have vital force, which force emanates from God and, as such, there is a constant relationship and reciprocal influence between the vital forces. One's personhood is also in one's relationship with the beings or forces in the hierarchy: family, relatives, and so forth. Tempels (1959, 36) echoes this inbuilt reality. The world is a communion and not a collection of individuals, which clearly indicates that rights are ultimately not an individual phenomenon, but a communal affair. We talk then of a living, active and dynamic totality of life, of human origins and destiny, and of ethical and social harmony.

The particular human being therefore cannot defend his or her rights by demanding or exacting them independently of the whole. Rights have never been private, and therefore never within the jurisdiction of an individual. They are a community affair, rooted in the very fact that one is born into a natural society and as a social being.

4.1.2. Duty and responsibility in human rights

One's exercise of a right should never diminish one's vital force and that of others. For example, if one has the right to express oneself, this does not mean that one may diminish another's vital force through sorcery or curses, or through insulting a spouse. To do so would endanger oneself and perpetrate a disgrace to society, the clan, etc. Someone like Cain who, after murdering his brother Abel, said that he was not his brother's keeper, will protest openly or tacitly that they were not responsible to society, but only to themselves. The Acholi will warn us, however, that we either remain society's keepers – and thereby enjoy our rights – or perish with it altogether. The Acholi acknowledge rights as being natural but not absolute. Since beings are tied together in a web of relationships in the ontological hierarchy, and the community outlives the individual, it follows that communal rights ought to come first, and individual rights second. This point then brings us to the question of duty, namely, one ought also to perform a duty in order to enjoy rights. So, a human being has the right to be respected only in so far as one performs duties to others and maintains *wilobo* (the world). Duty is a necessary reality if society is to attain its end of the good life. For example, we have the right to eat only in so far as we fulfil the duty of allowing others to eat too.

This therefore means that the morality of rights is predicated on duty and equality, and is centred on the understanding of fairness. The ethic of rights is the balancing of the self and the other self. It is an ethic of responsibility towards the helpless, the vulnerable, and the weak, with an attitude of mercy, compassion, work and performing for society.

The following section invites the ICC to take heed of this reality, and to begin to engage in understanding the Acholi community if its operation in Northern Uganda is truly to benefit the people.

5. RELIVING ACHOLI TRADITIONAL JUSTICE MECHANISMS: PLANT ACHOLI IN AN ACHOLI GARDEN

5.1. THE ACHOLI CONCEPT OF *DANO* AS A FRAMEWORK FOR RECONCILIATION

The Acholi concept of *dano* (human being) is not only an ontological being as presence (an opposite of absence) in a biological way but, characteristically, *dano* is heavily founded on character, behaviour and conduct. As a result, an Acholi would cry out that 'you are not a human being', not because you have suddenly changed into a cabbage but that your character, behaviour and conduct do not indicate any human being in you. That means, the concept *dano* is deeper and reaches rather to the very reality of what makes you a human being, namely, humanness.

Humanness therefore is the correct translation of the Acholi concept, *dano,* and this concept pervades the entire Acholi reality, including traditional justice mechanisms. *Dano* philosophy focuses on humanity and humanness for the purpose of constantly building a social harmony. *Dano* is therefore understood as good social or communal co-existence and being each other's keeper and neighbour. In this respect, one who kills, for example, loses humanness, and the Acholi would refer to him as *pe dano* (not a human being). The wrong he committed is called *ujabu* in Acholi, which means, evil. Consequently, one with *ujabu* cannot live among people because that would bring evil spirit to the society. Until rituals are performed he will be ostracized as a misfit or an outcast. The individual wrong becomes a social problem in the families, clans and even the tribe, that needs the amicable restoration of human and social relationships and not just an individual restoration. As a result, the Acholi do not use the term, 'crime', but 'wrong' to denote a social problem that needs the restoration of humaneness through a humane solution. That means the Acholi emphasis on humanness forms a strong social incentive that drives forgiveness and reconciliation.

Here we should mention that it is unacceptable to pay wrong with wrong, or to inflict an equivalent suffering as caused on the victim. It follows that one may not be sentenced to death because of committing the wrong of killing. That is not being *dano* but *lee* (animal). Instead, for such a wrong, intentionally committed, after a series of rituals, the perpetrator and the victim are taken through the process of *mato oput*. The rituals will be performed after payments for compensation are made, either in terms of cows or goats, in such numbers as may be determined according to the capacity of the clan from which the perpetrator comes. The idea of payment represents two things: social punishment (by making hefty payments for the wrongs committed) and reparation. In some cases, if a man were killed, the family of the one who committed the murder would give a girl as a wife to the family of the victim, in the hope that she would produce a replacement for the deceased. This act is not as widely practised now as in the past, because of the dynamics of Acholi society and values.

Following compensation, a series of rituals will be performed, including the provision of a ram and a bull by the offender's family, and a goat by the deceased's family. When these animals are offered, elders and the clans of both the deceased and the perpetrator gather in a chosen area for the ritual. However, traditional practices have been adjusted to reality. Whereas it was not traditional for non-clan members to give animals for use in the rituals, civil society organisations have been allowed to provide these animals on several occasions. It is estimated that between 2004 and 2006, the Northern Uganda Peace Initiative (NUPI), through Ker Kwaro Acholi, supported about fifty four rituals and ceremonies (Latigo 2008, 105). The ritual is conducted, however, only when the perpetrator demonstrates remorse and repentance. While gathered, the chief elder invokes the presence of God while saying: "*This man whose fault brought us here today... has repented of his evil deed... We now beseech you our ancestors to let the two families resume a brotherly relationship...*" (Latigo 2008, 104). These invocations climax with pounding an extract from the root of the *oput* tree. The liquid is given to the perpetrator and a representative of the deceased to drink simultaneously from the same vessel (usually a calabash), while the women ululate (to indicate a successful reconciliation and restoration of humanness).

As this process reaches its climax, the chief elder or his delegated member, ritually spears the bull that had earlier been brought by the clan of the person who killed. The meat of the slaughtered bull is roasted and shared by both clans. Immediately thereafter, other foods are served to everyone,[13] and the families may now interact freely (ibid., 105).

---

13 The Acholi have a very strong belief that once you have shared a meal with your enemy, such a person ceases at once to continue being your enemy. If you continue to hold or treat him as an enemy even after sharing a meal, you bring curse onto yourself and your family.

Other rituals performed are *nyono tong gweno* (stepping on an egg) as intended to welcome one back to his or her family or clan members. There is also *moyo kom* (the cleansing of the body) to become blameless, and *moyo piny* (cleansing of the area), which includes the sacrifice of a goat to appease the ancestors and send away evil or bad spirits which could haunt people as a result of the murder committed.

5.2. JUSTICE AND SYSTEMIC THINKING: RETURNING THE ICC TO THE CLASSROOM

The ICC should appreciate that the Acholi traditional justice system is not only a practice and an act of social redress, but a means for bestowing upon society the dignity and security of living, and the connecting of generations. It is not just a practice but is established in the ontology and cosmology. It has meaning and wisdom, and is consequently a conscious frame for social healing.

The saying, 'justice must be done', means that the concept and practice of justice is not an external activity but comes from within the people or community it hopes to serve, and fulfils the aspiration of its seekers. It is from this that the phrase 'returning the ICC to the classroom' makes sense, namely, the ICC must appreciate this value not from their own perspective but from the perspective of its originators.

It is therefore necessary to emphasize that Acholi traditional justice does not condone a wrong, but deals with it through a different framework and orientation. It does not support impunity since it condemns wrong, and finds a way of solving it with a view not to convict and punish but to restore. By its constitutive parts, the ontology and cosmology is communal and sensitive to religious and human rights. The importance of considering this ontology and cosmology can be explained by referring to systemic thinking. Systemic thinking emphasizes an appreciation of the complexity of social living and an interpretation of the phenomenon. It indicates the variety of issues, as in the case of the LRA; the culture and tradition of the people, their values, philosophies and socio-economic milieu. Below is a diagram that clarifies the systemic thinking.

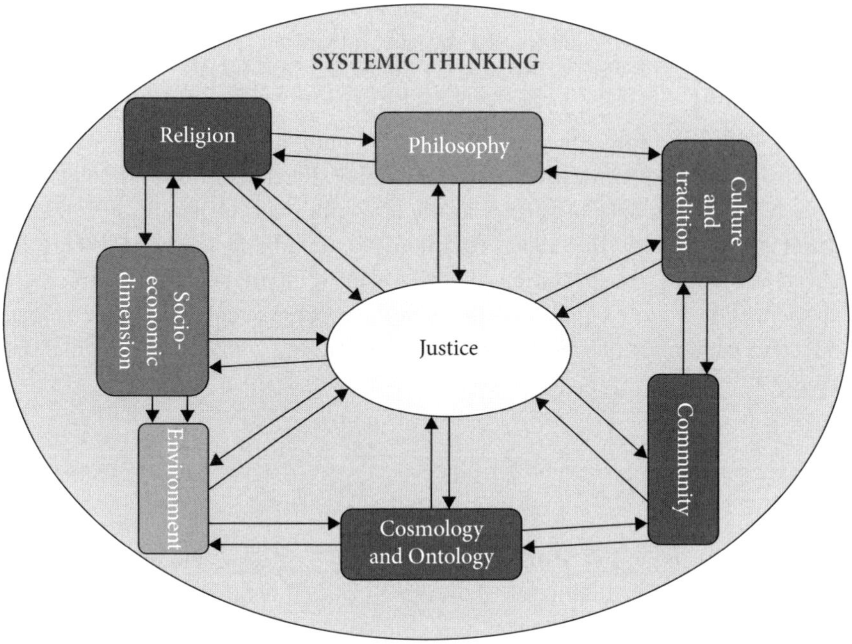

Adopted from Elly Musafiri (et al.), *Great Lakes Programme (GLP) workshop on curriculum development and capacity cooperation* – UPEACE Africa Programme, 2010.

Unlike the value-free conception of justice that the ICC would wish us to believe in, the core emphasis of systemic thinking is that the meaning and practice of justice must interact with – and therefore be affected by – the people and their living experience. This means that one cannot deal with justice as though it were a spaceless and atemporal value but that it should be the outcome of a general view of situations, environment and the community.

This, in effect, resonates with a stronger call for the ICC to make a careful appreciation about what justice means and to consider Acholi traditional justice. Like the flowering of a plant that is greatly assisted by environmental conditions, authentic justice should begin and end with the user. This means that we cannot assume a standardized frame of justice that is not accepted by the Acholi people, when they have their own system in which generations have participated.

In any event, Acholi justice has not claimed universal application. Instead, it seeks to validate itself as applicable to its own society. The communities neighbouring Acholi, however, as in other parts of Africa, have their own systems of traditional justice. Hence, the Acholi system is limited to the Acholi, and only at the level of inter-tribal conflict are joint justice mechanisms necessary. For example, atrocities committed by the LRA (which is predominantly composed of

Acholi) in Lango, Teso and West Nile (in northern Uganda) have, on several occasions, been jointly addressed by an integrated system of traditional mechanisms.

Consequently, an authentic justice system should not look for an objective standard to which communities regardless of their lived historicity are subjected. As with the multiplicity of species in the biological world, there is an intrinsic advantage of diversity. This allows communities to find and appreciate their own collective identity in opposition to the 'other', and to begin to share their experiences on a more equal basis through the process of collaborative dialogue and conversation, which will lead to understanding without privileging the other.

6. CONCLUSION

The ongoing competitive debate on justice and justice practice has opposed emphatic interest for differences, diversity and fragmentation to the dominant discourse that believes and takes for granted that justice necessarily means retribution.

This paper questions whether there should be one, comprehensive understanding and practice of justice and showed that the understanding and practice of justice is not uniform, but is specific to a particular culture and tradition. This makes justice more than a mere instrument: it is a human and organic phenomenon.

As Ingelaere (2008, 58) emphasized, living together is a practice that is forged locally and not at the level of the international community. As the paper intimated, a global and externally imposed system of justice and peace is bad and unnecessary, because justice and peace are found from within. Building from this, we are called to appreciate the 'within': the capacity of local resources to establish justice and peace.

This is the heartbeat of this paper, taking us through the Acholi restorative justice system, rooted within their cosmology and ontological hierarchy. This cosmology and ontology may not be generalized, but is at the core of Acholi justice, and is one of the fundamental reasons why the Acholi concept of justice is at odds with the ICC justice concept and thus with its operation in northern Uganda.

Resonating with the Acholi system, the paper calls upon us to broaden our perspective of justice so as to include not only retribution but other forms of settlement. It is only then that we can truly build a global knowledge on justice, without preference or competitive dialogue, but with a hermeneutic that seeks to understand, not from our own perspective but from the perspective of the narrator.

This is the discipline that we have to build: pluralism in the generation of knowledge, not a closed and rigid system, but one that is open-ended, allowing for a cooperative dialogue and conversation. This conversation will help the ICC to reconstruct a justice mechanism that truly reflects the will and interests of the Acholi community.

BIBLIOGRAPHY

Allen, T. (2005)
War and Justice in Northern Uganda: An Assessment of the International Criminal Courts Intervention, Draft Report.

Allen, T. (2006)
Trial Justice: the International Criminal Court and the Lord's Resistance Army, London: Zed Books Ltd.

Anyanwu, K.C. (1984)
African Philosophy: an introduction to the main philosophical trends in contemporary Africa, Rome: Catholic Book Agency.

Appiah, K.A. (1992)
In My Father's House, New York: Oxford University Press.

Bartlet, M. (2009)
Forgiveness, Reconciliation and Judicial Process in Northern Uganda: The Lord's Resistance Army and the International Criminal Court, *Africa Peace and Conflict Journal*, Vol. 2 (2), 42–57.

Batard, A. (2005)
Punish Impunity in Northern Uganda, *New Vision Sept.*

Bernstein, J.R. (1978)
The Restructuring of Social and Political Theory, Philadelphia: University of Pennsylvania Press.

Bernstein J.R. (1983)
Beyond objectivism and relativism. Science, Hermeneutics and practice, Philadelphia: University of Pennsylvania Press.

Braithwaite, J. (ed.) (1989)
Restorative Justice: Philosophy to Practice, Aldershot: Ashgate.

Cavadinio, M. and Dignan, J. (1997)
The *Penal System: An Introduction*, London: Sage.

Cianci, G. and Eliot, T.S. (2007)
The Concept of Tradition, Cambridge: Cambridge University Press.

Christopher, J.C., Richardson, F.C. and Christopher, S.E. (2003)
Philosophical Hermeneutics. A Meta-theory to Transcend, Dualism and Individualism, Western Psychology, http://htpprints.yorku.ca/archive.

Cubit, P.C. (2010)
Sierra Leone's post-conflict reconstruction: a study of the challenges for building long term peace. Doctoral Thesis, Submitted to Department of Peace Studies, University of Bradford.

Descartes, R. (1937)
Meditations on First Philosophy: In Which the Existence of God and the Distinction of the Soul from the Body Are Demonstrated. Translated by Donald A. Cress (1993), Hackett Publication Corporation.

Diop, C.A. (1981)
Civilisation or Barbarism: An Authentic Anthropology, Translated by Yaa-Lengi M.N., New York: Lawrence-Hill Books.

Finnstrom, S. (2003)
Living with Bad Surrounding: War and Existential Uncertainty in Acholiland, Northern Uganda, Uppsala: Uppsala University Press.

Fischer, F. (1990)
Technocracy and the Politics of Expertise, California: Sage Publications.

Gade, B.N.C. (2010)
Ubuntu and the South African Truth and Reconciliation Process. Master Thesis.

Gorringe, T. (1996)
God's Just Vengeance: Crime, Violence and the Rhetoric of Salvation, New York: Cambridge University Press.

Gross, D. (1992)
The Past in Ruins: Tradition and the Critique of Modernity, Massachusetts: University of Massachusetts Press.

Gyekye, K. (1995)
An Essay on African Philosophical Thought: The Akan Conceptual Scheme, Philadelphia: Tempel University Press.

Hegel, F.G.W. (2004)
The Philosophy of History. Translated by J. Sibree, Dover: Dover Publications.

Heidegger, M. (1957)
Identity and Difference, Chicago: University of Chicago.

Hoffman, M. (2001)
Secret Societies and Psychological Warfare, Idaho: Independent History and Research.

Honderich, T. (1969)
Punishment, The supposed justifications, London: Hutchinson and Co.

Hountondji, P. (1996)
African Philosophy: Myth and Reality, Bloomington, Indiana University Press.

Huyse, L. and Salter, M. (eds.) (2008)
Transitional Justice and Reconciliation after Violent Conflict: Learning from African Experiences, Stockholm: International IDEA.

Ingelaere, B. (2008)
The gacaca courts in Rwanda, in: Huyse, L. and Salter, M. (eds.) *Traditional Justice after Violent Conflict. Learning from African experiences*, Stockholm: International IDEA, 25–59.

International Center for Transitional justice and the Human Rights Center (2005)
Forgotten Voices: A Population-Based Survey of Attitudes about Peace and Justice in Northern Uganda, Berkeley: University of California.
International Criminal Court (2007)
Interest of Justice, www.iccnow.org/?mod=interestofjustice.
Jankiewicz, H.
The Concepts of Rhetoric, http: // web.syr.edu/hjjankie/209/cncpts.rhet.html.
Kant, I. (1999)
The Metaphysical Elements of Justice, Indianapolis: Hackett Publishing Company.
Kebede, M. (2006)
Africa's Quest for a Philosophy of Decolonization, *African Studies quarterly, the Online Journal for African Studies*, Vol. 8 (4).
Latigo, J.O. (2008)
Northern Uganda: tradition-based practices in the Acholi region, in: Huyse, L. and Salter, M. (eds.) *Traditional Justice after Violent Conflict. Learning from African experiences*, Sweden: International IDEA, 85–120.
Laudan, L. (1981)
Science and Hypothesis: Historical Essays on Scientific Methodology, Dordrecht: Reidel.
Levi-Strauss, C. (1962)
The Savage Mind, Chicago: University of Chicago Press.
Levy-Bruhl, L. (1966)
How Natives Think, New York: Washington Square Press.
Machiavelli, N. (1970)
The Prince, Hammondworth: Penguin Books.
Martien, J. (2005)
The English Legal System, London: Hodder Arnold.
Mill, J.S. (1978)
On Liberty, Indianapolis: Hackett Publishing Press.
Masolo, D.A. (1994)
African Philosophy. In Search of Identity, Indiana: Indiana University Press.
Mosley, A. (1995)
African Philosophy: Selected Readings, New York: Prentice Hall.
Mudimbe, V.Y. (1988)
The Invention of Africa: Gnosis, Philosophy and the Order of Knowledge, Indianapolis: Indiana University Press.
Pattie, L. (1991)
Getting Smart: Feminist Research and Pedagogy within the Postmodern, New York: Routledge.
Pease, B. (2001)
A Man's World? Changing Men's Practices in a Globalized World, London: Zed Books.
Peirce, C.S. (1974)
Collected Papers, Vol. 2, Hartshorne and Weiss (eds.), Cambridge: Harvard University Press.

Plato (1964)
The Republic. Translated by Francis MacDonald Cornford, London: Oxford University Press.

Seidman, S. and Wagner, G.D. (eds.) (1992)
Postmodernism and Social Theory, Cambridge: Blackwell.

Senghor, L.S. (1966)
Negritude: A Humanism of the Twentieth Century, in: Hord, F.L. and Lee, J.S. (eds.) (1995) *I am because we are: Readings in black philosophy*, Amherst, MA: University of Massachusetts Press, 45–54.

St. Augustine (1958)
City of God, Translated by Walsh G.G. et al., New York: Image Books.

Sturm, D. (1975)
Autonomous Morality and the Question of the Decrepitude of Justice, Blucknell University, www.jstor.org/pss/1202076.

Tempels, P. (1959)
Bantu Philosophy, Paris: Présence Africaine.

Toulmin, S. (1992)
Cosmopolis: The Hidden Agenda of Modernity, Chicago: Chicago University Press.

Tsenay, S. (1994)
The Hermeneutics of African Philosophy: Horizon and Discourse, New York: Routledge.

Van Binsbergen, W. (2002)
Sensus Communis or Sensus Particularis? Immanuel Kant in Africa. A Social Science Comment, www.shikanda.net/general/ gen3/Kant_Afrika.htm.

Volquartz, J. (2005)
ICC Under Fire Over Uganda Probe, www.icc.joselinevolquart2.

Walsh, G.G. and Zema, D. (1985)
Nuclear Ethics And Options: Perceptions And Reflections, www.globalsecurity.org/ wmd/library/report/1986/ODE.htm.

CHAPTER VII

REVISITING THE LEGAL AND SOCIO-POLITICAL FOUNDATIONS AND (WESTERN) CRITICISMS OF *GACACA* COURTS

Felix Mukwiza NDAHINDA and Alphonse MULEEFU

1. INTRODUCTION

The *gacaca* courts in Rwanda have provided a very prolific source of inspiration for discursive writings on how to best deal with the legacy of violent conflicts. It is increasingly rare to read a book, chapter or article of a general (theoretical) character on transitional justice that does not mention or elaborate on the *gacaca* courts. Numerous monographs, articles and expert opinions – penned by individuals ranging from renowned academics in various legal and social sciences to aspiring young researchers in quest for a hot topic for their dissertation – have taken up the task to explore, investigate or validate theories or hypotheses on a wide range of aspects of societal reconstruction in the aftermath of conflict (Clark 2007 and 2010; Ingelaere 2006, 2008 and 2009; Waldorf 2006a, 2006b and 2011; PRI 2010b). Moreover, there are countless informed and uniformed journalistic accounts or internet postings describing or expressing opinions about the *gacaca* courts and their societal significance for Rwanda and beyond.

The *gacaca* courts are a community-based and tradition inspired dispute settlement mechanism established in 2001 by the Rwandan government to deal with the heavy legacy of the 1994 genocide. A preliminary determination of circumstances and responsibilities in the commission of crimes is initiated at the hill (Cell) level for purposes of collecting relevant information and categorizing suspects into one of the initially four then three categories of suspects. Categorization is based on the gravity of the committed crimes, the level of participation or the particular position of the suspect in society. Based on the information gathered in the preliminary phase and on the categorization of suspects, the actual trial takes place before a *gacaca* court at the Cell (3rd category cases), Sector (2nd and some 1st category cases) or ordinary courts (some 1st category cases). *Gacaca* hearings involve the population where the crime was committed and take place before a bench composed of lay judges elected from the population. The process encourages confessions, guilty pleas and demands for forgiveness in exchange for substantial reduction of sentences; a suspension of sentences and/or a commutation of sentences into community service.[1]

Predictably, the focus of the various elaborations on *gacaca* courts varies from one study to another. Some writings consist of balanced descriptions, assessments and critical appraisals of the *gacaca* system from mono or multidisciplinary perspectives. Others are essentially very opinioned pamphlets expressing views on the *gacaca* system based on preconceptions about the inherent limits of a mechanism that departs from what are considered as universal(ised) standards of the criminal judicial process. The major focus of elaborations on *gacaca* courts has, indeed, been on the perceived deviant aspects of the mechanism *vis-à-vis* the so-called ordinary or classic court system of Western inspiration. They mostly relate to: the veracity of confessions encouraged under the mechanism; the reconciliatory power or potential of *gacaca*; political interferences in the process; the focus on the crime of genocide rather than on all possible crimes committed during the country's civil war, including by the former fighting forces of the RPF/A – Rwandese Patriotic Front/Army; relatedly, the perceived generalization of the Hutu guilt or persecution of the Hutu by a Tutsi-dominated post genocide government; and, more generally, the (non-)compliance with due process guarantees in criminal proceedings.

Like any other complex mechanism intended to address equally complex issues such as the Rwandan genocide, the *gacaca* process has its share of supporters and

---

1 Organic Law No. 40/2000 of 26 January 2001 Setting up "Gacaca Jurisdictions" and Organizing Prosecutions for Offences Constituting the Crime of Genocide or Crimes against Humanity Committed between 1 October 1990 and 31 December 1994, Official Gazette, No. 6 of 15 March 2000. Organic Law No. 16/2004 of 16 June 2004 Establishing the Organisation, Competence and Functioning of Gacaca Courts Charged with Prosecuting and Trying the Perpetrators of the Crime of Genocide and other Crimes against Humanity, Committed between 1 October 1990 and 31 December 1994, Official Gazette, No. Special of 19 June 2004. Organic Law No. 10/2007 of 1 March 2007 Modifying and completing Organic Law No. 16/2004 of 16 June 2004 establishing the Organisation, Competence and Functioning of Gacaca Courts Charged with Prosecuting and Trying the Perpetrators of the Crime of Genocide and other Crimes against Humanity, Committed between 1 October 1990 and 31 December 1994, Official Gazette No. 5 of 1 March 2007. Organic Law No. 13/2008 of 19 May 2008 Modifying and completing Organic Law No. 16/2004 of 16 June 2004 establishing the Organisation, Competence and Functioning of Gacaca Courts Charged with Prosecuting and Trying the Perpetrators of the Crime of Genocide and other Crimes against Humanity, Committed between 1 October 1990 and 31 December 1994, Official Gazette No. 11 of 1 June 2008.

critics. Due to the global proliferation of expertise on Rwanda in general and on *gacaca* courts in particular, there is a wide variety – in terms of depth and substantiation – of expressed views for or against (particular aspects of) the *gacaca* courts. While there are those who consider the mechanism as an innovative and effective process in dealing with the huge caseload of the genocide, critics insist on its limits in terms of jurisdiction, perceived lack of independence and practical challenges that arguably hinder rather than foster reconciliation in the country (Clark 2010, 4 et seq.; Thompson and Nagy 2011).

Very few would argue that the mechanism is immune from criticisms. In fact, the identification of shortcomings of an essentially experimental *gacaca* process often lead to several amendments of the initial law establishing – and providing for the functioning of – the *gacaca* courts. Yet, in spite of many efforts to improve the mechanism, there are those who consider it as irredeemably tainted by its departure from what is considered as the orthodoxy in normative and procedural criminal law (as discussed in Chakravarty 2006). While it is more than legitimate to highlight and elaborate on the shortcomings of the mechanism, some conclusions on how the process impacts on the country's future (in terms of peace and reconciliation) – even when they are purportedly based on empirical evidence – seem hastily drawn (as elaborated in Ingelaere 2009; Waldorf 2011). Only time can allow for sound conclusions to be drawn as to whether *gacaca* courts have achieved (some of) their stated objectives since even after the official closure of proceedings, society will still be marked by the process as long as (the majority of) convicts are not yet reintegrated in their communities.

From the outset and subsequently, Rwandan authorities listed a number of reasons justifying their move to institute *gacaca* courts to hear cases about responsibilities in the commission of the genocide. Such reasons have historical, legal, political and cultural dimensions. These dimensions are precisely the main source of domestic and mostly Western criticisms of the *gacaca* process. Some of the criticisms of the *gacaca* process are substantive: they relate to the shortcomings of the mechanism *vis-à-vis* its stated objectives or fundamental human rights norms. Others focus on the mainly procedural and institutional distinctive features of the *gacaca* process in comparison with criminal justice norms, procedures and institutions rooted in the West. The various criticisms of *gacaca* courts are labelled as Western because, whether expressed by individuals from the global West or from other continents including Africa, they are mostly framed taking as referents norms, institutions or ideals rooted or embedded in Western legal and socio-political thought, even where some of them might have acquired a universal (human rights) stamp.

The analysis to follow will revisit the reasons behind the establishment of the *gacaca* courts, their historical, legal, socio-political and cultural legitimacy and the various criticisms of this unique mechanism. It is argued that while some of the *gacaca* criticisms are legitimate, others are a result of misconceptions about, or ideological rejection of, a mechanism perceived as contravening to the established foundations of the globalised criminal justice mechanisms of Western inception. Furthermore, in spite of evident shortcomings of the mechanism, it is argued that the tendency in some studies to generalize their conclusions based on limited findings from specific geographies or the hasty predictions about the legacy of a mechanism still in motion are more a result of subjective than objective evaluations of the process.

2. LEGAL AND SOCIO-POLITICAL UNDERPINNINGS OF *GACACA* COURTS

2.1. PROSECUTING GENOCIDE CASES IN POST-GENOCIDE RWANDA

It is a widely documented fact that the Rwandan genocide ended with a military victory of the RPF/A over former governmental forces and militia that supervised the execution of the genocide (Prunier 1999; Mamdani 2001; Melvern 2004) The new post-genocide authorities faced numerous challenges of rebuilding a country and society torn by nearly four years of civil war and one of the most efficient, destructive and intimate genocides of recorded human history. With estimated 800,000 to one million persons killed and more than two million Rwandan refugees scattered in neighbouring countries and around the world, many of whom were forced into exile by former Rwandan authorities (UNHCR 2000, 250), it should always be recalled that the odds of bringing back some level of stability were very slim. It goes beyond the scope of the present inquiry to revisit the overall reconstruction process as well as the refugee crisis and its linkages to the Congo wars (see: Mamdani 2001, 234 et seq.; Prunier 2008; Lemarchand 2009; Turner 2007). One should only mention that from the outset, not only genocide survivors but also the new Rwandan authorities insisted that criminal accountability was a prerequisite for any form of lasting peace and stability in the country (Lierop 1997, 898). In the aftermath of the genocide, there were some suggestions that instead of, or in combination with, criminal prosecutions, the pursuit of reconciliation required some form of amnesty or the institution of a Truth and Reconciliation Commission (TRC) inspired from past dynamics in Latin America and the contemporaneous South African model adopted in dealing with crimes of the apartheid era (Mackintosh 1997, 473; Bradley 1998, 138–147). However, given the nature, magnitude and historical background that nurtured the genocide, Rwandan authorities, genocide survivors and some non-

Rwandans disputed the wisdom of the reconciliatory power of any proposed alternatives to criminal prosecutions for genocide suspects (Schabas 1996).

The new Rwandan authorities made a calculated political choice of pursuing the path of prosecutions. With the help of foreign partners, they undertook to rebuild the judiciary and led reflections and consultations on the appropriate course of action in holding perpetrators of the genocide accountable (Digneffe and Fierens 2003; Schabas and Imbleau 1997, 22 et seq.). It took nearly two years to clear the hurdles and put in place the needed normative and institutional infrastructure for putting in motion criminal prosecutions of genocide cases. In the meantime, Rwandan authorities requested and obtained from the United Nations Security Council the creation of an International Criminal Tribunal for Rwanda (ICTR) (Akhavan 1996; Morris 1996–1997) which, for over fifteen years has commendably achieved a lot in establishing responsibilities in the genocide and defining certain crimes, but only managed to process a little less than 100 cases.[2] The new legislation providing for prosecutions of genocide cases introduced features that departed from the traditional Rwandan Criminal Justice (1996 Genocide Law).[3] Suspects were classified in four categories based on their suspected role in the planning and level of participation in the execution of the genocide (Articles 2–3 of the 1996 Genocide Law). They were encouraged to confess and plead guilty to their crimes; a procedure that was accompanied by substantial reductions of otherwise applicable sentences (Articles 4–18 of the 1996 Genocide Law). These two features remained the cornerstone of genocide prosecutions in Rwanda as they eventually became the central ideas upon which the *gacaca* mechanism was erected (see Articles 54–63 and 68–75 of the 2001 *Gacaca* Law).

Arguably, the Rwandan authorities did not fully appreciate the magnitude of the task they were undertaking, namely, to put to trial all persons suspected of having played a role in the genocide. The establishment of Specialized Chambers within the existing judiciary (twelve Tribunals of First Instance and four Appeal Courts) to handle the workload of genocide cases did not certainly foresee the fact that to be somewhat exhaustive, the judicial system had to process more than one million cases. By early 2005, it was estimated that only some 10,000 cases were tried before the Specialized Chambers (Schabas 2008, 218). Rwandan authorities and observers of the process estimated that it would take more than a century to try some 135,000 detainees (estimate by 1999) and certainly many more years to deal with all genocide suspects, including those still at large

2 See International Criminal Tribunal for Rwanda (ICTR), www.unictr.org/Cases/tabid/204/Default.aspx, visited on 12 May 2011.

3 Organic Law No. 08/96 of 30 August 1996 *On the Organization of Prosecutions for Offences constituting the Crime of Genocide or Crimes against Humanity committed since October 1, 1990*, Official Gazette, Year 35, No. 17, September 1996.

(Schabas 2005, 888; Fierens 2005, 897–898; HRW 1998, 13).[4] As they came to terms with the fact that ordinary courts were unable to fulfil their mandate of dealing with all the caseload of the genocide, Rwandan authorities were left with three possible options:

1) they could have abandoned prosecutions and instead granted a general amnesty or reverted to a South African type of TRC;
2) they could have chosen to proceed with selective prosecutions of persons suspected of bearing the highest level of responsibility in the planning and execution of the genocide (others would be granted amnesty, through a TRC or not); or
3) they had to look for alternative processes in dealing with the overall caseload of the genocide.

Determined to bring accountability for all perpetrators of the genocide, Rwandan authorities engaged in deliberations that led to the establishment of the *gacaca* courts in 2001 (Urugwiro Report 1999). The historical, legal and socio-political reasons that dictated this course of action are explored below.

2.2. MOTIVATIONS FOR THE ESTABLISHMENT OF THE *GACACA* COURTS

Sarkin argues that since the new post-genocide Rwandan government came to power following the overthrow of the former regime – rather than through internal reform or through some compromise – it had the '*widest discretion to decide how it should deal with the past, including unfettered power to bring the perpetrators of human rights abuses to justice*' (Sarkin 2001, 146). Naturally, principles of legality, equity and the societal legitimacy were expected to act as safeguards in the exercise of the discretionary power that the new authorities held. Furthermore, their reliance on foreign (mostly Western) assistance for the much needed finances and human resources in the reconstruction process constrained their freedom of action. Yet, the course of action undertaken by Rwandan authorities reflected their determination to dictate the agenda on how to move forward.

The choice to dig into the country's history and tradition in a quest for alternatives to criminal prosecutions by ordinary courts was certainly part of a process of reinventing the Rwandan identity itself. Beyond the debate as to whether the unprosecuted killings that surrounded the country's accession to

4 For figures on detainees and persons tried before Specialized Chambers, see: www.inkiko-gacaca.gov.rw/En/Generaties.htm, visited on 12 May 2011.

independence (1959–1964) amounted to a genocide, Rwandan history did not have precedents from which the new authorities could draw inspiration in dealing with this particular tragedy. History could only serve as an inspiration in designing a mechanism that certainly has several novel features. Thus, some analysts' insistence on the idea that the "*'new' gacaca courts are in the truest sense an 'invented tradition*'" (Ingelaere 2008, 32) somehow ignore the fact that even the records of debates that led to the creation of the *gacaca* courts show that the conceptualizers of the mechanism established a distinction between the 'old' *gacaca* and the 'new' *gacaca* and viewed the former as only a socio-cultural inspiration for the latter (Urugwiro report, at 53 et seq.). Various writings on the *gacaca* courts have extensively described the organizational structure and the functioning of the mechanism under the successive *gacaca* laws (Lahiri 2009; Clark 2010; Clark 2007; Meyerstein 2007). It would therefore be superfluous to re-engage into a detailed description of the mechanism. The following elaboration dwells on those features perceived as embodying the very foundations of the *gacaca* process. It is worth noting that the stated objectives of the *gacaca* courts – namely: 1) to reveal the truth about what happened; 2) to eradicate the culture of impunity; 3) to speed up the genocide trials; 4) to reconcile the Rwandans and reinforce their unity; 5) to prove that the Rwandan society has the capacity to settle its own problems through a system of justice based on the Rwandan custom[5] – reflect the historical, legal, political and socio-cultural motivations that informed the process of setting up the *gacaca* courts.

2.2.1. Socio-legal dimensions

By 1999, Rwandan authorities and their foreign partners agreed on the undesirability of keeping several dozens of thousands of genocide suspects in jail without the possibility of trying them in a short run. The continued detention amounted to a violation of the presumption of innocence – until one is found guilty by a competent court – recognized under Rwandan and international law (on the presumption of innocence in then applicable Rwandan law see: Schabas and Imbleau 1997, 47 and 176). In addition, not all persons incarcerated upon denunciations were certainly guilty of crimes they were suspected to have committed. An evaluation of proceedings before specialized chambers by *Avocats sans Frontières* found that between 1998 and 2000 around 20% of accused persons were acquitted (ASF 2000, 16). The most basic principles of justice and equity dictated that their situation be clarified as swiftly as possible, instead of keeping them indefinitely in detention. On the other hand, releasing all suspects and sending them back to the hills to freely live in the same neighbourhoods as the few survivors whose relatives they were suspected to have decimated was certainly not the best option to achieving peace and reconciliation.

---

5 Inkiko-Gacaca, www.inkiko-gacaca.gov.rw/En/EnObjectives.htm, visited on 12 May 2011.

Inasmuch as it was unjustifiable and tragic for a wrongly suspected person (mainly Hutu) to spend several years in very poor prison conditions without trial, it was similarly unbearable and traumatizing for survivors (mostly Tutsi) to live a normal life next to suspected rapists or killers of their mothers, fathers, brothers, sisters, relatives or neighbours. Even if the traditional *gacaca* had never had to settle similar cases as those arising from the genocide, the governmental decision to shoulder the burden of determining the responsibilities in the genocide on the general population at the hill level was rather a creative move in tackling the otherwise insurmountable caseload of the genocide.

Contextual realities pertaining to the committed crime, the level of popular participation and the intermingled habitat of Rwanda's Hutu and Tutsi rendered the Latin American or South African models of truth for amnesty quite inappropriate. For some Rwandans (and non-Rwandans) who lived through the contradictions of Rwandan society since the end of the genocide, empathized with the situation of survivors and fully appreciated the dilemmas of post-genocide authorities, it is hard to imagine – some 17 years later – how the Rwandan society would have been better off without determining individual responsibility, not only to answer survivors' demand for justice, but also to diffuse or reduce a generalization of responsibility on the Hutu population (PRI 2010a, 26–27).

2.2.2. Socio-political considerations

There is a tendency in transitional justice literature to denounce a perceived predominance of retributivism over restoration in the *gacaca* process (Waldorf 2006a, 422; Ingelaere 2008, 32). As the story goes, pursuit of retribution in combination with other shortcomings of the process annihilates the advocated goal of achieving reconciliation through this mechanism. In the era of (inherently retributive) internationalization of criminal justice for perpetrators of crimes that include genocide, the denunciation of perceived *gacaca* retributivism seemingly suggests that punishing perpetrators of genocide is the wrong course of action that undermines the greater goal of societal reconciliation. Part of the retribution versus reconciliation debate is rooted in a very optimistic projection – by some Rwandan and foreign actors or analysts – on what the *gacaca* process alone may be able to achieve in reconciling the Rwandan society or eradicating the culture of impunity. The debate is also informed by differing historical narratives over what happened in Rwanda between 1990 and 1994.

Rwandan authorities' reading of the immediate historical antecedents to the genocide goes as follows: after decades of exile, descendants of people who fled the country in the 1950s and 1960s took up arms in 1990 after they were denied to peacefully return to their homeland. For nearly four years, they fought and talked with the Habyarimana regime which, instead of pursuing a peaceful resolution to the conflict, increasingly radicalized and repeatedly retaliated against civilian, mainly Tutsi populations but also some Hutu opposed to the regime (generally referred to as moderate Hutu). Extremists crafted a plan to eliminate all Tutsi and started to carry it out following the downing of former president Habyarimana's plane. In the course of the civil war and the fighting that resumed after the start of the genocide, civilians were killed by individual RPF/A soldiers. Such killings, RPF/A officials argue, were never part of a concerted policy and many of those responsible for committing such crimes were punished (Clark and Kaufman 2008, xxiv). Rwandan authorities' position is therefore that people should avoid establishing any (criminal or moral) equivalence between the genocide and possible crimes committed by individual RPA soldiers.

There are several, some still emerging, alternative narratives over what happened in Rwanda in 1994. Most proponents of alternative narratives agree with the characterization of the targeting of Tutsi as a genocide, but argue that the RPF/A engaged in large-scale atrocities (Philpot 2004; Lemarchand 1998; Reyntjens 2004). There are those who even suggest that the RPF committed atrocities comparable (Rusesabagina 2006, 14–15)[6], if not greater, proportions than the genocide (Péan 2005, 260). In the latter case Pierre Péan for instance deplored the fact that it was not yet acceptable to talk about double genocide in Rwanda or to say that there were more Hutu than Tutsi killed since 1990 (Péan 2005, 260). These narratives have in common the idea that lasting peace and genuine reconciliation requires that suspects from 'both sides' be either prosecuted (or amnestied in some cases). While some of these narratives are animated by a genuine pursuit of justice for all, other appeals for prosecutions of 'both sides' hardly mask the underlying characterization of events that took place in Rwanda in 1994 as constitutive of inter-tribal killings or interethnic violence.

Certainly all victims – Tutsi, Hutu and the often forgotten Twa – deserve justice. Debates over the non-inclusion of RPF/A crimes in the mandate of the *gacaca* courts (or their prosecution in general) will be revisited in subsequent sections. It is worth noting here that less disputed facts and figures about RPF/A crimes (Des Forges 1999, 726–31; Prunier 1999) do not allow for the establishment of equivalence between them and the genocide. In any case, appeals for prosecutions of RPF/A crimes do not diminish the importance of survivors' quest for justice and, indeed societal demand for retribution. However appealing the ethnocracy

---

6 *The Grinding machine: terror and genocide in Rwanda: Keith Harmon Snow talks with Paul Rusesabagina, the ordinary man who inspired the film Hotel Rwanda*, at http://allthingspass.com/uploads/html-191TheGrindingMachine.InterviewwithPaulRusesabaginaFINAL.htm, visited on 7 July 2011; F.M. Ndahinda, *Genocide revisionism in the Hague's Peace Palace*, at www.newtimes.co.rw/index.php?issue=14164&article=6145, visited on 7 July 2011.

argument may seem – meaning the perceived lack of socio-political legitimacy for a Tutsi dominated government to prosecute the Hutu masses however massive the participation in the genocide may have been – it does not address the question as to what alternatives would have better answered the concerns of survivors and suspects.

In spite of the growing importance of restorative justice, most (Western-inspired) criminal justice systems remain predominantly retributive. Furthermore, transitional justice elaborations on the linkages between post-conflict healing and non-pursuit of retributive justice have not so far generated standard models to be applied in every context. There are simply no conclusive studies demonstrating that at the inter-personal level, whites and blacks in post-apartheid South Africa are more reconciled than Hutu and Tutsi in Rwanda, because of lack of criminal prosecutions in the former context. Anyhow, with all its flaws, the *gacaca* mechanism embodies more restorative features than most criminal justice systems of Western inspiration. A reading of the evolution of the *gacaca* laws on sentencing (commutation of sentences), mostly for people who (spontaneously) confessed, pleaded guilty, repented and asked for forgiveness, clearly shows that retribution was not the main goal pursued by the process (Articles 13–14 the 2007 *Gacaca* Law and Articles 16–21 of the 2008 *Gacaca* Law). The mere fact that a notorious murderer [Article 11(1) of the 2007 *Gacaca* Law] could only end up incurring a prison sentence of 24 years of which only 4 would be spent in custody [Article 14(3) of the 2007 *Gacaca* Law), the rest being commuted into a suspended sentence and community service (with a possibility of converting even the 4 years of imprisonment into another community service for convicted persons who exemplarily served their previous part of the sentence) displays normative leniency and hence, a quest for restoration/reconciliation rather than retribution once some conditions were fulfilled. It should always be noted that under then applicable Rwandan law (of Western, mainly Belgian, inspiration), the qualification of a crime as (aggravated) murder would have resulted into the pronouncement of a death sentence. The death sentence was eventually abolished in 2007.[7]

In many ways, it remains premature to fully appreciate the impact of *gacaca* on lasting stability, peaceful coexistence between Hutu, Tutsi and Twa without aggregated data on the activities of *gacaca* courts nationwide. It is even more difficult to determine the impact of *gacaca* on reconciliation in Rwanda – whatever the contextual meaning of this fashionable concept is in terms of who should be reconciled with whom – without the healing passage of time necessary for society to digest the outcome of the *gacaca* process. The closure of activities

---

7 Organic Law No. 31/2007 of 25/07/2007 *Relating to the abolition of the death penalty*, *Official Gazette* No. special of 25 July 2007.

of *gacaca* courts that has been pushed back on several occasions (HRW 2011, 24–25) has been announced for April 2012.[8] Even after the closure of activities of *gacaca* courts it will possibly require many more years before the real impact of the process can be fully assessed since that chapter of Rwandan history cannot be considered to be closed as long as most convicts are still serving their sentences. Understandably, many non-Rwandans – including some development partners of Rwanda – were very uneasy with the idea of addressing the complex caseload of the genocide through a mechanism hitherto unknown to them that featured lay (some illiterate) judges. However, faced with an unprecedented task, Rwandan authorities were justified in pushing an unpopular course of action in light of the absence of credible alternatives. Some of the proposed alternative included the involvement of foreign actors in proceedings in Rwanda. However, *"the Rwandan government made it clear that it did not want foreign jurists to work within its judicial system as judges or other officers of the court"* (Schabas 1996, 528). In a way, the government was somewhat vindicated since the experience of international(ised) tribunals has shown their limitations in dealing with a considerable number of cases. The determination to move forward with the *gacaca* process in spite of dominant international objections was informed by the background to and configuration of the Rwandan conflict but also the perceived need to reinvent the Rwandan society as a whole.

2.2.3. Socio-cultural motivations

Besides the undertaking to reveal the truth about the genocide, to speed up genocide trials, to tackle the culture of impunity and to foster reconciliation, the *gacaca* courts undertook to 'prove that the Rwandan society has the capacity to settle its own problems through a system of justice based on the Rwandan custom' (*supra*, Section 2.2). This objective clearly fitted into RPF's narrative on the need to re-invent a new, inclusive Rwandan society. Such narrative is built on the idea that with its flaws, the pre-colonial Rwandan society was certainly not equal but less divided. Ethnicities were mapped and antagonized by colonial authorities for self-serving purposes and perpetuated by short-sighted post-colonial administrations. The RPF emerged by the end of the 1980s as a movement advocating not only for the return of (mainly Tutsi) refugees to Rwanda but also fighting for social justice (Prunier 1998; Prunier 1999, 90–120). From its years in the bush (1990–1994), the movement professed inclusiveness and vowed to fight for an end to ethnicity-based politics. The failure of the international community to successfully oversee the implementation of the peace accords, the genocide and the lack of foreign intervention to save lives somehow reinforced RPF leadership's resolve to ban ethnicity in the public realm and

---

8 Igihe, *Irangizwa ry'inkiko gacaca ryimuriwe umwaka utaha* (The closing of activities of Gacaca Courts has been postponed for next year), see www.igihe.com/spip.php?article19375.

reinvent a nationalism that promotes the shared Rwandan identity over 'Hutuness', 'Tutsiness' and 'Twaness'.[9] Aware of the paramount importance of shared history and culture in the process of recreation of a Rwandan identity transcending ethnicity, they revived a number of traditional institutions that, together with *gacaca*, were perceived as likely to foster reconciliation. In a report to the African Commission on Human and Peoples' Rights, Rwandan authorities contended that *"[t]he right to self determination encourages home grown and needs based initiatives. Inspired by its [tradition] culture, Rwanda has developed local values and initiatives that seek to strengthen citizenship, development, justice, good governance, rule of law, unity and reconciliation among others"* (Republic of Rwanda 2009, para. 106). The institution of *gacaca* courts therefore fits into a broader scheme of promoting institutions and structures perceived as reinforcing the sense of togetherness among Rwandans. Many legalistic critics of *gacaca* courts fail to capture this broader context in which it operates.

3. (WESTERN) CRITICISMS OF *GACACA* COURTS

No legal system can claim to be perfect and it would be too much to expect or assume that with more than 12,000 courts scattered on every hill in the country comprised of more than 170,000 *Inyangamugayo* (judges), *gacaca* was going to be perfect.[10] On the eve of the election of *gacaca* judges, Rwandan President Paul Kagame stated "*... if the gacaca Courts function as we anticipate, it will be an important contribution to the understanding and advancement of international law*" (Mibenge 2005, 410). Reflecting on this statement, Usta Kaitesi rightly remarked that the use of 'anticipate' reflected the uncertainty about the outcome of *gacaca*, even for those who introduced it.[11] It was also an indication that *gacaca* courts were instituted at a juncture when Rwandans desperately needed some breakthrough to start other reconciliatory initiatives. In other words, *gacaca* was not going to be an end in itself; it was just necessary to deal with an unprecedented reality.

Achievements of *gacaca* are generally buried into criticisms levied against the mechanism since its inception (Thomson and Nagy 2011, 11). It should always be noted that there are contextual differences between various conflict and post-

---

9 The imperative of 'reconstituting the Rwandan Society' is among other expressed aims pursued in creating the *gacaca* courts as it appears in the Preambles of the 2001 and 2004 *Gacaca* Laws.

10 Statistical information provided by Denis Bikesha, Director of Training and Sensitization of the National Service of *gacaca* Courts on 13 May 2011.

11 Comments by Usta Kaitesi made on the launch of the book *The Gacaca Courts, Post-Genocide Justice and Reconciliation in Rwanda: Justice without Lawyers* by Phil Clark Kigali, Rwanda, Kigali 21 April 2011.

conflict situations: Rwanda differs from Sudan, Sierra Leone, Iraq or Afghanistan. It is therefore very intricate to analyse *gacaca* – a process created to deal with a situation of mass victimization – using a general theory about transitional justice or general principles of criminal law.

As repeatedly stated, the *gacaca* mechanism has its flaws. Even Rwandan proponents of the mechanism denounce instances of false accusations, evidence based on hearsay, leniency of sentences, corruption of judges and witnesses or favouritism in deciding some cases. On a daily basis, the national Service of *Gacaca* Courts – the body coordinating and supervising their functioning – has had to deal with unexpected difficulties and challenges that would otherwise derail their smooth functioning. This dynamism and the experimental nature of the *gacaca* process contributed to practical solutions where other justice mechanisms were judged inadequate. The frequent amendments of *gacaca* laws were precisely aimed at addressing unforeseen realities that arose throughout the process. Major changes form the initial 2001 *Gacaca* Law related to, among others: the structure of *gacaca* courts; the number of judges and composition of the bench; the removal of compensation claims from the jurisdiction of *gacaca* courts, as well as the inclusion of rape and sexual torture within their jurisdiction. Moreover, references to the "*imprescriptibility of war crimes and crimes against humanity*" (preamble para 11 and Article 1a) were removed; most likely to avoid any ambiguities as to whether the *gacaca* courts had jurisdiction over war crimes, including purported crimes committed by the RPF/A. Compensation was set aside, pending the adoption of another law (Article 96 of the 2004 *Gacaca* Law).

The next section reviews (Western) criticisms of *gacaca* courts based on existing literature and on our personal involvement in the functioning of the *gacaca* courts.[12] The aim here is not to justify or legitimise the shortcomings of the mechanism but rather to provide an additional perspective on the ever-expanding *gacaca* scholarship.

3.1. NON-INCLUSION OF RPF/A CRIMES IN THE *GACACA* PROCESS

The dominant criticism of the *gacaca* process relates to the exclusion of war crimes in the mandate of the popular courts. It generally affirms that such exclusion was intended to shelter RPF/A suspects from prosecution (Waldorf 2006b, 1221–1277). However valid such argument may be, it fails to capture the

---

12 Alphonse Muleefu worked as a Legal Officer of the National Service of *gacaca* Courts from 3 April 2007 to 30 April 2009 and Felix Ndahinda participated in the training of *Inyangamugayo* in April and May 2002.

whole complexity and reality of the matter since the exclusion of war crimes is not synonymous with crimes committed by the RPF/A. In fact, such perception obliterates the responsibility of other soldiers who were somehow involved in the Rwandan conflict. Instead, it leads to the simplified views about *gacaca* as a process aimed at prosecuting (and hence persecuting) the Hutu only (Thomson and Nagy 2011, 20 and 23; Haile 2008, 29). In addition to RPA soldiers, available records on the civil war and the genocide suggest that war crimes may have been committed by ex-FAR (*Forces Armées Rwandaises*), Zairian contingents sent by Mobutu to fight the 'invading rebels' and the multiple interventions by French soldiers in the country (Prunier 1999, 281 et seq.; McMillan 2008; Dallaire, Manocha and Degnarain 2005; Republic of Rwanda 2007).

It is a documented and quite acknowledged fact that some RPA soldiers committed crimes against civilians between 1990 and 1994. There has never been any systematic investigation into alleged crimes committed by the RPF during the civil war and the genocide or after it took power. Uncorroborated sources suggest that between 25,000 and 60,000 were killed by the RPF/A and in the immediate aftermath of the genocide (see various sources in HRW 2008, 89; Prunier 1999). Equally documented – and in spite of related criticism – is the fact that there are RPA soldiers who were prosecuted for crimes committed during the civil war, the genocide and aftermath, including revenge killings (International Federation for Human Rights 2002, 16 and 64–70; Waldorf and Haskell 2011, 61 et seq.). In a response to the pressure from human rights organisations to act on alleged RPF/A crimes, the prosecutor of the International Criminal Tribunal for Rwanda stated: "*[i]n 2007, the Prosecutor General at my request provided me with particulars of several military officers who had been prosecuted before military courts for offences committed against civilians in connection with the genocide of 1994. According to his report to me, out of a total of 42 RPF soldiers on this list, 19 were actually prosecuted for offences committed in 1994 falling within the jurisdiction of the ICTR with the rest being prosecuted for offences committed post 1994 against civilians suspected of being genocidaires*" (Jallow 2009). There are indications to the fact that there were other forms of accountability by RPF soldiers in light of Rwandan President Kagame's affirmation that "*[w]hile some rogue RPF elements committed crimes against civilians during the civil war after 1990, and during the anti-genocide campaign, individuals were punished severely according to the RPF's internal procedures of the day*" [Clark and Kaufman 2008, xxiii].

The departure from the existing legal regime in prosecuting genocide and related crimes in post 1994 Rwanda was presented by Rwandan authorities as a result of institutional incapacity to handle the overall caseload. From the 1996 legislation to the various *gacaca* laws, the focus was on prosecution of genocide (*itsembabwoko* or *jenoside*) and related crimes against humanity (*ibyaha byibasiye inyoko muntu*). Until the adoption of the Law *repressing the crime of genocide, crimes against humanity and war crimes*,[13] the latter category of war crimes (*ibyaha by' intambara*) did not expressly feature as a distinctive category prosecutable before Specialized Chambers or *gacaca* courts. Any crime committed during the course of the civil war, the genocide and the aftermath that could not be categorized as genocide or crime against humanity was to be submitted to ordinary courts which were still considered as competent and capable. From Rwandan authorities perspective and in spite of debates over legal characterization of allegedly crimes committed by the RPF/A; nothing justified non-subjection of the latter to the jurisdiction of ordinary (mostly military) courts.

Questions remain as to whether the list of prosecuted RPF/A officers is representative of the crimes allegedly committed and, if not, whether there are possibilities for future prosecutions. But the recurrent question raised in analyses over post-genocide justice in Rwanda is whether prosecutions through *gacaca* courts would have been more suitable and effective avenue for war crimes than Rwandan military courts. In other words, would the inclusion of RPF/A crimes have better served the interests of victims and reconciliation in Rwanda? It is not quite clear whether the inclusion of RPF/A in the *gacaca* process would be aimed at ensuring their effective prosecution or at creating an ethnic balancing though prosecution by the same body of crimes committed by 'both sides'. For the sake of consistency, arguments for inclusion or exclusion of war crimes in the *gacaca* process should always take into account other possible perpetrators such as the FAR, the French or the Zairians. Furthermore there are a number of practical considerations that are not taken into account in calls for the inclusion of war crimes – including in the mandate of *gacaca* courts. Among other pillars of the *gacaca* process is the idea that "*crimes were publicly committed in the eyes of the population, which thus must recount the facts, disclose the truth and participate in prosecuting and trying the alleged perpetrators*" (preamble of the 2004 *Gacaca* Law). The structuring of activities of *gacaca* courts – the role of Cells and Sectors in collecting information and trying suspects respectively – was premised on the assumption that communities had first-hand knowledge about the circumstances of the commission of the crimes subjected to their jurisdiction.

The majority of RPA soldiers were members of the Rwandan Diaspora; many of whom had never been to Rwanda before the civil war and the genocide and thus, were generally unknown to Rwandans living where they operated. If some may well be identified, it would be extremely difficult if not practically impossible for ordinary citizens to accurately identify most RPA soldiers who might have

13 Law No. 33*bis*/2003 of 6 September 2003 *Repressing the crime of genocide, crimes against humanity and war crimes*, *Official Gazette* No. 21 of 1 November 2003.

committed certain crimes. The subjection of RPF/A crimes to *gacaca* jurisdiction might have led to a similar situation as in cases concerning crimes committed by the internally displaced persons who were in camps in the outskirts of Kigali far from the neighbourhoods where they ordinarily lived (mainly the Northern provinces occupied by the RPF/A) or crimes committed by *Interahamwe* who operated in areas where they were not known. Many such files were classified without trial because perpetrators could not be identified as they were simply known as refugees or under their nicknames. One may predict that there might have been a similar outcry if war crimes had been included in *gacaca* jurisdiction but many dossiers ended up being unprosecuted because most of the authors were unknown. Thus, beyond advocacy for judicial ethnic balancing, it should always be borne in mind how more challenging it is to establish criminal responsibility of individual RPF/A soldiers in the commission of war crimes than it is for genocide suspects. In spite of huge pressure from various sources, including human rights organisations[14] and notwithstanding the assumed higher level of judicial independence in comparison with proceedings in Rwanda,[15] the International Criminal Tribunal for Rwanda has so far opted for cooperation with Rwandan judiciary (military courts prosecutions) rather than using its prerogative of primacy over the latter in prosecuting RPF/A crimes.

Imperatives of justice and reconciliation as well as the interests of all victims require that all crimes be prosecuted and punished. In accordance with applicable procedures, aggrieved parties can, in principle initiate proceedings. Where facts are documented and actors are identified, there is no sound argument that can be made against prosecution of actors who committed war crimes, including RPA soldiers. But for practical reasons, translating this ideal into reality is always challenging, not only in such a very complex context as Rwanda. In many conflict situations, including conflicts where presumably better trained and equipped Western armies have been involved, debates persist as to whether particular incidents are constitutive of war crimes or whether deaths were 'merely' unavoidable collateral victims of war under the application of the principle of proportionality (Watkin 2005, 19).[16] Debates surrounding the

14 Letter by Kenneth Roth of HRW. Read it together with the ICTR Prosecutor's response both available at www.hrw.org/en/news/2009/08/14/letter-ictr-chief-prosecutor-hassan-jallow-response-his-letter-prosecution-rpf-crime, accessed 20 May 2011.

15 According to Article 15 al. 2 of the ICTR statute states that "*The Prosecutor shall act independently (...). He or she shall not seek or receive instructions from any Government or from any other source*" (ICTR Statute, S/RES/955 (1994), of 8 November 1994, as amended up to date) while the ICC statute stipulates that "*(...) The Prosecutor shall act independently (...) and shall not seek or act on instructions from any external source*" (42 al. 1, The Rome Statute, A/CONF.183/9 of 17 July 1998).

16 For relevant information, see: Protocol Additional to the Geneva Conventions of 12 August 1949, and relating to the Protection of Victims of International Armed Conflicts (Protocol I), 8 June 1977, at www.icrc.org/ihl.nsf/full/470?opendocument, accessed on 10 May 2011.

controversial decision by the International Criminal Tribunal for the former Yugoslavia (ICTY) not to assume jurisdiction over purported crimes committed by the North Atlantic Treaty Organization (NATO) during an air campaign against the Federal Republic of Yugoslavia in 1999 attest to the difficulty in scrutinising the conduct of actors favoured by the course of history (International Criminal Tribunal for the former Yugoslavia; Amnesty International Report 2000; Wuerzner 2008).

3.2. NON-COMPLIANCE WITH DUE PROCESS GUARANTEES

In addition to non-prosecution of war crimes attributed to the RPF/A, *gacaca* is also frequently castigated for non-compliance with internationally recognised minimum standards of fair trial. Substantively, *gacaca* courts are criticised for violating the *nullum crimen sine lege* principle (or the prohibition of post-facto criminalisation); the prohibition against trial by special tribunals and the reliance of the system on lay judges (Haile 2008, 21–25; Meyerstein 2007; Fierens 2005). The present analysis will not dwell on arguments about post-facto criminalisation since there is a rich literature debating the existence of legal grounds for prosecuting genocide due to prior ratification of the genocide convention by Rwanda (Schabas and Imbleau 1997, 167; Digneffe and Fierens 2003, 31–43). Similarly, arguments about the constitutional prohibition of establishing special tribunals were outweighed by the imperatives of prosecuting persons responsible for such serious crime as the genocide (Haile 2008, 22–24). The remaining and most recurrent criticism of *gacaca* relates to its perceived non-compliance with due process guarantees.

Arguably, arguments over the fairness of the *gacaca* process should not solely be based on standards of other systems – (mainly Western) criminal procedures. In addition to its traditional roots, the *gacaca* process combines different theories of justice: restorative or community justice, punitive or retributive justice, and rehabilitation or reintegration of the offender. It has principles that are applicable in common law while other principles are found in civil law systems. It is absolutely possible for someone from either legal tradition to consider the whole system as somewhat an oddity (as elaborated in Haveman 2008; Haveman and Muleefu 2011). While comparisons are more than legitimate, examinations of the fairness of *gacaca* should mostly be based on its own principles and values (or, as Meyerstein 2007, 470 puts it, *gacaca* as *gacaca*). In other words, the focus should not be on whether non-lawyers are able to fairly render justice outside the formal structures of contemporary criminal justice systems. In many African societies including Rwanda, traditional justice mechanisms survived the invasion of state structures erected through colonisation. Without idealising traditional processes of justice that predate – and some survived – the colonial order, there are indications to the fact that their pillars revolved around social conceptions of fairness.[17] It would be quite paternalistic to simply assume that their jurisdictional restriction to simple disputes renders them somehow incapable of handling more serious matters which they handled prior to the advent of modern structures.

Analyses of the *gacaca* process have all the legitimacy to raise questions as to whether the functioning of the courts complies with the key principles upon which the mechanism is erected: have the communities fairly served as both prosecution and defence; has the National Service of *Gacaca* Courts provided them with adequate legal advice, training, administrative and logistic support without interfering into the determination of the outcome of particular cases or to what extent has the truth about the genocide emerged and if not why. The variety of perspectives in answers to these questions in various analyses of the *gacaca* process suggest that it is quite difficult to authoritatively and satisfactorily address them as long as the process is still underway and, in the absence of aggregated data, it is still not possible to have a clear nationwide perspective thereon. While the situation may differ from one place to another, hearings during the various stages of the *gacaca* process are inherently contradictory. Possible shortcomings of the *gacaca* process in specific settings should not lead to simple generalisations about its inadequacy in dealing with the caseload of the genocide.

3.3. LACK OF JUDICIAL INDEPENDENCE

Judicial independence is a concept that remains hard to clearly define. As one American legal practitioner eloquently stated: "*Judicial independence is more than the creation of a judiciary or tenure and salaries ... it embodies the concept that a judge decides cases fairly, impartially, and according to the facts and law, not according to whim, prejudice, or fear; the dictates of the legislature or executive, or the latest opinion poll*" (Abrahamson 2003, 3–4). She conceded that "*[n]ot all judges reason alike or necessarily reach the same result even when presented with the same facts and the same law*" (ibid.). More close to the Rwandan context, another author stated that judicial independence contributes to the sustainability of rule of law and democracy (Rugege 2005, 411). The starting point is, indeed, to acknowledge the fact that a clear separation of powers, that guarantees judicial independence, characterises any society that claims to be democratic and

17 For instance, in Kinyarwanda they say "*uca urubanza rw'abavandimwe arararama*" (if you are a judge in a matter involving relatives – in a narrow and broad sense – you avoid taking sides). Similarly, in Luganda they say "*Tosaala gwa kawala nga towulidde gwa kalenzi*" (you cannot decide on a conflict based on one party's story).

governed by the rule of law. Where judicial independence is still an aspiration, there should be clear signs of efforts made to create conditions for its achievement.

While this understanding should guide any inquiry into the level of judicial independence in the *gacaca* courts, there is a need to broaden the debate to the overall contextual realities of pre-genocide and post genocide Rwanda. The broader question should investigate how much judicial independence there was in Rwanda prior to the genocide and whether there has been any improvement or instead, if the country has been on regression during the 17 post-genocide years. The position of many Western writers and Human Rights Organisations such as Amnesty International and Human Rights Watch is that there is no judicial independence in Rwanda (Thomson and Nagy 2011, 24; Waldorf 2011; HRW 2009; AI 2007 and Redress 2008 for a relevant discussion). The perceived lack of judicial independence does not only relate to genocide cases but also to any other criminal matters, such as the perceived misuse of the judiciary to crush dissent by figures opposed to the government.[18] The most denounced channels of political influence into the *gacaca* process are the local leaders and the staff of the National Service of *gacaca* courts (PRI 2010a, 14, 17 and 44–45; Thomson and Nagy 2011, 24; HRW 2009). Reports of coercion of the population to participate in the *gacaca* process and of corruption of *gacaca* judges – partially blamed on the unpaid character of their work – are further used to reinforce the idea of a total lack of independence, but more generally, of the flawed nature of the process (Sosnow 2008; Clark 2010, 4 et seq.). Several of these claims of irregularity in the *gacaca* process are indeed illustrated by concrete examples, either recorded by researchers or officials in charge of the process. However, other studies suggest that while there are real cases of official interference in the judicial process and examples of shortcomings that taint the judicial independence, they are not characteristic of the overall process (Clark 2010, 133 et seq.; Meyerstein 2007, 478 et seq.). Rwandan officials argue that the responsibility of the National Service of *Gacaca* Courts is not to interfere in the determination of the outcome of cases but to rather to supervise and coordinate activities of *gacaca* courts and ensure that the functioning of the courts complies with applicable norms. Again, there are no conclusive studies that can authoritatively lead to credible projections about the overall system. This probably explains the divided opinions, views or conclusions from various analyses, reports or dissertations on a *gacaca* process that is still in motion. But beyond the sole *gacaca* mechanism, the erection of institutions that can sustain a democratic Rwanda characterized by the rule of law and a high degree of separation of powers is still a process that will take more

18 HRW: Rwanda: End Attacks on Opposition Parties, Intimidation of Political Opponents Increases in Advance of Presidential Election 10 February 2010, www.hrw.org/en/news/2010/02/10/rwanda-end-attacks-opposition-parties, accessed on 21 February 2011.

time. It is likely that it will take several years before Rwanda can attain a level of judicial independence that fully or mostly complies with the underlying ideals. Thus, most criticisms over lack of judicial independence in the *gacaca* process have been, and possibly are still, levied against other Rwandan judicial institutions (Meyerstein 2007, 473).

4. CONCLUSION

Roughly one decade since the institution of *gacaca* courts, the multiplicity of opinions, projections, research data and analyses on their short-term and long-term significance for Rwandan society (for some even beyond) makes it quite difficult to determine whether they have achieved (some of) their stated objectives beyond the hardly disputed speeding up of genocide trials. Since the *gacaca* process is still in motion and cannot be expected to generate tangible results in some domains – it will take some years to fully appreciate the impact of the mechanism – it is indeed quite pretentious to make far-reaching projections on its achievements or legacy. Most criticisms of the *gacaca* courts have revolved around perceived non-compliance with (internationalised) principles of Western inspiration governing the administration of criminal justice. Some of the criticisms relate to the very essence of the *gacaca* mechanisms as an inappropriate forum to deal with such serious matters as the determination of criminal responsibility in one of the most horrendous criminal acts namely genocide. Such criticism nonetheless fails to prescribe viable alternatives that would be acceptable to perpetrators, survivors and the Rwandan society in general. Others criticism highlights shortcomings in terms of achievement of its assigned objectives. Undoubtedly, the various criticisms of the essentially experimental *gacaca* mechanism have contributed to its improvements. One can only hope that other legitimate issues raised may equally be addressed so that the stated objectives of the *gacaca* courts are, as much as doable, met. In the end, only history will judge whether the legacy of the *gacaca* courts was mostly positive or negative for Rwanda's recovery after the genocide.

BIBLIOGRAPHY

Abrahamson, S.S. (2003)
Thorny Issues and Slippery Slopes: Perspectives on Judicial Independence. Keynote Address delivered at the Ohio State University on March 21, 2002, 64 *Ohio State Law Journal* 3.

Akhavan, P. (1996)
The International Criminal Tribunal for Rwanda: The Politics and Pragmatics of Punishment, *The American Journal of International Law* 90 (3), 501–510.

Amnesty International (2007)
Report 2007, Rwanda, available at http://report2007.amnesty.org/eng/Regions/Africa/Rwanda (accessed August 2008).

Amnesty International Report (2000)
NATO/Federal Republic of Yugoslavia, 'Collateral Damage or Unlawful Killings?. Violations of the Laws of War by NATO during Operation Allied Force' (AI INDEX: EUR 70/18/00), Summary.

Avocats Sans Frontières (2000)
Justice Pour Tous Au Rwanda: Rapport d'activités 2000, at www.grandslacs.net/doc/3577.pdf (accessed on 9 June 2011).

Bradley, E. (1998)
In Search for Justice – A Truth in Reconciliation Commission for Rwanda, *Journal of International Law and Practice* 7: 129–158.

Chakravarty, A. (2006)
Gacaca Courts in Rwanda: Explaining Divisions within the Human Rights Community, *Yale Journal of International Affairs* 1(2): 132–145.

Clark, P. (2010)
The Gacaca Courts, Post-Genocide Justice and Reconciliation in Rwanda: Justice without Lawyers, Cambridge: Cambridge University Press.

Clark, P. (2007)
Hybridity, Holism, and "Traditional" Justice: The Case of the Gacaca Courts in Post-Genocide Rwanda, *George Washington International Law Review* 39(4): 765–837.

Clark, P. and Kaufman, Z. (eds.) (2008)
After Genocide: Transitional Justice, Post-Conflict Reconstruction and Reconciliation in Rwanda and Beyond, London: Hurst and Company.

Dallaire, R., Manocha, K. and Degnarain, N. (2005)
The Major Powers on Trial, *Journal of International Criminal Justice* 3: 861–878.

Des Forges, A. (1999)
Leave None to Tell the Story: Genocide in Rwanda, New York–Paris: Human Rights Watch and International Federation of Human Rights.

Digneffe, F. and Fierens, J. (eds.) (2003)
Justice et Gacaca: L'Experience Rwandaise et le Genocide, Namur: Presses Universitaires de Namur.

Fierens, J. (2005)
Gacaca Courts: Between Fantasy and Reality, *Journal of International Criminal Justice,* 3: 896–919.

Haile, D. (2008)
Rwanda's Experiment in People's Courts (Gacaca) and the Tragedy of Unexamined Humanitarianism: A Normative/Ethical Perspective, University of Antwerp, Institute of Development, Policy and Management, Discussion Paper/2008.01.

Haskel, L. and Waldorf, L. (2011)
The impunity gap of the International Criminal Tribunal for Rwanda: Causes and consequences, *Hastings International and Comparative Law Review* 34: 49–85.

Haveman, R. and Muleefu, A. (2011)
Gacaca and Fair Trial, in: Rothe, D. et al. (eds.) *Crimes of the State,* Rutgers University Press.

Haveman R. (2008)
Doing Justice to Gacaca, in: Smeulers, A. and Haveman, R. (eds.) *Supranational Criminology. Towards a Criminology of International Crimes*, Antwerp: Intersentia, 359–400.

Human Rights Watch (2011)
Justice Compromised: The Legacy of Rwanda's Community-based Gacaca Courts, R, www.hrw.org/en/reports/2011/05/31/justice-compromised-0 (accessed on 17 June 2011).

Human Rights Watch (2009)
World Report. Chapter Rwanda, Events of 2009, available at www.hrw.org/en/node/87596 (accessed on 16 May 2011).

Human Rights Watch (2008)
Law and Reality: Progress in Judicial Reform in Rwanda, Report, at www.hrw.org/node/62098 (accessed on 11 June 2011).

Ingelaere, B. (2009)
Does the Truth Pass across the Fire without Burning? Locating the Short Circuit in Rwanda's *gacaca* Courts, *Journal of Modern African Studies* 47(4): 507–528.

Ingelaere, B. (2008)
The gacaca courts in Rwanda, in: Huyse, L. and Salter, M. (eds.) *Traditional Justice after Violent Conflict. Learning from African experiences*, Stockholm: International IDEA, 25–59.

Ingelaere, B. (2006)
Changing Lenses and Contextualizing the Rwandan (Post-) Genocide, *L'Afrique des Grands Lacs. Annuaire 2005–2006*, 389–414.

International Criminal Tribunal for the former Yugoslavia
Final Report to the Prosecutor by the Committee Established to Review the NATO Bombing Campaign against the Federal Republic of Yugoslavia www.icty.org/x/file/About/OTP/otp_report_nato_bombing_en.pdf (accessed on 12 May 2011).

International Federation for Human Rights (2002)
Victims in the Balance: Challenges ahead for the International Criminal Tribunal for Rwanda, Report, n° 329/2.

Jallow, H.B. (2009)
ICTR letter n° Ref/OTP/2009/P/084 by Jallow, H.B., Chief Prosecutor, of 22 June 2009 to Human Rights Watch www.hrw.org/node/85068 (accessed on 18 May 2011).

Lahiri, K. (2009)
Rwanda's "Gacaca" Courts: A Possible Model for Local Justice in International Crime?, *International Criminal Law Review* 9(2): 321–332.

Lemarchand, R. (2009)
The Dynamics of Violence in Central Africa, Philadelphia: University of Pennsylvania Press.

Lemarchand, R. (1998)
Genocide in the Great Lakes: Which Genocide? Whose Genocide?, *African Studies Review* 41(1): 3–16.

Mackintosh, A. (1997)
Rwanda: Beyond ethnic conflict, *Development in Practice* 7(4): 464–474.

Mamdani, M. (2001)
When Victims become Killers: Colonialism, Nativism and Genocide in Rwanda, New Jersey: Princeton University Press.

McMillan, N. (2008)
'Our' Shame: International Responsibility for the Rwandan Genocide' in *Australian Feminist Law Journal* 28, 3–28.

Melvern, L. (2006)
Conspiracy to Murder: The Rwandan Genocide, London: Verso.

Melvern, L. (2004)
Conspiracy to Murder: The Rwandan Genocide, New York: Verso.

Meyerstein, A. (2007)
Between Law and Culture: Rwanda's Gacaca and Postcolonial Legality, *Law and Social Inquiry* 32(2): 467–508.

Mibenge, C. (2005)
Enforcing International Humanitarian Law on National Level: The *gacaca* Jurisdictions of Rwanda, in: *Yearbook of International Humanitarian Law*, Vol. 7 – 2004, 410–424.

Morris, M.H. (1996–1997)
The Trials of Concurrent Jurisdiction: The Case of Rwanda, *Duke Journal of Comparative & International Law* 7: 349–374.

Office of the President of the Republic of Rwanda (1999)
Report on the Reflection Meetings Held in the Office of the President of the Republic from May 1998 to March 1999.

Péan, P. (2005)
Noires fureurs, blancs menteurs: Rwanda 1990–1994, Paris: Mille et Une Nuits.

Penal Reform International (2010a)
The contribution of the Gacaca jurisdictions to resolving cases arising from the genocide. Contributions, limitations and expectations of the post-Gacaca phase, Final Monitoring and Research Report on the Gacaca process.

Penal Reform International (2010b)
Eight Years on: A Record of Gacaca Monitoring in Rwanda, www.penalreform.org/files/WEB.english.gacaca.rwanda-5.pdf (accessed on 15 June 2011).

Philpot, R. (2004)
Ça ne s'est pas passé comme ça à Kigali, Paris: Editions Duboiris.

Prunier, G. (2008)
African's World War: Congo, the Rwandan Genocide, and the Making of a Continental Catastrophe, Oxford: Oxford University Press.

Prunier, G. (1999)
The Rwandan Crisis: History of a Genocide (2nd ed.), Kampala: Fountain Publishers.

Prunier, G. (1998)
The Rwandan Patriotic Front, in: Clapham, C., *African Guerillas*, Oxford/Kampala/Bloomington: James Currey/Foutain Publishers/Indiana University Press, 119–133.

Redress (2008)
Extraditing Genocide Suspects from Europe to Rwanda: Issues and Challenges. Conference report, www.redress.org/africa/rwanda (accessed on 12 May 2011).

Republic of Rwanda (2007)
National Independent Commission charged with the collection of evidence on the involvement of the French state in the genocide committed in Rwanda in 1994, Final Report, Kigali.
Republic of Rwanda (2009)
The 9th and 10th Periodic Report of the Republic of Rwanda under the African Charter on Human and Peoples' Rights, www.achpr.org/francais/state_reports/Rwanda/rwanda_9-10_report.pdf (accessed on 18 May 2011).
Reyntjens, F. (2004)
Rwanda, Ten Years On: From Genocide to Dictatorship, *African Affairs* 103(411): 177–210.
Rugege, S. (2005)
Judicial Independence in Rwanda: Paper presented at the Judicial Independence and Legal Infrastructure: Essential Partners for Economic Development, *Pacific McGeorge Global Business & Development Law Journal* 19: 412–425.
Rusesabagina, P. (2006)
Compendium of RPF Crimes – October 1990 to Present: the Case for Overdue Prosecution, www.taylor-report.com/articles/Compendium_of_RPF_Crimes.pdf (accessed on 15 June 2011).
Sarkin, J. (2001)
The Tension between Justice and Reconciliation in Rwanda: Politics, Human Rights, Due Process and the Role of the *Gacaca* Courts in Dealing with the Genocide, *Journal of African Law*, 45(2): 143–172.
Schabas, W.A. (2005)
Genocide Trials and Gacaca Courts. *Journal of International Criminal Justice*, 3: 879–895.
Schabas, W.A. (1996)
Justice, Democracy, and Impunity in Post-Genocide Rwanda: Searching for Solutions to Impossible Problems, *Criminal Law Forum*, 7: 523–560.
Schabas, W.A. and Imbleau, M. (1997)
Introduction to Rwandan Law, Québec: Yvon Blais Inc.
Sosnow, M. (2008)
The Adjudication of Genocide: Gacaca and the Road to Reconciliation in Rwanda, *Denver Journal of International Law and Policy*, 36(2): 125–153.
Thomson, S. and Nagy, R. (2011)
Land, Power and Justice: What Legalism Fails to Address in the Functioning of Rwanda's *gacaca* Courts, *International Journal of Transitional Justice* 5: 11–30.
Turner, T. (2007)
The Congo Wars: Conflict, Myth and Reality, London/New York: Zed Books.
United Nations High Commission for Refugees (2000)
The State of The World's Refugees 2000: Fifty Years of Humanitarian Action – Chapter 10: The Rwandan genocide and its aftermath.
Vandeginste, S. (1997)
Poursuite des Présumés Responsables du Génocide et des Massacres Politiques devant les Juridictions Rwandaises., L'Afrique des grands lacs: annuaire 1996–1997 / Centre d'étude de la région des grands lacs d'Afrique, Paris: L'Harmattan.

Van Lierop, R.F. (1997)
Rwanda Evaluation: Report and Recommendations, *International Lawyer (ABA)*, Vol. 31(3): 887–910.

Waldorf, L. (2011)
A Mere "Pretense of Justice": Complementarity, Sham Trials, and Victor's Justice at the Rwanda Tribunal, *Fordham International Law Journal* 33(4): 1221–1277.

Waldorf, L. (2006a)
Rwanda's Failing Experiment in Restorative Justice, in: Sullivan, D. and Tifft, L. (eds.) *Handbook of Restorative Justice: A Global Perspective*, London/New York: Routledge/Taylor & Francis Group, 422–434.

Waldorf, L. (2006b)
Mass Justice for Mass Atrocity: Rethinking Local Justice as Transitional Justice, *Temple Law Review* 79(1): 1–88.

Watkin, K. (2005)
Assessing Proportionality: Moral Complexity and Legal Rules, in: McComack, T. and McDonald, A. (eds.) *Yearbook of International Humanitarian Law*, The Hague: T.M.C. Asser Press.

Wuerzner, C. (2008)
Mission impossible? Bringing charges for the crime of attacking civilians or civilian objects before international criminal tribunals, *International Review of Red Cross* 90(872): 907–930.